The Odyssey of
IBN BATTUTA

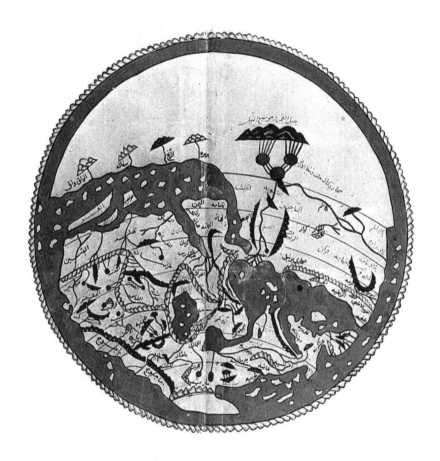

Map of the world by the twelfth-century geographer al-Idrisi.

The Odyssey of

IBN BATTUTA

UNCOMMON TALES OF A MEDIEVAL ADVENTURER

David Waines

THE UNIVERSITY OF CHICAGO PRESS

David Waines is Emeritus Professor of Islamic Studies at Lancaster University. He wrote the bestselling textbook *An Introduction to Islam*, now in its second edition, and edited a volume entitled *Patterns of Everyday Life* in the Formation of the Classical Islamic World series. He has also written many articles on the medieval Arabic culinary and dietetic traditions.

Published in Great Britain in 2010 by I.B.Tauris & Co. Ltd
6 Salem Road, London W2 4BU
www.ibtauris.com

Published in the United States and Canada in 2010 by The University of Chicago Press, Chicago 60637

19 18 17 16 15 14 13 12 11 10   1 2 3 4 5

ISBN-13: 978-0-226-86985-8 (cloth)
ISBN-13: 978-0-226-86986-5 (paper)
ISBN-10: 0-226-86985-7 (cloth)
ISBN-10: 0-226-86986-5 (paper)

Library of Congress Cataloging-in-Publication Data

Waines, David.
  The odyssey of Ibn Battuta : uncommon tales of a medieval adventurer / David Waines.
    p. cm.
  Includes bibliographical references and index.
  ISBN-13: 978-0-226-86985-8 (cloth : alk. paper)
  ISBN-10: 0-226-86985-7 (cloth : alk. paper)
  ISBN-13: 978-0-226-86986-5 (pbk. : alk. paper)
  ISBN-10: 0-226-86986-5 (pbk. : alk. paper) 1. Ibn Batuta, 1304–1377. Tuhfat al-nuzzar fi ghara'ib al-amsar wa-'aja'ib al-asfar. 2. Ibn Batuta, 1304–1377—Travel—Islamic Empire. 3. Travelers—Islamic Empire—Biography. 4. Travel, Medieval. 5. Islamic Empire—Description and travel. I. Title.
  G370.I2W35 2010
  910.92—dc22

                                                          2010001037

Typeset in Adobe Caslon Pro by
A. & D. Worthington, Newmarket, Suffolk
Printed and bound in Great Britain by
CPI Antony Rowe, Chippenham

Mixed Sources
Product group from well-managed forests and other controlled sources
www.fsc.org Cert no. SGS-COC-002953
© 1996 Forest Stewardship Council

❧ ❧

Contents

やゃ ゃゃ

Illustrations

Preface and Acknowledgements

Several generations of scholars and writers have contributed to a growing understanding and appreciation of Ibn Battuta and of his only work, known simply as *The Travels*. They continue to fascinate readers to the present day, evidenced by the publication of a newly edited, abridged English translation in 2002. The latest edition of the multi-volume Arabic original was published, fittingly enough in Morocco, in 1997. Purists might claim that there is no substitute for reading the entire *Travels* in the original language. Yet reading Ibn Battuta in one of the dozen or so languages into which he has been translated is a valuable second option for a far wider readership.

The present work on Ibn Battuta's odyssey has, of necessity, a more modest aim. Like an abridged translation, the material presented here has had to be selective. Moreover, in the spirit of an abridged translation, the object here has been to allow the reader to 'listen' as far as possible to Ibn Battuta's own descriptions of his experiences. For this purpose his own words have been highlighted in italics in the text. The words of other persons quoted in the travels by Ibn Battuta himself have not been so treated and appear as quotations in roman type.

The selection of the chapter themes, on the other hand, is entirely my responsibility. In Chapter 1, Ibn Battuta is briefly placed in the context of medieval travel writers, both Christian and Muslim, and especially with Marco Polo, his older contemporary. Notably, each of their travel accounts was a conscious collaborative venture between the traveller and his 'editor'. This was perhaps the medieval version of 'ghost writing', except that the ghost's name was known in both cases although the actual contribution of each to the finished work is a matter of controversy among modern critics. The remainder of the chapter deals with modern critics of Ibn Battuta's narrative. Chapter 2 is intended to initiate the reader unfamiliar with Ibn

Battuta's travels to the places he visited and what he experienced along the way; it emphatically reminds us that medieval travel bore no resemblance to the modern concept of a ten-day 'away break' in Thailand. The remaining chapters, on food, spiritual travel and a broad category of the 'other' that includes women, are not topics systematically treated by Ibn Battuta under specific headings but are rather concerns or interests of his sprinkled throughout the narrative; taken together, however, they comprise a significant proportion of the text.

The excellent translation of Gibb and Beckingham provided the English rendering of the Arabic text which I used in the recent edition by Abd al-Hadi al-Tazi. I have taken liberties with the English translation where slightly different readings seemed appropriate. Transliteration of Arabic into English can be a nightmare for non-specialist readers, so I have avoided the inevitable clutter of signs and squiggles by abolishing all diacriticals.

Several friends and colleagues contributed to the final outcome of this work. In debates with the publisher over an appropriate title for this volume, discussions with Lancastrian friends, Dermot and Trish, resulted in the key word 'odyssey', which indeed has characterized the whole project. Professor Manuela Marin of Madrid kindly read Chapter 3 on food and hospitality, a subject we have closely collaborated on during our mutual research on medieval Arab culinary culture. Professor Remke Kruk of Leiden read the whole manuscript and made a number of valuable suggestions, especially on the final chapter. It has been a real pleasure to work again with Alex Wright of I.B.Tauris who expertly oversaw one of my earlier books. Gillian Taylor's help was invaluable in delivering the illustrations electronically to the publisher, as my computer skills have progressed little beyond the typewriter era. And finally, as a major supporter who read the entire manuscript, made numerous comments and who cheerfully coped with Ibn Battuta's constant presence in our lives for so many months, this volume is dedicated to Kauser.

I have indeed – praise be to God – attained my desire in this world, which was to travel through the earth, and I have attained in this respect what no other person has attained to my knowledge. The world to come remains, but my hope is strong in the mercy and clemency of God, and the attainment of my desire to enter the Garden of Paradise.

Ibn Battuta

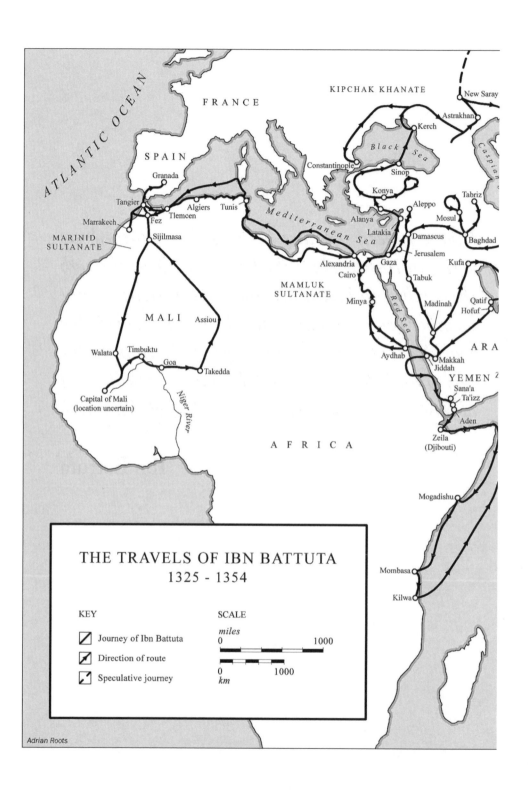

ATLANTIC OCEAN

FRANCE

KIPCHAK KHANATE

New Saray

Astrakhan

Kerch

SPAIN

Granada

Black Sea

Constantinople

Sinop

Caspian

Tangier

Algiers

Tunis

Konya

Aleppo

Tabriz

Marrakech

Tlemcen

Alanya

Mosul

Fez

Mediterranean Sea

Latakia

Damascus

Baghdad

MARINID
SULTANATE

Sijilmasa

Alexandria

Cairo

Gaza

Jerusalem

Kufa

MAMLUK
SULTANATE

Tabuk

Minya

Madinah

Qatif

Hofuf

MALI

Assiou

Red Sea

A R A

Walata

Timbuktu

Goa

Takedda

Aydhab

Makkah
Jiddah

YEMEN

Niger River

Sana'a

Ta'izz

Capital of Mali
(location uncertain)

Aden

Zeila
(Djibouti)

AFRICA

Mogadishu

Mombasa

THE TRAVELS OF IBN BATTUTA
1325 - 1354

Kilwa

KEY

Journey of Ibn Battuta

Direction of route

Speculative journey

SCALE

miles

0   1000

0   1000
km

Adrian Roots

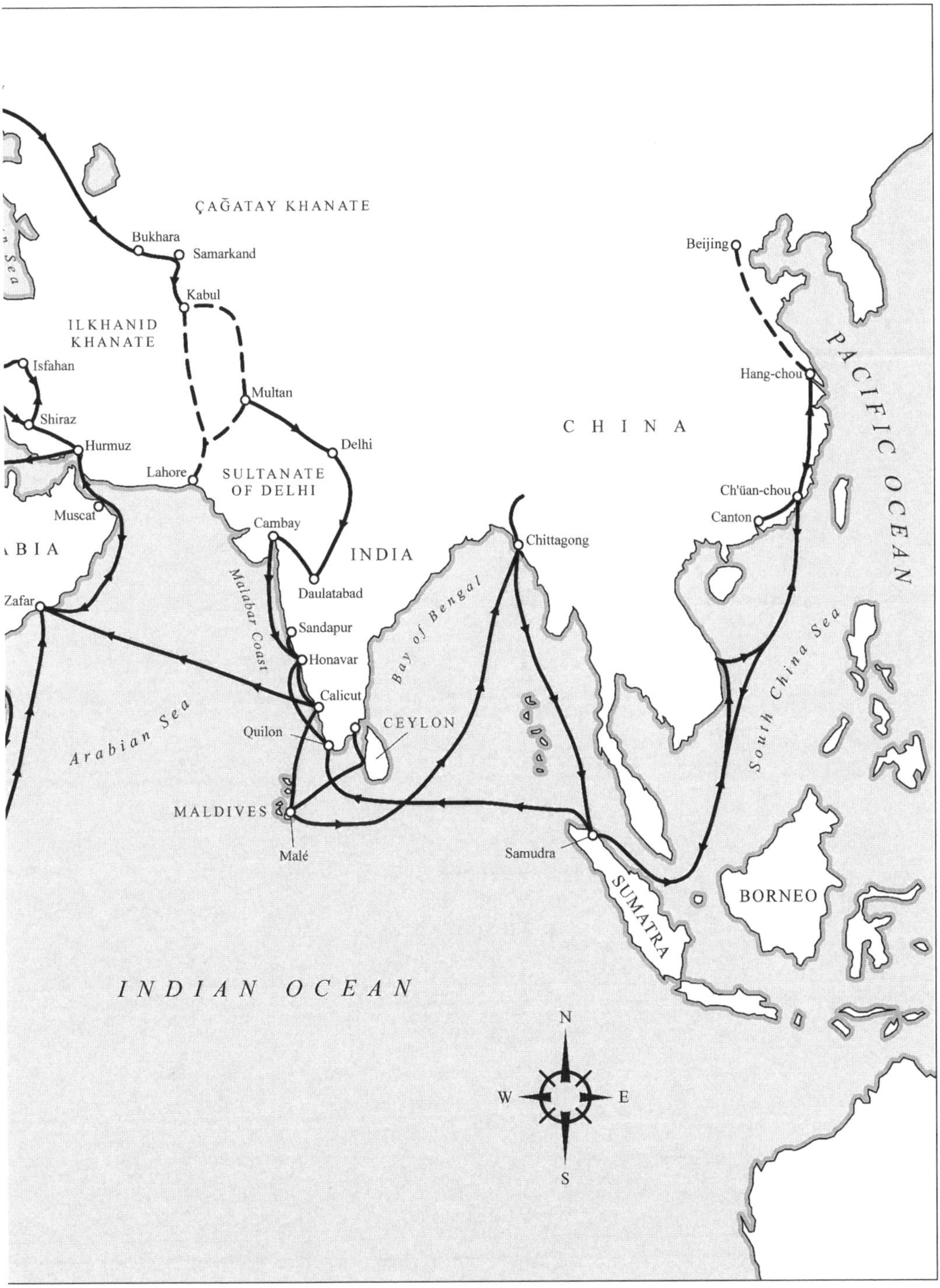
ÇAĞATAY KHANATE
Bukhara
Samarkand
Kabul
ILKHANID KHANATE
Isfahan
Shiraz
Hurmuz
Multan
Delhi
Lahore
SULTANATE OF DELHI
Muscat
BIA
Cambay
INDIA
Daulatabad
Zafar
Malabar Coast
Sandapur
Honavar
Calicut
Quilon
CEYLON
Bay of Bengal
Arabian Sea
MALDIVES
Malé
Chittagong
CHINA
Beijing
Hang-chou
Ch'üan-chou
Canton
PACIFIC OCEAN
South China Sea
Samudra
SUMATRA
BORNEO
INDIAN OCEAN
N
W
E
S

CHAPTER 1

Travel Tales, Their Creators and Critics

The medieval world was a world in motion. European or Middle Eastern, everyone risked similar dangers on land and sea, travelling in groups, large or small, but rarely alone. People set out on short or longer journeys for a variety of reasons. Merchants moved goods while kings, sultans and popes moved armies. Ambassadors and their entourages were dispatched on missions of political concern while missionaries ventured abroad to win souls for the faith. Laymen travelled in search of work or in pursuit of family matters. The pilgrim's quest, often shared with the scholar's, was a search for enrichment of the spirit, or simple curiosity to see and experience other places and things, as Chaucer's 'wanderinge by the weye' might suggest. Crucially, support for these movements came from the skills and labour of travel guides and transport experts who manned the varied types of craft that traversed the rivers and seaways, or the caravans, themselves veritable societies in motion, that crossed landscapes linking one realm or continent to the next. The medieval traveller, in short, included both the rich and the restless. The largest-scale movement of all, although more strictly defined as migration than travel, was the periodic shift of whole tribes and peoples from regions of the East into the Middle East and Europe: the Huns into the Roman Empire, and Turks and Mongols into the Abbasid Empire are but two examples.

Compared with the multitude that travelled, few individuals left accounts of their experiences. Indeed, travel itself did not have a literary or intellectual purpose, and only those literate, educated persons with a desire or inducement to record their journeys did so. Throughout Muslim domains travel did mould the lives of many a scholar, literate merchant or scholar/merchant. One aim of their journeys, if not the sole objective, was the acquisition of knowledge, whether religious or mundane. A religious goal entailed a 'searcher of knowledge' seeking out men and women, wherever they resided, to draw upon their fund of religious learning. This could include their knowledge of Muslim scripture, the Quran, and its commentaries, or of traditions related orally about the Prophet Muhammad's life. That objective was an end in itself and did not necessarily act as a stimulus for travellers to recount the experiences of their quest. Travel alone, of course, opened broader horizons of thought that served other ends. The historian al-Masudi (d. 957), for example, alludes to the extent of his travels in his surviving works, especially the *Muruj al-Dhahab* (*Meadows of Gold*), although he left no separate account of them. His method of historical research displayed a rejection of the extremes of scepticism and credulity, as well as an uncritical imitation of the conclusions of his predecessors; his extensive travels contributed to this method through experience derived from direct and constant observation that informed many of his judgements on peoples and nations of the past.[1] Born in Baghdad, he ventured as far afield as India, taking in various parts of Arabia including pilgrimage to the Holy Cities of Mecca and Medina and thence to islands off the East African coast.

Al-Masudi's younger contemporary, the geographer al-Muqaddasi, was a native of Jerusalem. Little is known of his life but for what he mentions in his pioneering geography of the Islamic dominions (*mamlakat al-islam*). He lived until at least 990. His book's title *Ahsan al-taqasim fi marifat al-aqalim* (*The Best Divisions for Knowledge of the Regions*) reflects a systematic structure: the Islamic world is divided into 14 provinces or regions, six Arab and eight non-Arab, each section covering the distinctive features of a province, including its climate, products and specialities, currency and customs, and ending with a list of the main routes within or across it. The method adopted in his book, he noted, was informed by three sources, namely, from 'what I myself have witnessed, from what I have heard from persons of confidence and what I have found in books devoted to this subject and others'.[2] Except for the Iberian peninsula (al-Andalus in the Arabic sources) he claimed to have visited every region described in the work. But for all that, it does not constitute a travel narrative. Rather, it has been called a literary atlas of Islam. As with al-Masudi the historian, travel was essential to Muqaddasi's enterprise as a geographer, for each aimed to surpass his predecessors' methods by the classification of information based upon observation and inquiry.

So great travellers did not make travel writers, great or otherwise. Indeed, travel accounts were actually few in number and may have been fewer still but for fortuitous circumstances, or the incentive and dedication of others than the travellers themselves. The point can be illustrated from early medieval Europe by the Latin narratives of certain Christian pilgrims to Jerusalem who travelled shortly after the rise of Islam in the seventh century CE. Adomnan, the Abbot of Iona between the years 679 and 704, one day received an unexpected visit from a bishop from Gaul. On his return by ship from the holy places in Palestine, Bishop Arculf had been driven by a fierce storm onto the shores of Britain. Adomnan was delighted to hear Arculf's first-hand adventures and decided to preserve them for the benefit of posterity, saying, 'I first took down his trustworthy and reliable account on tablets; this I have now written on parchment in the form of a short essay.'[3] Another instance is that of the English pilgrim Willibald who travelled to Syria and the Holy Land between 724 and 730. Returning to Europe he eventually became a bishop in Germany and dictated his lively experiences to a nun named Hugeburc. It was not until half a century later, however, that she produced the account of the life of, by now, St Willibald. The loyal nun concluded her account on a note of apology, familiar to many medieval travel narratives, in order to quell comments by the sceptics: 'We heard his story at his dictation in the monastery of Heidenheim. I had as my witnesses his deacons and several other clergy of his. I say this in order that no one ever again shall say it is all nonsense.'[4] By such good fortune, a violent storm or a nun's lasting devotion to her bishop, were these narratives ever set down in the first place. A somewhat different survival curiosity is the account of travels, *c.*1173, from the Iberian peninsula to the Middle East. The anonymous Hebrew text is attributed, by the equally anonymous author of its brief preface, to one Benjamin of Tudela. Scholars have accepted the attribution as genuine without possessing any corroborating detail that would confirm the traveller's identity. Where, when and how the preface became attached to the text is also a mystery.

Contemporaries: Marco Polo and Ibn Battuta

These acts of 'collaboration' were fortuitous. Other travel accounts, in contrast, survived by means of a conscious, close collaborative partnership.

The two greatest travellers of the entire medieval period produced their
renowned works in this fashion. Marco Polo, the Venetian, was 17 when,
in 1272, he embarked on his adventures among the Mongols in China and
was absent from Italy with his father and uncle for 23 years. He died aged
69 in January 1324, at the very moment when a younger Muslim contemporary, Shams al-Din Abu Abdallah Muhammad b. Abdallah b. Ibrahim
al-Luwati al-Tanji, better known as Ibn Battuta, was preparing to set out
on his own travels, initially on pilgrimage to Mecca and Medina. Ibn
Battuta left family behind in his birthplace, Tangier, in June 1325, aged
22. He returned home for good after nearly 30 years abroad. Both he and
Marco Polo had accumulated myriad tales of fascination for their respective future audiences, although, in the event, neither brought his adventures to light solely by his own efforts.

In 1298 Marco Polo found himself in a Genoese jail. There he met a
reputed writer of Arthurian romances for the English court, Rustichello
of Pisa, to whom he recounted his tales. In the brief opening passage of
the completed work, Rustichello explains that his companion felt it would
be a pity if others could not know of the things he had seen in the East
and learn from them while, at the same time, he wished 'to occupy his
leisure [in prison] as well as to afford entertainment to readers'.[5] Some 60
years later, around 1356, Ibn Battuta was relating his travels to the author
of works on poetry, Islamic law and theology, Muhammad Ibn Juzayy. He
had been appointed as Ibn Battuta's collaborator by 'exalted command'
of the reigning Marinid Sultan of Morocco, Abu Inan Faris (1348–58).
Ibn Juzayy's commission, set out in his prolix introduction to the travels,
was to assemble from Ibn Battuta's dictation 'a compilation which should
comprehend what was of profit in them … giving care to the pruning
and polishing of its language and applying himself to its clarification and
adaptation to the taste of readers, that they may find enjoyment in these
curiosities and that the profit to be derived from their pearls should be
increased in stripping them from their shell'.[6] These terms of reference,
expressed in more extravagant prose than Rustichello's, equally describe
the latter's task, namely to convert a mass of information based upon both
travel notes and discussions with his informant into a coherent and read-
able account. Rustichello's remark in the prologue said of Marco Polo,
could have applied equally to Ibn Juzayy on Ibn Battuta: 'But what he told
was only what little he was able to remember.' What *little* each was able

to recall of their wandering years was indeed remarkable. In Ibn Battuta's case, the material he provided Ibn Juzayy resulted in a work several times greater in volume than the travels of Marco Polo. The travellers' shared ambition was to entertain, inform and impress those who would read or have read to them their works in order to learn of the 'various races of men and the peculiarities of the various regions of the world' (Rustichello) or of 'the rulers of countries, of their distinguished men of learning and of their pious saints' (Ibn Juzayy). As with the nun Hugeburc, Rustichello and Ibn Juzayy each justified his editorial labour and affirmed the authenticity of the account in which each had been engaged.

The travelogue and the critic

By their very nature, travel narratives of distant, unfamiliar, even unknown places would have stirred mixed reactions among their first audiences, who absorbed these accounts through reading or listening to them read aloud. Some received them, as intended by their authors, as diversionary entertainment; others felt they had learned about exciting new and mysterious worlds. But there were inevitably the sceptics, as Hugeburc knew well enough. Marco Polo's contemporary audience greeted his account with mixed reactions. In part, the travels were viewed as simply a collection of curious tales. At a deeper level, Europeans found it difficult to accept the existence of another world, hitherto unknown to them in detail, as China was, that possessed major cities enriched from trade and commerce without parallel to anything in their own European societies. Modern critical opinion, on the other hand, is both more radical and nuanced in its reception. Concern has been broadly expressed over Polo's trustworthiness as a reporter. Among Sinologists, for example, there is disquiet over Marco's claim even to have been to China; some say the jury is still out on the matter, while another view dismisses Polo's claim out of hand. Discrepancies have been discerned between Marco's description of northern China, which appears genuine, and that of southern China, which, it is held, could only have reached him at second hand. Marco's account of Japan is described by a critic as strewn with error, although it is in fact the only mention of the region in a European source before the sixteenth century. A more radical revisionist assessment, moreover, argues that Marco had never been in prison and that Rustichello had not written the travels in French or Franco-Italian as is currently accepted, but had rather translated it from Marco's original Venetian version. Unfortunately, the original manuscript is not extant; hence the language in which it was written cannot be conclusively determined. In a recent major study where these problems are discussed, John Larner concluded the real contribution of Polo's work was that '[N]ever before or since has one man given such an immense body of new geographical knowledge to the West.'[7]

Thus modern scholarship advances our understanding of the past, here by subjecting a classic of medieval travel and its creators to close scrutiny. Ibn Battuta was no exception to this process. In his own day, there were those who also received his stories with reservation. At a gathering in the presence of his patron Abu Inan, Ibn Battuta spoke of the many marvels he had witnessed, dwelling at length upon his experiences in India. *'The ruler of the Delhi Sultanate, Muhammad Shah,'* he said, *'was noted for his generosity to the public. When he embarked upon a military campaign each man, woman and child was given provision for six months while his return to the city was greeted by the entire populace upon whom sacks of money were catapulted.'*[8] Mutterings of disbelief at this tale spread among the assembly, resulting in Ibn Battuta being labelled a liar. A witness to the event was the young historian Ibn Khaldun (d. 1406). One day he conveyed his own concerns about Ibn Battuta's veracity on India to the sultan's *wazir*. He replied that incredulity often arises over reports, exaggerated or not, relating to the government of a country one has never personally visited. He said it was rather like the story of a high government official who had been imprisoned by his king for years together with his son who had grown up from infancy in the same confined environment. Now a youth, he asked his father what meat they were fed by the prison authorities. The father described a sheep which of course the boy had never seen and hence concluded that it must belong to the same species as the prison rats!

Ibn Battuta's reception in Europe

Judging by the number of extant manuscripts of his travels, some 30 in all, Ibn Battuta had nevertheless posthumously enjoyed some popularity in the Middle East, especially in the Maghrib (present-day Morocco). In Europe his importance appears to have been first recognized only when two famous traveller-explorers to the Arab world, Ulrich Jasper Seetzen

(1767–1811) and Johan Ludwig Burckhardt (1784–1817), had purchased abridged copies in manuscript acquired on their travels in the Middle East. In the next stage, several European scholars translated portions of the travels from similar abridgements. Samuel Lee published his *Travels of Ibn Battuta Translated from the Abridged Arabic Manuscript Copies* in London in 1829. In their bits and pieces the travels were stimulating a wider interest in Europe and were, in general, favourably received in scholarly circles. It was not until the French conquest of Algeria in 1830 that several Ibn Battuta manuscripts, some complete, were 'liberated' and brought to Paris where they were housed in the Bibliothèque Royale so that study of the work as a whole could commence in earnest.

The task was undertaken by two scholars of Arabic, C. Defremery and B.R. Sanguinetti. They had five manuscripts to work with, two of which were complete. The travels were originally conceived in two parts. In modern geographical terminology, the first part covered Ibn Battuta's journeys from Morocco to the Indus valley, taking in Egypt, several pilgrimages to Mecca, Syria, Iraq, East Africa, Turkey, Iran and Afghanistan. The second part included a long account of his sojourn in India, passing from there to the Maldive Islands, Ceylon, Bangladesh, Indonesia to China and then the return journey home from where he next visited southern Spain (al-Andalus) and finally Mali in West Africa. The most complete and accurate manuscript employed by the editors was dated 1180 of the Muslim era, 1776, which formed the base text for the first part of their printed edition. The oldest manuscript contained only the second part of the travels. It was, remarkably, dated 757AH (1356CE). In Europe at the time, the dating gave rise to the view that this was the very copy Ibn Juzayy had penned himself. Be that as it may, Ibn Juzayy died a few months after completing his commission, aged just 36. The manuscript ends giving the book's full title in rhymed Arabic that in English awkwardly reads, *Gift to Those Who Contemplate the Wonders of Cities and the Marvels of Travelling*. Or better, for short, *The Travels* (in Arabic *Rihla*).

Defremery-Sanguinetti's first printed version of the complete travels appeared in the Arabic original with French translation in Paris in four volumes from 1853 to 1858. Exactly a century later, the famous British orientalist H.A.R. Gibb published the first volume of his English translation (1953), finishing two further volumes before his death, with the final fourth volume, prepared by C.F. Beckingham, appearing in 2000. Ibn

Battuta has also been translated into a further dozen languages.

Ibn Battuta's modern critics

In the intervening century and a half since the Arabic-French version first saw light, Ibn Battuta's journeys have, like Marco Polo's, been critically discussed by modern scholars. A central problem, as with all medieval travel accounts, concerned the degree of reliability the reader could place in them. This covered a number of separate but inter-related problems. There was, first of all, the question of the narrative's complex chronology and itineraries: was Ibn Battuta actually in all the places he claimed to have visited at the times he said he was or, put more bluntly, had he been in all the places he claimed to have seen? A second major problem was the degree and nature of plagiarism in certain parts of the travels: were the descriptions of places he claimed to have visited actual first-hand accounts or were they borrowed directly from or based upon the works of earlier travellers, whether the particular source was acknowledged or not? This question will occupy our attention a little later but first let us focus on the matter of chronology.

What did Ibn Battuta really witness – and when?

The reason questions arose stemmed from textual errors in a number of the itineraries. Ibn Battuta had to rely primarily on his memory when dictating his travels, and confusions and slips were bound to occur. Gibb's view of this problem was both generous and critical: 'It is indeed remarkable that the errors are comparatively few, considering the enormous number of persons and places he mentions. The most serious difficulty is offered by the chronology of the travels, which is utterly impossible as it stands.'[9] Ibn Battuta's narrative of Palestine and Syria is a case in point. According to his own dating, Ibn Battuta travelled from Cairo to Damascus in 1326, taking the normal three weeks to cover the distance, while somehow managing the impossible task of touring all of Syria as far north as Aleppo and Antioch within the same period. The resulting perplexity has been explained as an example of a composite journey, that is, one based upon his later recollection of different excursions through the same region conflated into a single trip.

Another example occurs in the Anatolian narrative of 1331. Here Ibn Battuta appears to have inserted a lengthy 'detour' through Konya and Sivas to Erzerum in eastern Anatolia during his summer stay in Milas and Birgi, both located in the extreme west. He could not have completed such a long 'detour' and return in the course of a summer, so doubt was cast on this whole section of his travels. On the other hand, had he actually visited all of the places in Anatolia mentioned, it has been proposed that his real itinerary must have followed a quite different sequence and occupied a longer time. In another instance, it has been argued, and now generally accepted, that Ibn Battuta's expedition to Bulghar could not have taken place. The brief 1929 article by Stephen Janicsek bluntly inquired, 'Ibn Battuta's journey to Bulghar: is it a fabrication?' Bulghar was a famous city in the central region of the Volga River valley, which he claimed to have visited for three days during a journey there and back lasting only 20 days. Under prevailing conditions, however, the actual return journey would have required 60–70 days. Janicsek concluded that for this and other reasons, Ibn Battuta's 'journey' to Bulghar was beyond doubt pure invention. Opinion is divided, too, over whether Ibn Battuta ever journeyed to and visited Constantinople. The confusion over the itinerary, says Ivan Hrbek, is matched only by that of Ibn Battuta's travels in China. At the very best, he concluded cautiously, the evidence may be just sufficient to make it 'reasonably certain' that he had been present in the Byzantine capital.[10] Of the journey itself, Harry Norris noted that while some of it may be imaginary, it is a unique fourteenth-century Arabic account containing enough fact 'to vouch for its overall authenticity'.[11]

Of Ibn Battuta's China venture, Ross Dunn has remarked upon its problematic and unsatisfactory character in the travels. Others have doubted that Ibn Battuta ever got further east than Ceylon, arguing that he either fabricated these later sections or based them completely upon hearsay. Dunn's own judgement on this question is, nonetheless, that 'No one ... has made a completely convincing case that Ibn Battuta did not go to East Asia, at least as far as the ports of South China. The riddle of the journey probably defies solution.'[12]

Another example is the curious tale about the kingdom of Tawalisi. Ibn Battuta described this 'discovery' during a voyage on a Chinese junk from Java to the Chinese mainland. The kingdom has variously been identified as Cambodia, Cochin China or Tongking (Vietnam), Celebes

(Sulawesi), Brunei, an island in the Moluccas and Mindanao in the southern Philippines. The Japanese scholar Yamamoto Tatsuro connected the name Tawalisi with the princely title employed in Champa, a medieval kingdom also in modern-day Vietnam. No satisfactory identification has yet been made. However, a plausible explanation for the tale itself is offered in the concluding remarks of this volume.

On the matter of chronology in medieval travel accounts, it should be enough to observe that travellers were not overly concerned with specific dates, apart, perhaps, from the starting and finishing dates of their travels. In Rustichello's prologue to Marco Polo's adventures, he records one date, 1269, that marked the return of the brothers Niccolo and Maffeo Polo to Acre in Syria. From there they returned to Venice to complete their first journey. After an enforced wait of 'two years' or so, the brothers set forth again, this time accompanied by Niccolo's son, Marco. The second and only other date Rustichello offers marked the return of the Polo family to Venice in 1295. The book's editor, Robert Latham, writes that the period of this second Polo venture beginning in 1272 or thereabouts is described by Marco in a remarkably impersonal tone, since 'For the next twenty years the Polos appear to have remained in the East; but how they spent their time there we do not know. Very few incidents are mentioned in this book.'[13] And few incidents meant few dates.

Ibn Battututa could not be accused of creating an impersonal travel narrative in any sense. He provided the date of his departure and the date of the book's completion with Ibn Juzayy. His chronology, as we have noted, often failed the test of adequacy, even allowing that his memory was accurate in recalling when events mentioned did occur. He did cite, albeit infrequently, the day, month and the year of certain events such as his arrival at or departure from a location. More often he supplied the day and month only and left the year understood from the context, which was not always unambiguously evident. Then, he employed other date indicators. A religious celebration like the Feast of Ashura occurred on the tenth day of Muharram, the first month of the Muslim year; or, the religious feast at the end of the fasting month of Ramadan; or, the rites of pilgrimage during the pilgrimage season of Dhu-l Hijja. These are the most significant dates in the Muslim calendar and when they are mentioned by a traveller, the precise calendar dates can be determined. Christian travellers, especially churchmen, employed a similar method. The Franciscan

John of Plano Carpini (d. 1252) was a papal delegate sent to the Mongol headquarters in Central Asia and wrote the first account to reach Europe of their land, history, character, religion and military organization. To this he appended a brief account of his travels. He mentions few dates and they are expressed in terms of the Christian church calendar: the Feast of the Ascension (17 May), the Feast of St John the Baptist (16 June) or the Vigil of St Peter (28 June). Other markers of less assistance to the modern researcher would be the number of days a journey took between two locations, and the length of stay in them. Still more vague, but nonetheless helpful, are passing references to the season of the year, such as 'snow' or the 'fruit ripening' period. Even if all this data were available, the results could still be baffling when a sequence of dates covering a relatively long period is examined. Let us look at one example.

Ibn Battuta informs the reader that in September 1332 he performed the pilgrimage to Mecca, and one year later, September 1333, he arrived at the Indus River frontier into northern India. This was the event that brought the first volume of the travels to a close. The problem for Ibn Battuta's readers was that he had proclaimed his presence at the Feast of Ashura the same year in the Anatolian city of Bursa which also fell during September 1333. This implied, however, that he was nowhere near the Indus River on that date, but still many hundreds of miles to the west of it. The second volume commenced with the same information that ended the first volume: Ibn Battuta's arrival at the Indus on the day of the new moon of Muharram, the first day of the year 734AH, that is 12 September 1333CE. Critics are divided as to where the error lay. Gibb was inclined provisionally to accept the date of 1333 and question the date of the pilgrimage of 1332. He proposed instead that Ibn Battuta had begun his journey from Mecca to Anatolia a full two years earlier during October 1330, thus allowing for the elapse of three years to cover his journey to the East African coast, then back to Mecca and onwards to Anatolia before finally arriving at the Indus crossing. Hrbek, on the other hand, took the opposite view and accepted the pilgrimage of 1332 but questioned the date of the Indus crossing in 1333. And there the problem remains, since, in either case, Ibn Battuta's chronology cannot be resolved by appeal to external evidence which is, regrettably, inconclusive.

Plagiarism

The problem of chronology, fascinating or frustrating as it is, does not arouse scholarly indignation or wrath. The question of plagiarism does. It is uncertain what one critic had in mind when he mused that Ibn Battuta might have composed his entire travels, including those to distant India and remoter China, without ever having left the comforts of his Tangier home. Was it blatant plagiarism or rather a rich imaginative fantasy? Either way, the idea is not as far-fetched as it sounds, as the following example illustrates.

One of Ibn Battuta's European contemporaries was the creator of a vastly popular work known today as *The Travels of Sir John Mandeville*. In the book's prologue, 'Sir John Mandeville' claimed to be an English knight, born and raised in St Albans. He offered his book as a pilgrim's guide to Jerusalem, followed by a description of the Middle East stretching to India and beyond to the kingdom of the Great Khan. In his words, he set out in 1322 and travelled abroad for over 30 years. Upon his return, worn out by age and travel, he claimed to have set down his adventures as best he could recall them. The book was written around 1357 and became a medieval bestseller. It survives today in some 250 manuscripts, and before 1500 the work had already appeared in multiple printed editions translated into several European languages. The original French version is unfortunately lost. Mandeville's reputation survived unblemished for over two centuries and remained largely unchallenged until the late nineteenth century. Meticulous research by then had uncovered most, if not all, the unacknowledged sources the 'Mandeville' author had used to put together his travels. Some 20 works dating from the twelfth century to 'Mandeville's' own day were identified. Chief of these were the first-person accounts of the Dominican William of Boldensele, who travelled to Egypt and the Holy Land in the 1330s, and that of Friar Odoric of Pordenone, who travelled to India and China in the 1320s. Mandeville's compilation method was to rewrite the underlying texts of Boldensele and Pordenone by expanding and supplementing them with copious material borrowed from yet other sources so that the resulting narrative was far longer than either of the two original base texts.

Thus one solution to the problem was near to being resolved: the work evidently had been compiled in a library, sizable enough to contain the diverse sources employed, by an educated and cultured individual who had, in fact, never set foot in the lands he described. For some scholars doubts still lingered. 'Mandeville' clearly had never been to Persia, India or China, but could it be proven that he had never been to the Holy Land? Be that as it may, another problem has remained: Mandeville's actual identity. One view holds simply that it will forever remain shrouded in mystery. A cautiously more optimistic explanation suggests the unknown author was a Benedictine monk, writing in an abbey in northern France. Whoever he was, the book's reputation hit rock bottom after the exposure. It was condemned as a deliberate imposture and 'Mandeville' accused of conscious mendacity. The travel *persona* he had created nonetheless continued to fascinate the general reader and scholar alike. Ironically, the more that the author's truthfulness was put to the test, the more his literary artistry was showered with praise. 'Mandeville' unwittingly had compiled an enduring masterpiece.

While Defremery and Sanguinetti were labouring over the Ibn Battuta manuscripts, a young Scottish scholar, W. Wright, edited and published in 1852 the one-volume adventures of Ibn Jubayr (d. 1217). He had set out from Granada in 1183 on the pilgrimage to Mecca and Medina and journeyed the first stage by the Mediterranean route to Alexandria. He returned via Iraq and Syria, then by sea again and arrived home after an absence of just over two years. His itinerary was shared a century and a half later, notably in Syria, the Holy Cities and Iraq, by Ibn Battuta. Wright had been alerted by his two Paris colleagues that Ibn Battuta cited his famous predecessor in his own description of the cities of Aleppo and Damascus. Wright thought that Ibn Battuta had possibly borrowed from Ibn Jubayr 'in other parts of his Travels' as well. For the moment Wright had spotted a more serious offence of literary misappropriation by a contemporary of Ibn Battuta called Abu al-Baqa Khalid al-Balawi. He had also composed an account of his pilgrimage to Mecca from his home in al-Andalus that occupied the years 1336–40. Wright noted that a great part of the descriptions of Alexandria, Cairo, Medina and Mecca al-Balawi had been taken *without acknowledgment* from Ibn Jubayr. Wright was outraged: 'It is true that al-Balawi has given the matter a somewhat different form by altering the arrangement of the several paragraphs, omitting all that could easily betray him, interweaving scraps of poetry and tradition ... but still the theft is barefaced and impudent enough.'[14]

Mid-nineteenth-century moral indignation was a world apart from the bitter legal battles that capture today's media headlines. Dan Brown learned this in London's High Court in 2006, much to the cost of the two plaintiffs who accused him, unsuccessfully, of plagiarizing his 'international bestseller' *The Da Vinci Code* from their work *Holy Blood, Holy Grail*. Wright's grievance, from today's perspective, is more modestly based upon al-Balawi's dishonourable failure to acknowledge whose work he was pillaging, and then trying to cover his tracks by inserting a few couplets of poetry or a story about the Prophet Muhammad into the plagiarized passages.

True, Ibn Battuta or perhaps his editor Ibn Juzayy did acknowledge Ibn Jubayr in the descriptions of Aleppo and Damascus, but only in recent years has the extent of that reliance been discussed in detail. One noted modern scholar, Charles Pellat, who wished to defend the superiority of Ibn Jubayr's work over that of Ibn Battuta, charged Ibn Juzayy with unscrupulous and shameless copying from the earlier travels. Other medieval authors, he conceded, had also exploited Ibn Jubayr, including the Moroccan traveller Muhammad al-Abdari, whose work (*c*. 1289) the barefaced al-Balawi had also dipped into.[15] We shall return to al-Abdari below. Pellat's annoyance seems oddly out of place, as Ibn Battuta had remarked frankly that although no description would do justice to the charms of Damascus, '*nothing is more brilliant than the language of Abu'l Hasan ibn Jubayr in speaking of her*', before proceeding to quote a passage directly from his book. Moreover, he added that he knew of a contemporary scholar who had also cited Ibn Jubayr and who said of him, '*He has indeed expressed himself with beauty and elegance in his description of Damascus.*' Here, so-called 'plagiarism' was simply intended as a tribute to the literary skills of their honoured predecessor, both men in agreement with the disgruntled Frenchman Pellat!

To date the closest examination of Ibn Battuta/Ibn Juzayy's use of Ibn Jubayr is that made by the late John Mattock, building on the observations of Gibb, Ibn Battuta's English translator. Mattock makes several points. First, the account of Aleppo in northern Syria is *wholly* taken from Ibn Jubayr. Second, the description of Damascus is achieved by *adapting*, *rearranging* and *adding to* the earlier account. Additional material chiefly comprises anecdotes of personalities Ibn Battuta met along the way. Third, a very lengthy section covers descriptions of Mecca and Medina, followed by the northward journey across Arabia to Kufa in southern Iraq; here Ibn Battuta adds the technique of *compressing* Ibn Jubayr's material. Finally, the route from Kufa to Baghdad, then north to Nasibin and Mardin, is described using all these methods, especially compression and, as Mattock reiterates, this section is taken *almost entirely* from Ibn Jubayr. Mattock has little doubt that Ibn Battuta did actually visit the places mentioned, yet the extent of the borrowing is conscious and involves to some extent an effort to disguise the fact. The underlying motive for this behaviour nevertheless remains puzzling despite our knowledge that Arab authors in the medieval period frequently borrowed 'silently' from other writers. Exceptionally of all people, Mattock asks, surely a traveller would be anxious to convey his own first-hand experiences and not rely on those of others. Moreover, why risk being found out by employing occasional direct quotations?

These perfectly reasonable concerns, however, lead Mattock to a harsh concluding judgement. He states: 'One thing certainly emerges. Whatever may be the case with the rest of Ibn Battuta's travel writings … as far as the sections to which I have referred here are concerned [Aleppo, Damascus, Mecca, Medina], *he cannot be relied on for a contemporary account.*'[16] Mattock notes that Ibn Battuta failed at times to update Ibn Jubayr, who had written 150 years earlier. For example, in the particular case of Baghdad, Ibn Jubayr's description of 1185, he says, simply could not apply to Ibn Battuta's city of 1327. Felipe Maillo Salgado, in his excellent Spanish translation of Ibn Jubayr, agrees and extends this judgement as well to all passages borrowed by Ibn Battuta which, he notes, 'only offer information valid for the years 1183–84 and not for the 14th century'.[17]

An alternative approach

Possibly the problem can be viewed in another way. Analysis of Ibn Battuta's technique of borrowing, or perhaps, more accurately, that of his editor Ibn Juzayy, shows that these passages can be qualified and defended as contemporary. Briefly, we can look first at how the use of compression of Ibn Jubayr's narrative can, in most cases, preserve the feel and sense of a contemporary witness. When Ibn Battuta had completed the pilgrimage rituals for the first time, he set out from Mecca by caravan to cross the Najd, heading towards Kufa in southern Iraq. By comparing the two

itineraries from Medina to Qadisiyya, one sees they correspond almost
exactly, as they share 24 stages on the route while each mentions one
place name which the other omits. Ibn Jubayr usefully records that it took
three weeks to cover the entire distance. Ibn Jubayr's account is reduced
by perhaps three-quarters, while Ibn Battuta adds a minor new detail here
and there and he does name two Bedouin princes he encountered along
the way. Nonetheless, Ibn Battuta clearly conveys to the reader the caravan leaders' fundamental concern in following this ancient pilgrim route,
namely to ensure the availability of adequate water and provisions. The
same conditions had confronted both travellers despite the century and a
half that separated their respective journeys. Ibn Battuta's description is
as valid as his predecessor's.

A more subtle means of altering reports from Ibn Jubayr may be illustrated by the description of Akka (Acre) on the Palestinian coast. This is
again a case of heavily compressing even Ibn Jubayr's own brief account.
Ibn Battuta adds one detail about Akka, namely that it is where the tomb
of the prophet Salih, mentioned in the Quran, is found. More importantly, he describes the town as now in ruins (*kharab*), the same term he
applies to Tyre, the next town on his itinerary. In Ibn Jubayr's day both
had been going concerns.

Baghdad

Now we may examine the description of Baghdad, the capital of the
Abbasid caliphs. This had been newly established on the western and eastern banks of the Tigris shortly after the overthrow of the Syrian-based
Umayyad dynasty in 750. Throughout the first generations of cultural glory
which subsequent political ups and downs tarnished but failed to extin-
guish completely, nothing prepared the city for the extensive destruction
and massacre of its inhabitants. Mongol warriors, led by Hulegu, grandson of the World Conqueror Genghis Khan, had already left swaths of
neighbouring Persia ravaged and desolate. Moving relentlessly westwards,
the campaign culminated in 1258 with the fall of Baghdad and the cruel
murder of the reigning caliph, effectively ending the Abbasid line.

That was not, of course, the city Ibn Jubayr had visited in 1185. The city
he did witness had evoked in him a moving lament on the faded splendour
of a great metropolis. 'Even though this aged city continues to be the capi-

tal of the Abbasid caliphate … most of its traces have gone leaving only a famous name. … In comparison with its former state, before misfortune struck it and the eyes of adversity turned towards it, it is like an effaced ruin, a remain washed out, or the statue of a ghost.'[18] As though seeking solace from the city's distressing ambiance, including the overweening vanity, corruption, lack of charity and hospitality of its inhabitants, Ibn Jubayr recounts at length his attendance at the assemblies of several religious jurists and preachers. They were unrivalled among all he had ever heard in the power they possessed over listeners' souls.

For his part, Ibn Battuta addressed the city ironically in the official manner as *Dar al-Salam* (the Abode of Peace) and as the capital of Islam. Then remarkably he continues, acknowledging Ibn Jubayr, to quote verbatim the very passage excerpted above. A long intervention follows from Ibn Juzayy who inserts selections from poets including the famous and long-deceased Abu Tammam (d. 845), whose verses uncannily seemed to foretell Baghdad's ultimate fate. Ibn Battuta resumed, repeating Ibn Jubayr's figure of 11 congregational mosques on both sides of the city that served the needs of the Friday prayer and sermon. But he adds that many other ordinary mosques and religious colleges by then all lay in ruins, whereas in his day Ibn Jubayr had noted the mosques could not even be estimated let alone counted and each of the 30 colleges all on the eastern shore rivalled princes' palaces.

Ibn Battuta echoes Ibn Jubayr's remark that the first quarters of Baghdad to be constructed on the west bank of the Tigris lay almost entirely in ruins. The mosque of the caliph al-Mansur, noted by Ibn Jubayr, still stood but the enormous hospital described as in full use in the earlier account was, according to Ibn Battuta, totally destroyed. The eastern side of Baghdad appeared to have fared better, with its famous Tuesday market still functioning. Both travellers mention the famous Nizamiyya college but, in addition to that, the newer Mustansariyya college, built after Ibn Jubayr's visit, is described briefly but fully by Ibn Battuta.

The contemporaneous nature of Ibn Jubayr's report is best reflected in the portrayal of the sumptuous but dramatically reduced circumstances of the caliph's existence. He had no *wazir* or first minister but only someone who supervised his property and another who inspected his harem. The army commander was a youthful eunuch whom Ibn Jubayr once saw in public. The caliph too had been spotted when he ventured out upon the river. His costly Turkish attire concealed the true state of affairs of his having to live on a fixed stipend.

Ibn Battuta's description closes with two significant and contemporary observations. First, he gives a list of all the Abbasid caliphs whose tombs were found in the Rusafa quarter of the city. The last was al-Mutasim, butchered, he recalls, by the Mongols who brought the caliphate to an end. The second point is that in the neighbourhood of Rusafa the domed tomb of Abu Hanifa (d. 767) was located. He was founder of one of the four Muslim schools of legal practice. Food was still provided for those who came and went but now, says Ibn Battuta, there exists no other place in all Baghdad where sustenance is provided as customary charity. Both notices symbolically marked the dramatic and violent end of an era – for the city itself and for Muslims generally. Ibn Battuta's report on Baghdad should, therefore, be read as a whole, taking into account its several components: borrowing from Ibn Jubayr, both verbatim and in other details, Ibn Juzayy's poetic interlude, and Ibn Battuta's independent sketch. Taken together, they indisputably express an authentic contemporary viewpoint.

The same approach may be applied to the descriptions of Aleppo and Damascus. Each commences with a passage, acknowledged and cited verbatim from Ibn Jubayr, together with other details, followed by a lengthy poetic interlude by Ibn Juzayy and then Ibn Battuta's own contribution. It is worth noting here that Ibn Juzayy's interventions throughout the travels overwhelmingly occur in two concentrations: according to Defremery-Sanguinetti's four-volume translation, the first concentration comprises the editor's comments scattered across volume one and the second occurs in the latter half of the final volume. Together the two groups contain 42 out of a total of 52 references to Ibn Juzayy.

Mecca and Medina

Let us now turn to Ibn Battuta's descriptions of Medina and Mecca. These include the most extensive portions borrowed from Ibn Jubayr. On Medina, Gibb noted two relevant sections of Ibn Battuta's account, one 'taken entirely from Ibn Jubayr but much abridged', the second 'for the most part abridged with some verbal changes' from the same source.[19] Together these two passages make up less than a quarter of Ibn Battuta's

account of the Prophet's city. In between the two abridged sections, he provides a potted history of the development of the holy mosque of Medina down to his own time, followed by a description of the mosque's pulpit (*minbar*), and then comments and anecdotes on the mosque's personnel and resident scholars of his own day. Ibn Jubayr's account is entirely original and contemporaneous. Ibn Battuta's is also original and contemporary *in its lengthy middle portion*. That section is framed between the borrowed, abridged descriptions of the sacred mosque and garden on the one hand and of the holy sanctuaries outside Medina on the other.

On Mecca, Gibb observed that the descriptions of the city and the religious ceremonies performed there are 'mostly taken from Ibn Jubayr, but with considerable rearrangement and some revisions'.[20] Concerning both Medina and Mecca Mattock asserts that 'with the usual qualifications of adaptation, rearrangement, and the addition of anecdotes and personalities, [Ibn Battuta's descriptions are] taken completely from Ibn Jubayr'.[21] As general observations neither is incorrect, but equally neither is sufficient. Ibn Battuta commences the lengthy chapter on Mecca with a very personal statement as to the spiritual significance for Muslims of their journey to the holy sanctuaries. From there, the structure of the narrative is strikingly similar to that just mentioned for Medina. That is, an original, middle section largely depicting contemporary personalities in Mecca is framed by abridged material from Ibn Jubayr placed before and after it. The 'before' section is complex and it is difficult to unravel the borrowed passages from Ibn Battuta's own interjections. The 'after' section easily traces the chief religious ceremonies through the months of Rajab, Shaban, Ramadan, Shawwal and Dhu-l Hijja, presented in a highly summary manner from the corresponding chapters in Ibn Jubayr's account. One interesting exception is a contemporary observation occurring in the final borrowed section of Ibn Battuta's Mecca narrative. His description of the Kaaba shrine's illustrious covering (*kiswa*), which by tradition was renewed annually, differs notably from Ibn Jubayr's account. Ibn Battuta describes the *kiswa* brought from Egypt as '*a jet black covering of silk lined with linen, and at the top of it is an embroidered band on which is written in white lettering: "Allah has made the Kaaba, the Sacred House, as a means of support for people"* [Q 5:98] *to the end of the verse*'. Ibn Jubayr describes the *kiswa*, supplied that year by the ruler of Iraq, as 'of a ripe green colour. ... In its upper part it had a broad red band (that ran around the Kaaba) upon which was written after "In the name of Allah, the first house of worship to be established for mankind was the one at Mecca" [Q 3:95]. On the other walls was written the name of the Caliph with invocations in his favour.'²² The difference in provenance of the *kiswa*, its colour and calligraphic decoration each reflected the altered Middle Eastern political conditions between the pre- and post-Mongol invasion periods.

Palestine

Pursuing the matter of 'plagiarism', we may now turn to a study that uncovered another source employed in Ibn Battuta's work. This is the travel book of the thirteenth-century Moroccan Muhammad al-Abdari briefly alluded to above. The analysis by Amikam Elad focuses upon four of the seven places in Palestine where both travellers' tracks coincided. In all instances al-Abdari's text is not acknowledged. The four locations are Hebron, Nabi Yaqin, Jerusalem and Ashkelon. Of the other three, two are near identical reports, while for Gaza, which lay on the frontier with Egypt, Ibn Battuta updates al-Abdari's very brief description. His very condensed version of al-Abdari's description of Hebron and nearby Nabi Yaqin still reveals its direct dependence. The same is true of Ashkelon. Ibn Battuta's description of Jerusalem, Elad states, contains only one authentic section which is the addition of names of scholars who lived there in his own times. He fails to note Ibn Battuta's claim that a patched cloak of a Sufi order had been bestowed upon him in Jerusalem. Nor does Elad draw attention to two additions made by Ibn Battuta, one relating to the destruction of part of the city's walls when the famous Muslim conqueror Saladin retook the city in 1195. The other detail concerned the provision of water to Jerusalem by the then governor of Damascus, Tankiz. Finally, the Israeli scholar omits Ibn Battuta's important initial point that Jerusalem contained the third-ranking mosque of Islam's Holy Cities after those of Mecca and Medina.

Depending upon how one imagines the territorial extent of Palestine in the mid-fourteenth century, there are at least eight other Palestinian towns mentioned by Ibn Battuta that were not visited by al-Abdari and cannot therefore be used for direct comparison. Elad's conclusion is thus strangely exaggerated. Leaving aside the parts Ibn Battuta borrowed from al-Abdari, he concludes, 'we are left with no more than two or three unconnected sentences, hanging in mid air … [thus] the majority of his descriptions of Palestine are not original'.[23] That is, like the parts Ibn Battuta borrowed from Ibn Jubayr, Elad argues that these sections also cannot be taken as contemporary accounts. True, Ibn Battuta's updating of al-Abdari appears less evident than his updating of Ibn Jubayr, with the exception of Jerusalem. Another exception, cited by Elad, requires further comment. In his description of the famous lighthouse in Alexandria harbour, Ibn Battuta begins with the observation that when he first saw it in 1325 one of its four sides was in ruins. On his return to Egypt years later, he described the lighthouse as being without access owing to its totally ruinous condition. The details borrowed from al-Abdari fall in between these two contemporary observations.

Despite the nature of the Gibb-Mattock-Elad conclusions which in effect can be misleading, the practice of borrowing among medieval authors in general remains an interesting if frustrating problem. To take only the handful of travellers discussed here: Why does Ibn Jubayr seem not to resort to the practice at all, except to make brief, attributed citations from al-Azraqi's *Meccan Annals* and Ibn al-Asakir's *History of Damascus?* Why do others, like al-Balawi, al-Abdari and Ibn Battuta (or perhaps Ibn Juzayy), borrow from Ibn Jubayr, with some passages acknowledged, others not? Why does Ibn Battuta openly borrow from Ibn Jubayr at times, but pass over al-Abdari in silence? It has also been suggested that there may exist a relationship between Ibn Battuta's travel narrative of Mali in central Africa and passages from a massive work by the famous writer-administrator Ibn Fadl Allah al-Umari (d. 1349). In the present state of our understanding of these texts, answers to these questions are not forthcoming. Elad appropriately reminds us that the verification of every detail of authenticity in Ibn Battuta would occupy several researchers each a lifetime. Yet, in the end, and judged by the standards of medieval convention, European or Middle Eastern, the charge of plagiarism seems beside the point: borrowing, re-writing or reworking, and invention in various guises, were widespread, accepted practices. Or, we may look at the matter from another angle and return to the example of 'plagiarism' in the *Travels of Sir John Mandeville*. That unknown author's reading list for his own work was formidable, possibly numbering as many as two dozen sources which he quoted from in greater or lesser degree.

His objective, nevertheless, was both consciously to borrow (or plagiarize) from contemporary and earlier European authors' works while, at the same time, attempt to create a travel account of interest and relevance to his own fourteenth-century audience. The key to the book's success, as C.W.R.D. Moseley has remarked, was in the handling of the author's *persona*.[24] If it seemed authentic to his first readers, the story he told would have been accepted as such as well. The same may be said of the *persona* projected by Ibn Battuta in his narrative. The succeeding chapters will set out to uncover for the modern reader that very aspect of *The Travels* by allowing the author, as far as is practicable, to speak for himself.

Ibn Battuta's odyssey

The matter of plagiarism has been dealt with in some detail above in order to show that while Ibn Battuta (and/or his editor Ibn Juzayy) did consciously borrow from earlier sources, observations of his own were equally consciously inserted into the narrative in order to retain its contemporary tone and character. The motive behind the choice to borrow any specific passage cannot, however, be determined. It may be the case, for example, that when the time came to dictate his adventures, the accounts of Ibn Jubayr or al-Abdari seemed convenient *aides mémoire* for the earliest journeys, those through Egypt, Syria and Arabia, of his three-decade odyssey. Moreover, borrowing from Ibn Jubayr's account of the Holy Cities may have been a silent tribute, just as borrowing for the account of Damascus was explicit, to his pious predecessor, fellow pilgrim, fellow North African Maliki and fellow traveller-reporter to the East. Ibn Battuta relied elsewhere, too, on oral rather than written sources. The account of the capture of Delhi and the history of the sultanate down to the time of his sojourn there was related to him by the grand *qadi* of Hind and Sind, Kamal al-Din Muhammad b. al-Burhan of Ghazna. His shorter account of Genghis Khan and the Mongol devastation of Transoxania and Khurasan likewise would have come from anonymous informants he had met.

Whatever Ibn Battuta's initial objective and motive for departing his native Tangier, whether as mere Mecca pilgrim or globetrotter-to-be, his travelogue, executed over 30 years later was inspired by a desire to inform and entertain his audience. His goal of giving pleasure and instruction was little different from that of his European contemporaries Marco Polo and John Mandeville, however contrasting in character these two were. And both were different from Ibn Battuta. Commentators and critics of Ibn Battuta's *Rihla* have, by and large, been content to debate various facets of the travels' authenticity. His desire to entertain and inform, and the way he chose to do so, have received as yet little attention.

A recent, brief reappraisal, full of fresh insight, takes a different tack and explores the *Rihla*'s 'conditions of intelligibility', that is, its principles of selection or 'what is worth telling and what is not'. In more technical jargon 'the grid disclosed by Ibn Battuta's techniques of representation … organize and delimit what he sees and how he sees it'. The author, Roxanne Euben, is, therefore, unconcerned with the text's authenticity but rather with what its author actually says. She conducts her inquiry into 'the ways in which Ibn Battuta represents the world and himself, [and] how these techniques of representation disclose a shifting sense of home and frontier, self and other'.[25] This is very helpful, as it allows Ibn Battuta to speak for himself – and about himself – and to be taken seriously. At a remove of several centuries, the modern reader will not, of course, receive the traveller's tales in the same manner as his original audience. Nonetheless, seen through Ibn Battuta's eyes at the time he dictated his adventures, today's audience may also enjoy and learn (hence the pedagogical goal of giving pleasure and instruction) much about the fourteenth-century world from the selections he has allowed us to participate in. Acknowledging Euben's stimulating analysis, the present treatment of the *Rihla* makes a further selection of Ibn Battuta's material and orders it in a manner quite different from Euben's while trying to remain within the spirit of that inquiry.

Ibn Battuta and his world

Nothing is known in detail of Ibn Battuta's early life and background apart from the allusions he disclosed in the *Rihla*. He was born in 1304 and was a native of Tangier in modern-day Morocco. He was, therefore, a Maghribi, or 'Westerner', as persons from that region of North Africa were known. He was a subject, too, of the ruler of the Marinid dynasty with its capital in Fez. Further, he was ethnically a Berber, a Sunni Muslim, trained in the Maliki tradition of Islamic legal practice, and acted in the capacity of *qadi* or religious judge on several occasions. He wrote in Arabic, the majority language of educated Muslims throughout the Middle East, and beyond; later, while in India, he claimed knowledge of spoken Persian as well. Together with his gender, this bundle of known characteristics constituted his identity, and he wrote foremost for an Arabic-reading North African public that would have included women.

Fourteenth-century Muslim domains (*Dar al-Islam*) occupied the middle portion of a longer period of dramatic expansion of the Islamic social order. Ibn Battuta was aware of Muslim losses in the West during the Christian *reconquista* of the Iberian peninsula (al-Andalus), yet was hopeful too of potential gains in the East which, indeed, were finally realized in Anatolia with the establishment of the Ottoman Empire. Symbolic of the historical ledger of geographic gains and losses were the conquest of Byzantine Constantinople by the Ottomans in 1453 and the fall of the last Muslim bastion in al-Andalus, Granada, to the Christians in 1492. Despite the gains and losses, during the half millennium between roughly 1000 and 1500, the *Dar al-Islam* on balance had expanded three-fold in size, well beyond its early Middle Eastern heartlands. Ultimately, a permanent Muslim presence – of greater or lesser significance – was established in regions which Ibn Battuta had visited in the course of his travels. In modern geographical terms, these areas included Central Asia, India, South East Asia, China and sub-Saharan Africa; he also managed a brief detour to Constantinople, the future Ottoman capital of Istanbul.

Ibn Battuta's life-share of the fourteenth-century world he encountered (he died in 1368) was politically one of relative calm and consolidation following upon the deluge of the Mongol invasions the previous century that culminated in the destruction of Baghdad and the Abbasid caliphate in 1258. The Mongol successor states, ruled by Genghis Khan's descendents who had converted to Islam, busily promoted conditions conducive to the movement of people, merchandise and ideas across highly porous cultural and linguistic frontiers. It was an era of an expanding common faith of Islam together with its own heterodox strands, coupled with vibrant minority communities of the two other Abrahamic traditions, Christianity and Judaism. Ibn Battuta also experienced Islam as a minority faith in India, where, however, Muslims were politically powerful and also where Islam was still marginal and not firmly grounded as in central Africa and in Sumatra and Java in South East Asia (modern Indonesia). In China, according to the Moroccan traveller, Muslims were found in their own merchant quarters in a few cities.

Drawing upon his lengthy and extended wanderings – his odyssey – what did Ibn Battuta finally judge worth recounting at journey's end? The traveller's view of the world was constrained to an extent by his background identity described above. In practice, it has been argued, there would be a continuing interplay between a sense of the familiar shaped by his native country (Morocco) and that of belonging to the much wider but less familiar Muslim community (*umma*) as the travel frontiers shifted ever further eastwards. Abderrahmane El Moudden addressed this matter in his essay on a traveller's awareness of integration into the *umma* as against his individual self-identity. Using later, sixteenth- and seventeenth-century Moroccan *rihla* narratives, he argued that through the *rihla* 'the traveller becomes more closely linked to the idea of the Muslim community as a whole, but at the same time learns what is specific to his own people and culture'. He concluded that the '*rihla* as text and as actual travel contributed to making both similarities and differences manifest, and left a sense of ambivalence that complicated what might be assumed to be a natural identification with the *umma*'.[26] One of the two travel narratives he examines is that of a well-known Moroccan traveller and scholar Abu Salim Abdallah al-Ayyashi (d. 1679). He journeyed to the Hijaz in 1649, 1653 and 1661 and remained for extended periods in Mecca and Medina as well as Cairo and Jerusalem. He set down his experiences in a two-volume travel narrative some time later. The final journey abroad lasted two and a half years, which seemed like a century, he said, so keen was he to return home. El Moudden concludes that 'Within the *umma*, therefore, al-Ayyashi felt closer identification to his own country and people, for the things that differentiated him from eastern peoples were exactly those that linked him to his compatriots in Morocco.'

As we shall see in subsequent chapters, ambivalence in Ibn Battuta's *Rihla* is less evident than this argument proposes. There are several reasons for this. First, the length of time he spent outside Morocco was about 28 years of near continuous absence, or 44 per cent of his life's span. Al-Ayyashi spent at best 20 per cent of his life abroad in three separate stages; he was always more at home – at home. Second, the geographical extent of Ibn Battuta's travels took him well beyond the Arab world to which al-Ayyashi's travels were confined. In fact, the Tangerine encountered two major Muslim language barriers, Turkish and Persian, during his travels, in the latter of which he acquired some competence; al-Ayyashi remained within the Arab-speaking world and hence his experience of the *umma* was restricted to it. In sharp contrast, after completing his first pilgrimage, Ibn Battuta began his venture to the fringes of the *umma*, first southwards to the East African coast and then on his journey through Anatolia, the Crimea and Afghanistan to India, where he remained for several years. After India, and an interlude in the Maldive Islands, he voyaged to Sumatra on the very eastern fringe of the *umma*. His return from China to Morocco was not the end of his travels. He was soon off again to visit the receding frontier of the Muslim presence in al-Andalus (Iberian peninsula) and then southwards again, this time into the West African Sudan. This was not a consciously conceived grand plan from the beginning but rather an enterprise that emerged from the travel experience itself. Once Ibn Battuta had decided that performance of the pilgrimage was not an end in itself – when and where that decision actually occurred is unclear – he, unlike al-Ayyashi, was constantly drawn to the *umma*'s frontiers, the very regions where the greatest differences from his native Morocco were found. Located as it was on the *umma*'s western-most fringe, he never rejected his Moroccan homeland but rather viewed it as one of several vital points on the perimeter of that greater formation of the *umma* that he had witnessed in his lifetime of travel.

To begin with, a question that might have been foremost in Ibn Battuta's mind as he commenced dictating his memories to Ibn Juzayy was how exactly to convey to his audience the trials and triumphs he had experienced during the many years and thousands of miles that had transformed his initial pilgrimage into a globetrotting odyssey.

CHAPTER 2

The Travels

The full title of Ibn Battuta's work highlights two separate but inter-related themes: cities together with their hinterland (*amsar*) and the journeys (*asfar*) to and from them. Focusing for now upon the second aspect, the journeys, we can inquire to what extent Ibn Battuta's narrative provides insight into the actual experience of travel. Coping with the forces of nature, the vagaries of fortune and of human behaviour, even descriptions of uneventful stages of a journey could combine to reflect those experiences and assist our imagining the living drama of medieval travel.

Not every traveller reveals himself the same way in the narrative. In some cases no 'personality' comes through at all. From among European travellers, one example is Benjamin of Tudela, noted briefly in the previous chapter, hailed as the greatest Jewish traveller of medieval times but who tells us nothing of himself or of his reactions to situations or people he met. Marco Polo's account is also impersonal, his lack of interest in relating anything about himself being 'one of the most obvious and remarkable characteristics of his Book'. John Larner adds that Polo's most striking feature is his 'silence about the difficulties and dangers he must have faced or about the character of the journeys he made'.[1] While we are made aware of certain risks along the way, such as shipwreck, piracy, brigandage or the threat from wild beasts, the dangers are only recorded in a second-hand, although at times entertaining, manner. The corsairs patrolling the coasts of Gujarat in India, he says, were the most notorious in the world, and he adds:

> Let me tell you one of their nasty tricks. You must know that, when they capture merchants, they make them drink tamarind and sea-water, so they pass or vomit up all the contents of their stomachs. Then they collect

all that they have cast up and rummage through it to see if it contains any pearls or precious stones. For the corsairs say that when merchants are captured they swallow their pearls and other gems to prevent their discovery.[2]

One of the most authentic voices of travel in this period was undoubtedly that of the Franciscan missionary Friar William of Rubruck. He preceded Marco Polo to the East and recorded for the Pope his journey to the court of the great Mongol Khan Mongke in 1253–55. The only detail of his personal appearance he notes is that he was always provided with a strong horse in view of his very great bulk. At the time, his party was crossing an arduous tract of empty steppe in late autumn and he expressly recalls this single occasion not daring to inquire whether his horse was proceeding at a comfortable pace or not:

> nor did I venture either to complain if it had difficulty in carrying me: each one of us had to bear with his lot. This gave rise to the most severe trials, in that the horses were very often exhausted before we could reach habitation, and then we would have to beat or whip them, or even transfer the clothing onto other pack-animals and exchange our mounts for packhorses, or sometimes two of us ride on one horse.

He continues:

> There is no counting the times we were famished, thirsty, frozen, and exhausted. We were given food only in the evening. ... Sometimes we were obliged to eat meat that was only half cooked or practically raw, since we lacked fuel for a fire: this happened when we were camping in the open country and halted at night, as then we were not really able to collect ox- or horse dung. We seldom discovered alternative fuel, except perhaps in some places a few briars.[3]

The first formal papal envoy to the Mongol court was William's Franciscan brother John of Plano Carpini, who had made the journey a few years previously, in 1245–47. He appended a brief account of his travels to his book *Historia Mongolorum* on Mongol customs and history. Remarkably, he was already advanced in years, aged 65, when he undertook his mission. In part, his age would explain the suffering he bore:

We feared that we might be killed by the Tartars or other people, or imprisoned for life, or afflicted with hunger, thirst, cold, heat, injuries and exceeding great trials almost beyond our powers of endurance – all of which with the exception of death and imprisonment for life fell to our lot in various ways in a much greater degree than we had conceived beforehand.[4]

This summary judgement on the entire two-year journey nonetheless lacks the vivid impact of William's attempt to convey something of the traveller's daily reality.

The travel account of Ibn Battuta's pilgrim predecessor Ibn Jubayr is singular for its descriptions of the perils at sea. He and his companion had contracted passage with the master of a Genoese boat headed for Alexandria in Egypt. They had safely and speedily sailed the near 400 miles from Minorca to Sardinia where the ship anchored for several days to take on fresh supplies. A short time after the resumption of their voyage, serious danger loomed, graphically described by Ibn Jubayr:

Early on the night of Wednesday the wind blew with violence upon us, throwing the sea into turmoil and bringing rain and driving it with such force that it was like a shower of arrows. The affair became serious and our distress increased. Waves like mountains came upon us from every side. Thus we passed the night, filled with despair, but hoping yet for relief in the morning to lighten something of what had fallen on us. But day came with increasing dread and anguish. The sea raged more, the horizon blackened, and the wind and rain rose to a tumult so that the sails of the ship could not withstand it and recourse was had to the small sails. The wind caught one of these and tore it, and broke the spar to which the sails are fixed and which they call the *qariyah*. Despair then overcame our spirits and the hands of the Muslims were raised in supplication to Great and Glorious God. We remained in this state all that day, and only when night had fallen did there come some abatement, so that we moved throughout it with great speed under bare masts, and came that day opposite the island of Sicily.

Once the ship had arrived safely to port in Alexandria, he uttered his gratitude for the divine assistance that had accompanied him thus far and prayed for continued guidance:

Praise be to God for the help and easement He bestowed. And Him, exalted is He, we petition to complete His benefactions in bringing us to our longed-for aim [pilgrimage to Mecca], and speedily restoring us, happily and in health to our native land. He indeed is the Benefactor. There is no God but He.[5]

Ibn Battuta nowhere describes in his narrative similar experiences of sea travel despite his quite lengthy voyages from southern Arabia to the East African coast and from India to China.

Ibn Battuta and Marco Polo were young men when they embarked on their adventures. In contrast to Marco who accompanied older male members of his family, Ibn Battuta initially set out alone. Years later, recounting his long absence abroad, he reflected upon the moment of departure to perform the pilgrimage at the Holy Sanctuary in Mecca and visit the tomb of the Prophet Muhammad in Medina:

> *I left my birthplace, Tangier, in June 1325. I departed alone, without the companionship of a fellow traveller, or in the assembly of a caravan. ... I resolved to leave my loved ones behind, female and male, and abandon my home as birds their nests. My parents were still alive and parting from them was a hardship I had to bear; indeed, we were all afflicted by the sorrow of separation. I was at the time twenty-two years old.*

On his return to Morocco in November 1349, just before reaching Fez, Ibn Battuta received the sad news of his mother's death from the plague. Such sentiment, simply expressed, is rare in the literature of the period. As we follow in his footsteps, there are numerous occasions along the way where his authorial 'I' commands the reader's attention as he reveals facets of himself as well as insights into the nature of fourteenth-century travel.

Ibn Battuta's first pilgrimage

The first stage of the journey ended with his arrival in Tunis. It was a testing introduction to travel overland: homesickness, illness and death accompanied him. The first major city mentioned is Tlemsen, where acquaintances advised him to join up with two official envoys who had just left the city heading east. He prayed, requesting God's guidance on the matter, spent three days procuring things he required, then set off in haste to catch up with the envoys in the city of Milyana. These were the dog-days of the year and the oppressive heat had struck them both down, causing a delay of ten days. Upon resuming their way, the condition of one seriously worsened. He died four days later and was quickly buried by his son in Milyana. Ibn Battuta then joined a party of merchants from Tunis heading home. They camped several days outside Algiers where they were rejoined by the remaining envoy's party. They then passed on to Bougie where the young Tangerine himself was attacked by a strong fever. He refused advice to rest saying that if God willed it, '*I will die on the road on my way to the Hijaz!*' The surviving envoy, a pious *shaykh* called al-Zubaydi, suggested Ibn Battuta sell his donkey and heavy baggage, enabling him to travel swiftly on another animal carrying only a tent, both of which al-Zubaydi would loan him. This was to avoid possible encounter with Arab bandits on the way. On the outskirts of Constantine, torrential rain forced them to abandon their tents and seek shelter in the city. The next day, the governor, one Abu al-Hasan, had noticed Ibn Battuta's dishevelled attire and ordered his clothes washed at home. He replaced the worn garment with a new one into which he had sewn two gold dinars. The gestures of al-Zubaydi and Abu al-Hasan were, Ibn Battuta gratefully noted, the first divine mercies and alms he had received on the pilgrim's path.

The first act of injustice he witnessed was the seizure of a sum of 3,000 gold dinars by the chamberlain of Bougie that was the property of one of the merchants of Tunis who had also suddenly died; he had entrusted the money to another merchant to pass on to his heirs in Tunis. At Bone some merchants decided to remain behind, fearing the rumoured dangers that lay ahead. The reduced party then headed in great haste towards Tunis, 150 miles distant. Once again fever struck Ibn Battuta and he was forced to tie himself into the saddle for fear of tumbling to the ground from weakness. It was all too much for the young traveller. On the outskirts of Tunis, a party emerged from the city to greet the well-known al-Zubaydi. Ibn Battuta was ignored, as he knew no one. A wave of loneliness engulfed him and he wept copiously. A fellow pilgrim comforted and accompanied him to lodgings in a *madrasa* in the city.

The next stage of the journey to Alexandria was – if anything – more eventful. In Tunis Ibn Battuta celebrated the feast at the end of the Ramadan month of fasting and joined in the communal prayers in an

open space outside the city. The head of the Hijaz caravan was chosen and
Ibn Battuta was put forward as its *qadi*, or religious judge, to give advice
on matters relating to the pilgrimage or other concerns brought to him.
His education in Tangier would have comprised study in the Quran and
traditions from and about the Prophet Muhammad. He would also have
read the standard books on Maliki legal practice which was then preva-
lent across North Africa and al-Andalus. One work may well have been
the legal tome entitled *Tabsira fi-l fiqh* of Abu al-Hasan al-Lakhmi, whose
tomb Ibn Battuta mentioned lying outside the city of Sfax. A hundred or
more horsemen accompanied the caravan from Qabis for a while and a
troop of archers was assigned to it for protection from marauding bandits.
On the road, before reaching the city of Tripoli, the second major religious feast, the Feast of Sacrifice, was celebrated, marking the end of the
pilgrimage rites at Mecca that year. Incessant rains and cold had dogged
the caravan and it remained in Tripoli for some time. During a brief
period before and after this stay in Tripoli, Ibn Battuta had contracted
and consummated a marriage with the daughter of a guild master from
Tunis, then separated from her following a quarrel with her father, then
contracted and consummated a second union with the daughter of a jurist
from Fez, for which occasion he threw a day-long feast for the whole
caravan. All of this was doubtless an attempt to seek some normalcy and
to overcome his continuing homesickness. Presumably with his new wife
in tow, for we hear no more about her, Ibn Battuta arrived in Alexandria, Egypt, in April 1326, almost ten months to the day after departing
Tangier.

The objective of the Holy Cities still lay before him. He decided to
adopt the land route to Mecca; that is, the one that ran along the west
bank of the Nile south from Cairo to the Red Sea crossing point at Aydhab
facing the Arabian port of Jiddah. Around this time, however, according
to his recollection years later, a change of heart concerning longer-term
plans in life was planted in his mind. This came about in a characteristic
Battutian way. He had stopped at Fawwa in the Nile Delta to visit the
tomb of a local *shaykh* and the hospice (*zawiya*) of another man of piety,
Abu Abdallah al-Murshidi. The *shaykh* greeted him warmly, offered him
food and generally treated him as an honoured guest among the others
present. He also asked Ibn Battuta to lead the prayers during his stay. At
bedtime the *shaykh* suggested that his guest sleep on the roof terrace in the

fresh night air freed from the oppressive daytime heat. Ibn Battuta dreamt that night of being swept away on the wings of a giant bird that bore him first to Mecca, then to the Yemen and finally towards distant Eastern lands before abandoning him in some dark and misty country. In the morning, after the other guests had left, the *shaykh* revealed his awareness of the dream which Ibn Battuta then related to him. Al-Murshidi's interpretation was that Ibn Battuta would visit the Holy Cities, wander about the Yemen, then Iraq, the lands of the Turks and India, where he would remain for some time, and meet his spiritual brother who would rescue him from danger. Ibn Battuta took his leave of the *shaykh*, who provided him with money and sweets for the road. Ibn Battuta observed, '*Since leaving him, I met nothing but good fortune on my journeys for the shaykh's blessed power* (baraka) *was always with me. I never met his equal anywhere.*'

Ibn Battuta's trip along the Nile from Cairo took about 18 days to reach Edfu. He stayed in other hospices and *ribats*, religious institutions that provided food and shelter for wayfarers or he accepted personal hospitality from pious *shaykhs* and judges. He preferred the shelter and company of religious colleagues both in Egypt and Syria to the more secular way stations or the merchants' hostelries (*funduqs* and *khan*s) such as those he saw while crossing the northern Sinai peninsula. Moreover, he notes that on the outskirts of Latakia in northern Syria there was a large Christian monastery, Dayr al-Farus, inhabited by many monks. Christians from all quarters came to visit, and Muslims too were welcomed with the standard fare of bread, cheese, olives, vinegar and capers. Further south along the Nile valley, at the city of Hu, Ibn Battuta lodged in another religious institution, a *madrasa* or college. There he met a famous man of piety, Abu Muhammad al-Hasani, who, upon learning the Tangerine's destination, predicted that he would not accomplish the sea crossing to Jiddah on this occasion but rather would complete his first pilgrimage only by way of the Syrian route from Damascus. Ibn Battuta chose to ignore the good *shaykh*'s caution. His two-week journey by camel across the desert with Arab guides to Aydhab was in vain. It was also, fortunately, uneventful, save for a night raid on their camp by hungry hyenas. When he discovered all available boats in Aydhab had been destroyed during hostilities between local forces and the Egyptian authorities, he perforce returned to the Nile at Qus and descended the river by boat to Cairo.

The weeks following were spent wandering through Syria as far north as Aleppo. The narrative of the itinerary is very confused and scholars explain its apparent randomness as a conflation of more than one journey later recalled by the traveller. As this portion adds little to our understanding of the travel experience, we rejoin Ibn Battuta in September 1326, when he did indeed set off from Damascus with the annual caravan to Mecca and Medina. In his eyes this was fulfilment of the *shaykh*'s 'miraculous' prediction rather than, more probably, the man's local knowledge of the Red Sea crossing. The traveller, now in his role of storyteller, was warming to his theme and we shall look to his account of miracles throughout his wandering years in another chapter. He had already expressed his conviction that Providence protects as well as provides; the *baraka* of pious individuals he met gave him a further comforting safety shield.

The caravan journey from Damascus to Mecca could take 45–50 days, including stopovers to water the camels and rest the pilgrims. Water, or the lack of it, was the travellers' constant concern, especially as south of Maan on the southern Syrian border the caravan entered a desert of which it was said '*whoever enters is lost, whoever exits is born (again)*'. Further south, four days were spent at Tabuk making preparation to cross a fearsome wilderness to al-Ula. Large reservoirs made of buffalo skins were filled to water the camels, and smaller water containers and bags made of goat skins were also filled; the ordinary pilgrim was charged a fixed sum for this service. The great caravan pressed on in haste from Tabuk, travelling night and day to pass through the so-called Valley of Hell and avoid the fate of many who in some years had perished from the hot, venomous wind called the *samum*. Ibn Battuta reports a rock inscription recording one occasion when the wind had dried every water source and the cost of a mouthful of the liquid reached 1,000 dinars, the last surviving vendor and buyer both perishing in the act of exchange. Al-Ula by contrast was a paradise of palm trees and springs. Pilgrims washed their clothes and prepared to leave behind in safe keeping any goods judged surplus to their needs. This was the furthest point permitted to Christian merchants from Syria for selling their goods to the pilgrims. Ibn Battuta does not say how long the journey had taken to the Prophet's city of Medina, nor when he entered Mecca for the first time. He only reveals the date of his departure from Mecca after completing the rites of his initial pilgrimage, which was in mid-November 1326.

Mecca revisited

It is evident from his description of the first pilgrimage that Ibn Battuta considered the whole journey from Tangier to Mecca as 'the road to the Hijaz'. Religious law stipulated that pilgrimage could be undertaken providing one had the material means and a sound constitution to endure the rigours of the venture. The pilgrim's experience commenced with the sincerely expressed intention to fulfil the obligation. Upon his first arrival at Mecca (and Medina), however, Ibn Battuta viewed the completed journey as something deeper, the fulfilment of an innate summons:

> *Of the wondrous doings of God Most High is this, That He has created the hearts of mankind with an instinctive desire to seek these sublime sanctuaries, and yearning to present themselves at their illustrious sites, and has given the love of them such power over people's hearts that none alights in them but they seize his whole heart, nor quits them but with grief at separation from them, sorrowing at his far journey away from them, filled with longing for them and purposing to repeat the visitation to them.*

Some pilgrims, therefore, decided to stay on in either of the Holy Cities for shorter or longer periods of time for reflection, to absorb the *baraka* of the holy site, to receive instruction from resident scholars or from those passing through, to instruct other visitors, or generally to enjoy the ambiance of continued contact with fellow Muslims from near and far. Those who stayed on were known as sojourners (sing. *mujawir*). They came from varied social and ethnic backgrounds and were supported from private resources, donations, charitable gifts or endowments.

When Ibn Battuta left Mecca in 1326, he may not yet have decided on the precise longer-term objective for his travels. He set out on the return leg of the Iraqi pilgrim route to Kufa (and thence Baghdad) which we have briefly touched upon in the previous chapter in comparing his description with that of Ibn Jubayr. During the next few months, he made excursions into Persia, visiting Shiraz, Isfahan and Tabriz, and from Baghdad he travelled to Mosul and Mardin in northern Iraq. Nonetheless his planning seems tentative, for by the time he reached Baghdad he was ready to return to Mecca on his second pilgrimage in 1327. He was no longer a novice wayfarer, although still just 23 years of age.

From Najaf, just outside Kufa, Ibn Battuta left the Baghdad caravan.

He joined a large convoy led by intrepid and powerful Khafaja tribesmen from whom he hired a camel and set out for Basra situated some ten
miles from the head of the Sea of Fars, or Persian Gulf. The precaution
was necessary, for as they passed through dense reed marshland, some
stragglers were picked off by Arab brigands and stripped of their possessions, including shoes and wooden bowls. The thieves then vanished into
the vast fortress of reeds. In Wasit, Ibn Battuta was guest of the founder
and head of the city's largest *madrasa*, who supplied him also with dates
and money. He took advantage of the caravan halt to visit the tomb of a
famous saint, a day's ride away, but found upon his return that his party
had just left for Basra, obliging him to chase after it.

The people of Basra, Ibn Battuta remarks, were noted for their acceptance of and generosity towards outsiders. The governor himself was
personally hospitable and treated him well. The party lodged in a *ribat*
named after Malik b. Dinar, a companion of the famous early ascetic
Hasan al-Basri (d. 728) whose tombs were also found in Basra. The *ribat*
normally had associations with frontier defence such as the fortresses built
along the shores of North Africa dating from the ninth century against
possible invading European Christian forces from the north shore of the
Mediterranean. Here Ibn Battuta clearly uses the term in the Moroccan sense, as an institution dedicated to the shelter of travellers and religious seekers. Another purpose was served by the *ribat* in the ancient city
of Nineva opposite Mosul on the Tigris. This was linked to the prophet
Jonas, whom people believed had prayed in its mosque. Worshippers from
Mosul sought the prophet's blessings and prayed there every Thursday
evening. Other *ribats* were found near Basra. Abbadan is described as a
large town built on a salt marsh with many mosques, shrines and *ribats*
for pious and devout worshippers. Ibn Battuta stayed in a *zawiya* next to a
ribat associated with the legendary al-Khidr and the prophet Elias. Before
arriving in Shiraz in south west Persia, Ibn Battuta describes a town on
the outskirts of which was located a *ribat* used by travellers; entrance
was only through an impregnable iron gate protecting the inhabitants,
visitors and shops, within which travellers were provided with all their
needs. Here is a hint of the fortress-type edifice of earlier times. The most
unusual building Ibn Battuta calls a *rabita* was found on top of a mountain on an island off the south Arabian coast, some four days' sailing from
the roadstead of Hasik.

The trip from Basra was made in a small boat, a *sunbuq*, sailing gently along the waterway linking the city to the sea. As they passed the sanctuary of another famous Sufi saint, Sahl b. Abdallah al-Tustari (d. 896), boat passengers scooped up bitter and salty water to drink, while imploring the saint's blessings. At Ubulla, Ibn Battuta changed to another small river craft (*markab saghir*) and sailed through the night, reaching Abbadan in the morning.

The *ribat* of al-Khidr and Elias was located on the bank of the waterway, just three miles from the town. Here Ibn Battuta learned of a renowned holy man who for years had come to fish nearby, securing sufficient food for a month and then vanishing until his next visit. Ibn Battuta searched the town and found him at prayer in a derelict mosque and sat beside him. When the holy man had finished, he took the young traveller by the hand and said, 'May God fulfill your wishes in this life and in the life to come.' That evening the group dined on a fresh fish sent by the holy man to Ibn Battuta. The thought came to him to remain the rest of his life in the *shaykh*'s service but, he says, a spirit of persistence towards his goal caused him to set the notion aside. Reflecting on the encounter while relating his adventures to Ibn Juzayy, Ibn Battuta remarked that he had indeed achieved his dream, travelling the earth to an extent greater than anyone else as far as he was aware. The unnamed man of piety had given Ibn Battuta his blessings that were fulfilled by God's protection, whose mercy he now sought during his remaining days on earth to enter paradise.

The journey through western Persia, forming a large loop on the map, was intended ultimately to bring Ibn Battuta to Baghdad. He reports that at every stage a hospice (*zawiya*) provided wayfarers with bread, meat and sweetmeats, food traditionally associated with Sufis. One followed a different custom by serving *harisa*, a cooked dish made from meat, wheat and clarified butter, eaten with thin, round flatbread. The hospice mission was different as well. Wayfarers were expected to stay a minimum of three days. Their wants were conveyed by the *shaykh* to the dozens of poor brethren associated with the *zawiya*, some married others celibate, who prayed together at the nearby tomb of the founding saint seeking God's mercy and generosity in meeting those needs. Most hospices were more modestly staffed but here, apart from a head *shaykh*, one summoned worshippers to prayer, another led the prayer, one tended to wayfarers' needs, while slaves and servants prepared the food. A city like Tustar had

a *zawiya* for poor brethren situated on the outskirts, while Ibn Battuta
stayed in the city itself at a *madrasa* which also had an adjoining *zawiya*.
This was a much larger establishment run by a descendant of the saintly
al-Tustari, assisted by a team of four men each in charge of a separate
function such as the *zawiya*'s income and expenditure, food supplies and
cooking. Each guest was given food enough for four persons which, in
addition to the standard fare, included peppered rice cooked in butter and
fried chicken. Ibn Battuta stayed for two weeks although unable to enjoy
fully the four-star experience it offered owing to a severe attack of fever.
Sadly, one of his companions died of fever and was buried there while a
second companion succumbed later.

The journey from Tustar to Idhaj, heading towards Isfahan, was
through '*lofty mountains*', but Ibn Battuta says nothing of the rigours the
company met along the way. In this portion of the narrative he evidently
confuses the first journey in 1327 with the one he took 20 years later.
However, on either or possibly both occasions, the region's current ruling
sultan gave him and his company money for expenses. Ibn Battuta had
been informed from a 'trusted source' that one of the pious sultans of
Idhaj had built 460 *zawiyas* throughout his realm, 44 alone in the capital.
In Isfahan he stayed for two weeks in a hospice that attracted many seeking the blessings of its founder, a student of the famous tenth-century
Sufi al-Junayd (d. 910). Ibn Battuta marvelled at its splendid marble baths
and walls lined with Qashani tiles; as it had been endowed for the service of God, one could enter and freely use its facilities. In Shiraz, a ten-
day journey from Isfahan, Ibn Battuta eagerly sought out its most famous
inhabitant, *shaykh* Majd al-Din Ismail in his own *madrasa*, the Majdiyya.
Majd al-Din's reputation for piety and generosity was widespread and Ibn
Battuta was no doubt grateful to receive his hospitality, including a fine
set of clothes and the offer of lodging in a small cell in the college.

From Shiraz, Ibn Battuta set out in the direction of Baghdad. Throughout his Persian interlude, he had been in constant contact with the memory
of saints past and present. The stories of the miracles (sing. *karama*) of the
shaykhs he met or was told about expand his narrative here well beyond
the sparser details devoted to his travel experiences. In the wake of these
adventures, Baghdad seemed dull by comparison. Ibn Battuta does not
say when he arrived, how long he stayed or where. The only *zawiya* offering food to wayfarers, he claims, was that attached to the tomb of the

famous jurist Abu Hanifa (d. 767); although he was in contact with *shaykhs* in the caliph's mosque on the eastern side of the Tigris, none is mentioned as having offered his visitor hospitality. Suddenly, however, he reports leaving the city to observe the mobile camp (*mahalla*) of the Sultan of Iraq, Abu Said. Several hundred persons were involved, from the sultan's troops, his ministers, mamluks and musicians, together with his wives, each accompanied by her own large entourage. The entire assembly would set out at dawn and encamp in the late forenoon. Ibn Battuta travelled for ten days with this armed court society and then joined one of the amirs for a further ten-day trip to Tabriz. Their visit was cut short with the amir's recall to camp, and Ibn Battuta laments that he had been unable to meet a single religious scholar in the famous city. Nevertheless, if all is well that ends well, Ibn Battuta had much to rejoice in. The amir informed the sultan of his companion's desire to journey again to the Hijaz. This resulted in gifts of garments, a mount and a written order to the governor of Baghdad to supply provisions and mounts for the next Baghdad caravan.

Over two months remained before the caravan's departure, so Ibn Battuta set off leisurely north to Mosul, camping overnight along the Tigris riverbank where in many parts continuous villages and cultivated fields made progress pleasant. At Mosul he was hosted at home by the governor who paid all his expenses while in the city. At Sinjar, to the west of the Tigris, he met a devout ascetic famed for his miracles, staying in a *rabita* on top of a nearby mountain. Ibn Battuta received his blessings and a gift of silver coins which he kept with him until infidel Hindus robbed him in India. Finally at Mardin, where he stayed with a *qadi*, he turned back towards Mosul where he joined a caravan of pilgrims heading for Baghdad. There he found the Hijaz caravan ready to depart.

As promised him, Ibn Battuta received half space in a camel litter with provisions and water for four persons – comfort enough if one were in a fit state to enjoy it. For about one month, from Kufa to Mecca, and during performance of the pilgrimage rites, Ibn Battuta suffered fits of diarrhoea. Several times a day he had to be lowered from the litter and then helped back into it. On arrival in Mecca he was able to perform the circuits around the Kaaba, although in his weak condition he could only do so seated; the ritual of 'running' between Safa and Marwa he managed on horseback. The station of Arafat that year was on 26 October 1327 and, as the assembly encamped at Mina, his strength began to return and he sensed he was on the mend. The cumulative effects of an earlier fever attack and a bout of diarrhoea in Isfahan, caused by eating preserved watermelon, combined with the strain of travel had made him susceptible to the more severe upset on the pilgrim road. His decision to remain in Mecca as a *mujawir* was therefore sensible. '*I lodged the entire year in the madrasa Muzaffariya*,' he says, '*while God cured me of my illness; life was pleasant devoting myself entirely to performing pious exercises and several lesser pilgrimages* (umra).' Sojourners like Ibn Battuta were heavily dependent for their subsistence upon the large sums of alms sent to the Holy Cities by the rulers of Egypt, Iraq and the Yemen.

In the event, Ibn Battuta stayed on in Mecca and completed the pilgrimages of 1328 and 1329 as well. During the pilgrimage season the following year, 1330, major disturbances broke out between the governor of Mecca and the head of the guard of the Egyptian sultan. Fighting spilled over into the sacred area of the Kaaba, prompting the *qadi, imams* and the *mujawirun* to protest against the violence and venturing into the fray with Qurans held above their heads in order to calm matters. Eventually pilgrims were able to enter the city, recover their belongings and depart. It was probably these troubles that determined Ibn Battuta's decision to leave as well. The next stage of his travels was about to commence, although the decision to undertake his great adventure eastwards to India lay ahead of him.

Southward bound

From Mecca to the Yemen Ibn Battuta had the choice between one of two land routes to the south or the open waters of the Red Sea. By opting to sail from the port of Jeddah, he reveals for the first time his unease about sea travel. He had good reason to be concerned. The type of vessel available was called a *jalba*, commonly used by pilgrims making the crossing to Aydhab opposite on the Egyptian coast; this was the place he had attempted unsuccessfully to sail from on his first pilgrimage. Ibn Battuta's famous predecessor Ibn Jubayr was well experienced with the craft and the crossing and has left a vivid description of both in his account covering the summer of 1183. The *jalba*'s hull was made of wooden slats sown together with cord made from the twisted threads of coconut fibre; the hull was caulked with palm wood shavings and then smeared with grease or shark oil to soften the wood as protection from impact against reefs. Nailed hulls were rigid and more liable to splinter upon impact. Ibn Jubayr notes further that the sails, woven from tree leaves, were by contrast badly designed and structurally unsound. There were other dangers in sailing these craft which had nothing to do with their manufacture. First was the avarice and indifference of the owners, who packed their boats with pilgrims 'like chickens in a coop'. A saying common among the owners was that since they produced the boats, pilgrims were responsible for their lives. The second danger was the weather, the shifting winds, sudden squalls and tempests that drove the boats every which way. In all, writes Ibn Jubayr, 'the journey from Jeddah to Aydhab is most calamitous for pilgrims save those few of them whom the Great and Glorious God preserves' and brings relief in their destitution.

We have seen how Ibn Jubayr's account was used by Ibn Battuta and his collaborator Ibn Juzayy. One could speculate that Ibn Battuta may have had occasion to read Ibn Jubayr's travels before setting out from Tangier on his own. Ibn Jubayr's descriptions of his Mediterranean journeys are unparalleled in the whole of medieval Arabic literature; an experienced seaman, he knew at first hand the terrors of storm, shipwreck and narrow escape which he repeatedly attributes to the Almighty's assistance. If Ibn Battuta had not had access to a manuscript copy, he would certainly have heard seamen's tales enough to make him wary of boats and the sea. The acquired sea lore might then have determined his initial choice to take the land route to Alexandria rather than Ibn Jubayr's more rapid but dangerous alternative sea route. As for his setting out from Jeddah, Ibn Battuta was at first put off boarding one *jalba* because a passenger was taking a number of his camels with him; he therefore embarked on another *jalba* in the company of some Yemenis carrying only their goods and provisions.

For two days all went well and then, as if on cue, '*the wind changed and drove us off our intended course. … The waves of the sea entered among us in the vessel, and the passengers fell grievously sick.*' Driven to the opposite African shore between Aydhab and Sawakin, the boat managed to reach shore safely where they discovered a reed hut in the form of a mosque; inside they found many ostrich shells filled with water to quench their thirst and which enabled food to be cooked. African Beja tribesmen escorted the party for two days until they reached Sawakin, from where they set

sail again for the Yemen. Owing to the danger of rocks and reefs in the
area, sailing was possible only during daylight hours and the anchor was
dropped from sunset until dawn. Six days' journey back across the Red
Sea brought them to the sheltered port of Hali which itself lay some
distance inland. Here Ibn Battuta was guest of the sultan, whom he had
met in Mecca on pilgrimage. Proceeding along the Arabian coast by boat,
Ibn Battuta landed at the roadstead leading to the major city of Zabid
and thence eventually, via Taizz and Sanaa, to the southern port of Aden.
Remarkably no mention is made of the mountainous nature or difficulties
of the journey from Zabid.

Indeed Ibn Battuta's account covering the next several months, until
his return to Mecca for the pilgrimage in 1332, is nearly void of mention
of travel experiences, although of course he relates many valuable details
of the places visited. This may seem the more remarkable as he sets off
on a major sea voyage from Aden to East Africa, stopping at Mogadishu, Mombasa and Kulwa, returning to Zafar on the south Arabian coast
situated about a month's journey eastwards from Aden overland through
desert. No dates are given except for the years he left Mecca (1330) and
next returned to it (1332). The sea voyage would have been made to accommodate the monsoon seasons, the north east winds in January–February
1331, enabling the journey south, and the south west winds in late April and
early May for the opposite direction. The total time lapse between leaving Aden and arriving at Zafar has been roughly estimated at six months.
After leaving Zafar, Ibn Battuta sailed along the southern Arabian coast
towards Oman. Thereafter, his itinerary from Oman to Mecca is very
confused, one likely solution being that he combines here reminiscences
from two separate journeys, that of 1331 and the later one in 1347.

One incident, however, is worth recounting. At the southern end of
Oman lay the anchorage and large village of Sur. From there Ibn Battuta
could see the city of Qalhat, actually some 10–15 miles away, although
it appeared to be but a nearby village. He decided upon a walk to spend
the night there. Ibn Battuta was accompanied by a fellow passenger and
pilgrim from India, together with a guide hired from among the boat's
crew. He left his belongings with friends on the boat, taking a few items
of clothing for the 'excursion', which the guide carried. Ibn Battuta notes
pointedly that he equipped himself with a spear, suspecting the guide's
intention of robbing them. In fact, their greater foes were thirst and

exhaustion, as they had to traverse river beds, hills and ravines, considerably increasing the distance covered. Night fell, the Indian pilgrim was ill and incapacitated and Ibn Battuta, although also worn out, was determined to put on a show of strength for fear of the guide. Ibn Battuta with spear at the ready stayed on watch the whole night and at daybreak he sent the guide to fetch water. More ravines and steep slopes lay before them and they arrived at Qalhat in total exhaustion. Ibn Battuta remarked, '*My feet had become so swollen in my shoes that the blood was almost starting under the nails.*' Fortunately, the governor was a man of generous nature and Ibn Battuta (and presumably the Indian) remained with him for a week, during which, says the Tangerine ruefully, '*I was powerless to raise my feet because of the pains they had endured.*'

The pilgrimage took place in September that year, 1332. In the intervening two years since his last performance of the rites, Ibn Battuta must have been seriously contemplating his future ventures; as the giant bird in his Egyptian dream had borne him from the Holy Cities, then south to the Yemen and thence to the East, he would have pondered how best to reach India, on the outer reaches of the Muslim world, from its spiritual centre in Mecca.

To the Indus valley: Anatolian adventures

'*When the pilgrimage ended, I went to Jeddah intending to sail to the Yemen and India. But that was not decreed for me.*' Thus Ibn Battuta begins the account of the next major stage of his travels. It is perplexing, however, because his stated intention contrasts with what actually happened. Had he initially wished to sail to India from Aden, he already knew it to be the port from which Indian merchants sailed home in great ships. He claims that he was unable to find a companion or guide to accompany him, an unlikely prospect in the wake of the pilgrimage season, at least as far as the Yemen. So he hung around Jeddah for about 'forty days', an expression simply meaning 'quite a while'. He was indecisive and becoming restless. A boat master he encountered wished to sail to the port of Qusayr on the Egyptian coast; Ibn Battuta went aboard to inspect its condition – it might have been a *jalba*, but he uses only the general term for boat, *markab* – and did not like what he saw. His decision to remain behind was, he said, '*an act of providence of Almighty God*' for the boat floundered in mid passage, the master and some merchants escaping in a small boat, while about 70 pilgrims perished in the treacherous seas. After that he sailed aboard a *sumbuq* to make the dreaded Aydhab crossing. Strong winds drove them south to a roadstead on the African coast which resulted in a nine-day overland trek – escorted again by Beja tribesmen – to their destination. Committing himself to this route, Ibn Battuta had decided to undertake the far longer journey overland to India, although this would take him to many important cities through lands within Muslim dominions.

From Aydhab, Ibn Battuta retraced his route of 1326 down the Nile valley to Cairo. There he met al-Hajj Abdallah al-Tuzari, who would become his travel companion for many years until his death in India. From Cairo they made their way across the Sinai and along the Syrian coast to Latakia. Here they boarded a Christian merchant vessel from Genoa. After some days with a favourable wind they landed at al-Alaya on the southern Anatolian coast in present-day Turkey. Ibn Battuta remarks on the Christians' generosity, not charging him or his Muslim companions passage for the journey.

In his day Anatolia was known as *Bilad al-Rum* (Land of the Greeks) and, in his own words, was *'one of the finest regions in the world; in it God has brought together the good things dispersed through other lands'*. Nevertheless, our traveller's Anatolian adventures do reflect another world and himself as one consciously crossing a frontier. It was his first venture into a land whose Muslim population was largely Turkish. Muslims overall were likely still a minority, perhaps the largest and a rapidly increasing one. The first migrations of Turkish pastoralists from inner Asia had begun to pass through Transoxania into Persia early in the eleventh century. Led by the Turkish clan of Saljuks, who were already Sunni Muslims, they entered Baghdad in 1055, ousted the caliphate's Shia rivals and thereby restored the dignity of Abbasid rule, if not its former power. Several branches of Saljuks came to dominate the Middle East, the longest surviving of them being the Saljuks of Rum based in southern Anatolia. Following a decisive defeat of a Byzantine army in 1071, the Saljuks founded their capital, Konya, the ancient city of Iconium, in 1081. Further penetration of Turkmen groups led to the creation of a number of separate principalities, chiefly in the interior Anatolian plateau. Another major defeat of Byzantine forces in 1176 effectively ended Christian hopes of restoring their former dominion over the whole of Anatolia. With the

Mongol invasions of the Middle East in the next century, the Sultan of Konya became their vassal from 1242 and in 1307 the sultanate collapsed in circumstances that remain obscure. William of Rubruck, who passed through the region in 1253, estimated Muslims then to be only a tenth of the population. Twenty years later Marco Polo said Anatolia, or 'Turkey' as he called it, was inhabited by three 'races': the Turkmen, a primitive people who worshipped Muhammad, spoke a barbaric tongue and lived off their flocks, and the Greeks and Armenians who mingled with the Turkmen in villages and towns and engaged in commerce and crafts as well as agriculture. A quarter of a century after the Saljuk downfall, Ibn Battuta observed that there were still large numbers of Christians in the region living under the protection (*dhimma*) of Turkmen rulers to whom the *jizya* and other taxes were paid. That an ethnic mingling and religious transformation of Anatolia had been long under way was certain, although it is impossible to judge the precise mix and religious composition of the population at any given stage.

It was not cultural shock Ibn Battuta experienced, as has been suggested. True, he was confronted suddenly by the strange ways of the Turks, but he describes his encounter first by the positive contrast expressed in the saying, '*Blessing* (baraka) *in Syria and kindliness* (shafaqa) *in al-Rum*', explaining that this referred to the people of the land, the Turks. He continued:

> *Wherever we stopped in this land, whether at hospice* (zawiya) *or private house, our neighbours, both men and women (who do not veil themselves) came to ask after our needs. When we left them to continue our journey, they bade us farewell as though they were our relatives and our own kin, and you would see the women weeping out of sorrow at our departure.*

He had not abandoned his critical temperament, however, as he roundly decried the Turks' widespread practice of consuming *hashish*.

For the first time in his travel narrative Ibn Battuta reports upon a Christian presence and does so in a matter-of-fact, detached manner. He saw them in a variety of contexts, and although direct contacts were sporadic the overall picture reveals several details of interest. In the great city of Antalia he notes that each group of inhabitants lived separately from the others. Foreign Christian merchants resided in the harbour quarter encircled by a wall, the gates being shut at night and during the Muslim

Friday congregational prayers. The ancient Greek Christian community lived in another quarter enclosed also by a wall, the Jews the same. The local Muslim ruler, his government officers and troops occupied a walled township set apart from Antalia itself. The remaining Muslim inhabitants lived in the city proper with its Friday mosque, college, bath houses and large bazaars. A great wall surrounded both this Muslim section and all of the others.

In Ladhiq, the ancient Greek city of Laodicaea, he marvelled at the renowned cotton fabrics made there. Most of the artisans were Greek women whose distinctive headgear was the large turban while the men wore tall pointed hats coloured red or white. Fine fabrics were also made in Arzanjan, whose population was mainly Armenian. Ibn Battuta admired a large church in Aya Suluq, the ancient Ephesus, a city and monument much cherished by Greeks. The city's Friday mosque was of *'unequalled beauty'* and had once been a church visited by Greeks from all over. In the small town of Kainuk, inhabited by infidel Greeks (*kuffar al-rum*), Ibn Battuta and his party could only escape the misery of cold and wet weather by renting accommodation for the night in the house of an elderly Greek lady (*kafira*). At Sanub on the southern shore of the Black Sea, he counted a number of Greek villages whose inhabitants lived under protection of the Muslim governor. From there his party hired a Greek vessel to take them across the Black Sea to the Crimean side. At an unscheduled roadstead they landed, found a church nearby occupied by a lone monk and spent the night within. The next morning one of the company hired a horse-drawn wagon from Turkish tribesmen who were Christian. The entire party proceeded to al-Kafa, the ancient Theodosia, a major Genoese trading centre. Once lodged in a mosque, there occurred a scene of burlesque heroics. In this city of infidels (*kuffar*) Ibn Battuta was startled out of his wits to hear for the first time in his life church bells, or rather clappers, 'ringing' all about. He rallied his companions to ascend the minaret, chant the Quran and loud praises to Allah and recite the call to prayer. At this, the local religious judge (*qadi*) appeared, armed with breastplate and sword, alarmed for the visitors' safety. The moment passed and with calm restored, Ibn Battuta sighed with relief that *'no evil befell us'*.

Exercising his critical tongue once again, Ibn Battuta condemned the inhabitants of Ladhiq for making no attempt to eliminate an especially odious practice exercised by '*the whole population of the region*', Muslims in particular, of buying beautiful Greek slave girls and plying them in prostitution, the girls paying a fee regularly to their masters. He was particularly incensed at the immoral behaviour that took place with the girls in the public baths. On the other hand, domestic slavery, which gave the master sexual access to his slave girls, was a widespread practice, one that no Mediterranean country was unacquainted with, yet without moral stain attached to it. He recorded purchasing two Greek slave girls, one in Aya Suluq who was a virgin (*bikr*) and the other in Baghama, named Marghalita.

In truth, Ibn Battuta was moving up in the world. The list of gifts presented to him personally, mainly by the rulers of towns and cities to whom he invariably gave the title of sultan, was evidence of his increasing material status. Money of unspecified amounts, horses, clothing, provisions and other vaguely termed 'hospitality-gifts' are commonly mentioned items. It was the custom of rulers to treat visiting scholars with deference and 'humility' (*al-tawadia*). Ibn Battuta's learning embraced knowledge of the Islamic sources but by now also included a fund of information gleaned from the people he met and the places he visited on his travels, especially the Holy Cities. His companions, of course, benefited as well. The Sultan of al-Laranda sent them quantities of food, fruit and sweetmeats in silver platters, together with candles, robes and horses. In Qaisariya, Ibn Battuta met the wife of a powerful prince in Anatolia, '*a generous and excellent princess*', who invited them to dine and afterward provided them with gifts of a horse, bridle, robe of honour and some money, with her apologies that it was not more. In Birgi they hit the jackpot. The sultan insisted on entertaining the company in two of his residences, one on a mountain retreat outside the city, the other in the city itself. Their stay of two weeks was with full board plus extras, and upon leaving Ibn Battuta alone was presented with 100 *mithqal*s of gold, 1,000 silver *dirhams*, a complete set of clothes, a horse and a second Greek slave called Mikhail; he had been presented with his first slave in Yazmir. The horse was possibly a replacement for the one he had lost during a bitterly cold night while visiting the sultan's mountain residence. The only other capital loss he mentions was a horse, saddle and bridle stolen by Turkmens they had camped with overnight in one of their pastures.

Ibn Battuta describes the Sultan of Bursa as the greatest, wealthiest

and most powerful of all the Anatolian Turkmen kings. He was Urkhan
Bak, son of the deceased Sultan Othman. He gave Ibn Battuta a considerable sum of money and in Yaznik he was entertained by the sultan's wife
who presented him with gifts as well. Ibn Battuta could not have known,
or even have imagined that about 120 years later, Urkhan's descendants
would conquer Constantinople (1453) and make it the illustrious capital
of the mighty Ottoman Empire. The Anatolian interlude seemed to pres-
age the prosperous years that lay ahead for him in the Delhi sultanate of
India.

Undoubtedly the most immediate and lasting impression of *Bilad
al-Rum* upon Ibn Battuta was made by the associations of the Akhiyya.
They were a special example of the quality of kindliness he claimed as
the essence of Anatolia. At the same time, they exposed the major sense
of difference or cultural barrier he experienced during these months, the
fact that he could not communicate in Turkish or, for that matter, in
Greek. Ibn Battuta's description of the Akhiyya, whose members were
called *fityan* and the leaders *akhi*s, highlights, moreover, a many faceted
phenomenon found

> in all the lands of the Turkmens of al-Rum, in every district, city and village.
> Nowhere in the world are there to be found any to compare with them in
> solicitude for strangers, and in ardour to serve food and satisfy wants, to
> restrain the hands of tyrants and to kill the agents of [corrupt] police and the
> thugs who join them. An Akhi, in their language, is a man whom the assembled
> members of his trade, together with others of the young unmarried men and
> those who have adopted the celibate life, choose to be their leader. That is also
> called al-futuwwa. The Akhi builds a hospice [zawiya] and furnishes it with
> rugs, lamps and what other equipment it requires. His associates work during
> the day and gain their livelihood, and after the afternoon prayer they bring
> him their collective earnings. With this they buy fruit, food and the other things
> needed for consumption in the hospice.

Their political activities suggest a distant or indifferent central authority
yielding space for the influence of these dedicated local urban groups.
Ibn Battuta's lodgings in Nakda was the hospice of a young *akhi* (*al-fata
akhi*) who was also governor of the city. Indeed, he notes that in places
where no sultan resided, an *akhi* was its effective master. *Akhis* themselves
could be from distinct social backgrounds: Ibn Battuta first met an *akhi* in

al-Alaya, a cobbler by trade, while, in contrast, the *akhi* of Qaisariya was a notable whose followers included many of the city's leading figures and their hospice was correspondingly rich in furnishings and lavish in hospitality. Ritual varied little from one hospice to the next, After a substantial meal, the recitation of the Quran was followed by group dancing and chanting (*sama*). These were emotional occasions for Ibn Battuta, who describes the beauty of the Quran reciters' voices that worked upon the soul, humbled the heart, made the skin tingle and brought tears to the eyes. He makes no specific comment on the dancing and chanting, judged by some scholars as of dubious spiritual value, if not altogether forbidden. One imagines Ibn Battuta swept along by the fervour of these occasions despite being unable to communicate with his hosts unless an interpreter were present.

The matter of the language barrier was a recurring problem. It had a lighter and darker side to it. In normal day-to-day intercourse, Ibn Battuta would rely on the presence of a religious scholar, whether Arab or Turk, such as a *qadi, khatib* or *faqih* (judge, preacher, jurist) whose knowledge of Turkish and Arabic permitted them to act as useful intermediaries. One occasion produced tri-lingual confusion at an *akhi* hospice. A Persian jurist whom the *akhis* believed spoke Arabic was called upon to interpret. He addressed Ibn Battuta in Persian but clearly did not understand his response in Arabic. So, to cover his ignorance, the Persian explained to his *akhi* host that Ibn Battuta spoke the ancient Arabic tongue while he knew only 'modern' Arabic! The *akhi* was suitably impressed and explained to his members that their guests spoke the language of the Prophet and must be treated with great respect. Alternatively, a Turk who had been on pilgrimage and had a basic grasp of Arabic was deemed a suitable translator. On the road to Qastamuniya Ibn Battuta had engaged one such pilgrim to act as interpreter for the ten-day journey. Provided with expenses for the family he left behind and with the promise of generous recompense, the man turned out to be a rogue. He converted surplus provisions into profit for himself and resorted to blatant theft of expense money. Totally dependent upon his Turkish, the company at last demanded to know how much he stole each day from the expenses. His frank answer of the precise amount caused laughter among the company – the only means of making the best of an impossible situation.

Travel on the road had its dramatic moments too. On one occasion a heavy overnight snow fall had wiped out all trace of the road to Maturni in mountainous northern Anatolia. Ibn Battuta's party followed on horseback in the snowy tracks of their Turkmen guide over the rugged terrain. Part way the guide demanded payment. Ibn Battuta gave him some *dirhams* and with that he fled and abandoned them to their fate. Sunset was approaching and Ibn Battuta decided to set out for help, as he alone possessed a strong mount. Through great good fortune, a providential God and an extraordinary coincidence in discovering an acquaintance who understood Arabic in a hospice of poor brethren, Ibn Battuta once again surmounted the language barrier and rescued his companions.

River crossings often spelled danger too. Ibn Battuta's party had witnessed a Turkish woman on horseback accompanied by a servant attempt to cross a river. The woman was thrown in midstream and the servant's effort to save her cost him his life. Would-be rescuers instructed Ibn Battuta to move downstream to the normal crossing point. There a contraption of four blocks of wood tied together carried the saddles, baggage and passengers as they were pulled across the river by men on the opposite bank; the horses were led across swimming.

Ibn Battuta was now nearing the end of his Anatolian journey, which had lasted an estimated 15 months in all. Before reaching the southern Black Sea port of Sanub (Sinope), a month or so was spent in the fine city of Qastamuniya. Ibn Battuta's company had by now increased to ten persons and fortunately the city was abundantly stocked with food at very low prices. At Sanub, as mentioned briefly above, they passed another few weeks and then awaited a favourable wind to carry them in their hired Greek vessel to the sea's north shore and out of Asia Minor. Ibn Battuta's last experience of this chapter of his travels was the violent storm that struck the ship in the open sea three days out of port and nearly drove them back to it. A second storm further delayed the crossing, but landfall was at last safely achieved. Ibn Battuta may have given a passing thought to a traveller of pious disposition he had met in Bursa, one Abdallah al-Misri. He had '*roamed the earth*', Ibn Battuta recalled years later in his travelogue, proudly adding that he had outdone the Egyptian by visiting distant places the other had never seen. But for the moment, China, Ceylon and West Africa lay well in the future. Even Constantinople was a distant prospect.

Guest of the Golden Horde

Ibn Battuta imagined the world politically divided among seven great and mighty rulers. The premier sovereign was, of course, the Sultan of Morocco who had commissioned the recording of his travels. Thereafter he lists the Mamluk Sultan of Egypt and Syria; the Sultan of the 'two Iraqs', that is Arab and Persian Iraq or, in modern terms, Iraq and Iran; the Sultan of Turkistan and lands beyond the Oxus River; the Sultan of India and the Sultan of China. Finally, there was the Sultan of the Golden Horde, Muhammad Uzbek, whose capital, New Sarai, was located on the lower Volga. It says much for the global impact of the Mongols' rise and rapid expansion that four of these seven leaders, sultans of the Golden Horde, the two Iraqs, Turkistan and China, were descendants of Genghis Khan.

New Sarai and Muhammad Uzbek became Ibn Battuta's first objectives of this next stage of his adventures. His natural curiosity, fed now by a confident ambition, decided this course of action. While in Baghdad, he reports seeing in public the youthful Sultan of the two Iraqs, Abu Said, *'the most beautiful of God's creatures in his features'*. Later he was introduced to him during his return from Tabriz to rejoin the sultan's large entourage (*mahalla*). This brief encounter, however, may also have planted in his mind the notion of meeting in person another of the great rulers of the age. He accomplished this end through the governor of the Crimea, Tuluktumur, who had honoured Ibn Battuta with gifts and, coincidentally, was about to set off to join his master, the Sultan of the Golden Horde. Ibn Battuta determined to join him.

As it turned out, Ibn Battuta did not travel immediately to New Sarai, but met the sultan in his camp at Bish Dagh. For the purpose he had purchased some wagons (sing. *al-ajala*) which the Turks called *al-araba*. These wheeled vehicles played an important role in the lives of the steppe and plain peoples at the time of the Mongol Empire. Ibn Battuta describes them having four large wheels, pulled by two or more horses, or by oxen or camels depending upon the wagon's weight, and guided by a driver mounted on one of the animals. The wagons also carried people's living and sleeping quarters. This consisted of

a kind of cupola made of wooden laths tied together with thin strips of hide. This is light to carry and is covered with felt or blanket cloth and in it are grilled windows. The person inside the tent can see others without their seeing him, and

*he can employ himself in it as he pleases, sleeping, eating, reading or writing
while he is still journeying.*

Other wagons carried equipment and provisions that were covered by a
similar kind of structure bearing a lock. Ibn Battuta bought wagons of
different sizes, one for himself and a slave girl, a smaller one for his travel
companion al-Tuzari, and a larger one for his other companions drawn by
three camels with a driver mounted on one of them. The Turkish travel
routine was similar to that of pilgrim caravans to Mecca: setting out
following the dawn prayer and halting by mid-forenoon, resuming after
noon and travelling until evening. It has been estimated that a wagon
train travelling between ten to 12 hours a day at about four kilometres an
hour might cover an average of 40–48 kilometres a day. When Ibn Battuta
at last encountered the sultan's residence (*ordu*) it was as a vast city on the
move, its inhabitants, mosques, shops and kitchens – for cooking on the
march was commonplace – all borne on hundreds of wagons, accompanied by thousands more on horseback, ranging from slaves to troops in
the sultan's service.

Sultan Uzbek's entire family, his wives, sons and daughter and their
respective retinues formed part of the massive mobile *ordu*. One of the
wives, Bayalun, was the pregnant daughter of the 'King of the Greeks',
the Byzantine Emperor. She sought the sultan's permission to travel
to Constantinople, visit her father, to give birth to her child and then
return. Not one to overlook such an opportunity, Ibn Battuta pleaded to
be allowed to join the princess's company. After an initial refusal, consent
was granted. His departure meant grants of gifts from the ruler and his
family, which in total amounted to '*a large collection of horses, robes, and furs
of miniver and ermine*', in addition to 1,500 gold dinars and silver ingots.
This more modest mobile party comprised, in Ibn Battuta's estimation,
about 400 wagons, 2,000 horses to draw them and for riding, as well as
some 300 oxen and 200 camels as draft animals. Protection was provided
by an army commander with 5,000 troops, in addition to the princess's
own escort of 500 Greek and Turkish troops. The journey to Constantinople was uneventful although the final third of the nine- to ten-week
trip was covered by horse and mule owing to the rough and mountainous
terrain; the wagons were left behind at a fortress on the edge of Byzantine
territory.

Ibn Battuta stayed in Constantinople for about five weeks, returning without Bayalun who remained with her father. She arranged for Ibn Battuta an escort of 500 Turks who wished to return to their own country. He parted company from them well inside Uzbek's territory and set out at last for the sultan's capital at New Sarai. The itinerary and chronology of the journey to and from the Byzantine capital is one of the most confused in the whole narrative. Nonetheless, his brief description of the return trip is noteworthy for the single hazard he encountered. The season was winter's frozen depths. He was obliged to wear three fur coats and two pairs of trousers, one quilted, and three types of footwear of wool, quilted linen, and on top boots of horse skin lined with bear skin.

> *I used to perform my ablutions with hot water close to the fire, but not a drop*
> *of water fell without being frozen on the instant. When I washed my face,*
> *the water ran down my beard and froze, then I would shake it and a kind of*
> *snow fell from it. The moisture that dripped from the nose would freeze on the*
> *moustache. I was unable to mount a horse because of what I was wearing and*
> *so had to be helped into the saddle.*

New Sarai was a sprawling, bustling, cosmopolitan city, comprising Muslims and Christians each divided into different ethnic groups. After an audience with the sultan, who arranged for their lodging and sustenance for some days, Ibn Battuta set about preparing for his next major destination. This was Khwarizm, 40 days' march across a desert, the city itself still within Uzbek's domains. Ten days out, at the city of Sarachuq, the horses were sold and replaced by camels to draw the wagons, owing to the scarcity of fodder and limited water holes along the route. The remainder of the journey was completed by forced marches, halting twice a day just long enough to have a simple meal. Once arrived in Khwarizm, '*the most beautiful and important city of the Turks*', Ibn Battuta and his party abandoned the wagons and he hired camels and purchased a double litter for himself and his companion al-Tuzari. The servants rode some of the horses, and horse-cloths were placed on the remainder as protection against the winter cold.

From Khwarizm the party entered a sandy wilderness and headed for Bukhara, some 18 days distant. From there Ibn Battuta set out for the camp of Sultan Tarmashirin, whose extensive kingdom and power marked him as another of the seven great rulers of the world. Ibn Battuta

stayed in his camp for nearly two months before journeying to Samarqand. By now the reader begins to sense that Ibn Battuta's 'political map'
of the seven rulers of the world may have a subtext advertising the traveller's ready welcome among this most exalted circle of sultans. Tarmashirin was the third sovereign he had met of this group. Those of India and
Morocco would follow in due course. How many could claim to have
met even five of the political world's contemporary 'giants', in addition
to having travelled an extensive portion of the known globe? A matter of
pride, certainly, but not one he was aggressively exhibitionist about.

After leaving Samarqand, Ibn Battuta adopts bare formulaic expres-
sions for his experiences on the road: for example, '*We set out from Samarqand … [and] then came to the city of Tirmidh … [then] next we crossed the
river Jaihun [Oxus] into the land of Khurasan … to the city of Balkh*', describing the beginning of a lengthy detour to the south and west almost as
far as the south coast of the Caspian Sea into what today is Iran. The
narrative then abruptly resumes in a region to the east of Balkh in neighbouring Afghanistan. Here the party camped for more than a month to
allow the camels and horses rest and pasture. A major obstacle before
reaching the Indus River lay before them – the Hindukush Mountains,
coupled with the season's cold and snow. '*We stayed until the warm weather
had definitely set in and crossed the mountain travelling all day from dawn to
dusk. We kept spreading felt cloths in front of the camels for them to tread on, so
they should not sink in the snow.*' Once across the mountains, they passed
through Kabul and Ghazna. Ibn Battuta's subsequent very brief description, however, makes it impossible to judge at what point they reached the
Indus and crossed over into India, whether from the north near Peshawar
or much further south in the lower Indus valley.

Here the narrative of the first volume ends. The date given is the first
day of the new Islamic year of 734AH, or 12 September 1333CE, a date all
critics agree is impossible if it implies that only a year had elapsed since
he had completed his last pilgrimage in September 1332. If the year 1333 *is*
correct, then the pilgrimage date is impossible, as critics also concur that
Ibn Battuta's adventures from Mecca to the Indus valley must have occupied about three years.

The second volume of Ibn Battuta's *Rihla* begins with the classical Islamic exordium. The narrative itself commences, '*On the day of the new moon of the holy month of Muharram, the first day of the year 734 [13 September 1333CE], we came to the river of Sind called Banj Ab which means "the Five Waters".*'

This second book differs in certain significant ways from the first. Over the space of 460 pages of the Defremery and Sanguinetti printed edition, Ibn Battuta's narrative concerns his lengthy stay in India (*al-Hind*) in the service of the Sultan of Delhi, Muhammad b. Tughluq. Close to 40 per cent of the entire *Rihla,* therefore, is dedicated to his ten years on the continent. Concerning the content of the Indian narrative, most is devoted to the person and rule of the sultan. A description of Delhi and a survey history of the sultanate are followed by two chapters on Muhammad b. Tughluq, and a third dealing with Ibn Battuta's personal account of his involvement with the sultan and his court. It will be recalled that the Sultan of Delhi is another of the seven leaders of the world enumerated by Ibn Battuta. Scholars acknowledge his contemporary account of the Delhi sultanate as a uniquely valuable source, and material from these sections will occupy our attention in subsequent chapters.

For the moment, Ibn Battuta's travel experiences remain the focus and in this respect another difference between this and the first volume can be noted. Ibn Battuta's travels in India are actually limited and cover only his initial journey from the Indus valley to Delhi and thereafter during his final departure from that city to south India along the western coast of Malabar. Although he would return to south India for a short but indeterminate stay after visiting Ceylon, the bulk of the remaining narrative covers voyages eastwards to modern Indonesia and China, followed by his return sea voyage to India and thence to Zafar on the southern coast of Arabia. These sea voyages are virtually devoid of detail in much the same way as his account from Aden to the East African coast and return to Zafar years before had been. From southern Arabia until his arrival in Fez, Morocco, the return journey westwards becomes more an itinerary of towns and cities he had visited during the first years of his travels. In other words, once related, Ibn Battuta saw little point in recounting his experiences on the way home, whether by land or sea.

Travel in India

Members of the sultan's intelligence service greeted Ibn Battuta's arrival at the river frontier. There a report was prepared, '*written with the utmost precision and fullness of description*', including the traveller's appearance and dress, the number in his party – slaves, servants and animals – '*his behaviour both on the move and at rest*', down to the last detail. This may seem the pernicious forerunner of modern profiling techniques at airports, but Ibn Battuta's attitude was quite upbeat. He remarks that visitors to India are honoured and judged only according to their actions and conduct, since no one was aware of the traveller's family or parentage! Moreover, it was the sultan's practice to welcome strangers, especially those of the *ulama* class, who stocked the ranks of his bureaucracy. The reports were then sent via the imperial postal service by horse relay that covered the normal 50-day journey from Sind province to Delhi in only five days. The traveller received the sultan's permission by return post in Multan, the capital of Sind.

One foreigner who served the sultan as governor of Lahari in Sind was the jurist Ala al-Mulk from Khurasan. Ibn Battuta joined him and his small fleet of 15 boats descending the Indus towards Lahari, located on the river's estuary just south of modern-day Karachi. The governor's vessel, presumably shared by Ibn Battuta, was called an *ahawara*, powered by about 40 oarsmen. Officialdom on the move required the pomp of musical accompaniment. Four other craft on either side of the *ahawara* bore instrumentalists, who performed on drums, trumpets, bugles and reed pipes, together with singers. After five days in Lahari and generously provided by the governor with travel necessities, Ibn Battuta set off again towards Multan. Another river crossing by boat lay on the way and, to Ibn Battuta's distress, the prospect of having his baggage closely searched. Fortunately a representative of the Multan governor was on hand who gave orders to spare the traveller from Tangier this indignity.

From Multan it was 40 days' march to Delhi. Leaving Abuhar accompanied by 22 horsemen, the party was attacked in open country by a much larger band of 'infidel' Hindu thieves on foot with only two horsemen. The attack failed, leaving a dozen bandits dead. Ibn Battuta suffered a minor arrow wound, as did the horse of a companion. It was, notes Ibn Battuta ruefully, the first attack he had experienced in India – indeed in his entire travels to date.

Fortunately they arrived safely in Delhi without further incident. The metropolis made an immediate impression upon the traveller. It was vast and magnificent, '*uniting beauty and strength. It is surrounded by a wall the equal of which is not found anywhere else, and is the largest city in India, nay, the largest of all the cities of Islam in the East.*' Over the course of nearly a decade, Delhi was Ibn Battuta's home base. He was again a sojourner, not this time as a pilgrim as in Mecca, but as a privileged employee of the Delhi bureaucracy. His reminiscences of these years appear oddly skewed towards financial concerns, first highlighting Sultan Ibn Tughluq's generosity towards his guest, granting him status, money, slaves and provisions, and, second, an account of his accumulated debts and other expenses which he sought to have settled by the sultan or other wealthy individuals.

The circumstances of his departure from Delhi for good are related in the briefest fashion, not helped by the uncertain sequence of events leading up to his departure. The sultan's suspicions had fallen upon Ibn Battuta when it became known that he had visited a Sufi *shaykh* who subsequently insulted Ibn Tughluq publicly. Ibn Battuta was left in fearful suspense as to his fate until released from close guard after the *shaykh*'s execution. It was apparently this incident that some time later led Ibn Battuta to withdraw from the sultan's service and join the company of a pious ascetic with whom he stayed five months performing rigorous spiritual exercises. The sultan learned of this and kindly summoned his return to service. Ibn Battuta refused and instead begged permission to journey to the Hijaz, which the sultan granted. Ibn Battuta resumed his devotions of prayer and fasting for another 40 days. The sultan then summoned him a second time, sending him gifts of horses, slaves, robes and money. During the ensuing audience the sultan, perhaps deliberately playing upon Ibn Battuta's known love of travel, proposed that he become his special envoy to the King of China. His task was to bear lavish gifts to China in return for the king's presents to the Delhi court.

It was a formidable challenge. Apart from comprising 1,500 pieces of the richest and varied fabrics, gold and silver vessels, the gifts included 100 thoroughbred horses, 100 male slaves, 100 Hindu singing and dancing girls, plus 15 eunuchs. Ibn Battuta was accompanied by a learned court dignitary, a eunuch in charge of the royal present, an amir with 1,000 horsemen to see them safely to a port whence they would embark for China, in addition to the 15 Chinese envoys their king had sent to Delhi. Throughout the following account, Ibn Battuta conveys his awareness that the customary Muslim division of the world neatly into the 'abode of Islam' and the 'abode of war' simply did not apply in India. Muslims and Hindus lived in geographically contiguous areas, as in the fortified towns and cities where Muslims chiefly lived, yet often even there as a minority. Infidels occupied the open countryside, the forests and hills, where rebels and bandits could assault Muslim travellers and convoys.

Barely a few days out of Delhi, near Aligarh, the sultan's party learned of infidel Hindus (*al-kuffar al-hunud*) besieging a town nearby and decided to intervene. The rebels were caught unawares and, despite their greatly outnumbering the sultan's armed escort, Ibn Battuta noted with satisfaction that '*we killed them to the last man and took possession of their horses and weapons. Of our party twenty-three horsemen and fifty-five foot soldiers suffered martyrdom.*' The conflict delayed immediate progress, as they decided to remain and assist local forces patrolling the district against the rebels. This led to a second, much graver incident, when Ibn Battuta fell into infidel hands. He feared for his life yet succeeded in talking his way out of immediate danger. But his ordeal was not over. He was obliged to wander about the countryside for more than a week, living off berries, mustard shoots, well water and sleeping rough. One night he found a well constructed with a dome over it and settled exhausted upon a layer of grass. He recalled that '*now and again I felt movement of an animal among the grass; I suppose it was a snake, but I was too worn out to pay attention*'. Another night he slept in a large vessel with an opening large enough for him to crawl inside. On top of the jar a bird flapped its wings most of the night and Ibn Battuta imagined it was frightened, so that '*we made a pair of frightened creatures*'. Salvation came when he stumbled upon a Hindu village with a Muslim governor. He rejoined his party only to encounter a great reluctance to proceed. But proceed they did and arrived on the Arabian Sea coast at the port of Cambay, an important city dominated by foreign Muslim merchants.

The voyage by boat southwards to the Malabar coast began, however, at Gandhar, a city with a Hindu sultan who acknowledged Muslim suzerainty. He provided two boats with water, provisions and forage for the horses. One carried 60 oarsmen who were protected by a roof during battle from flying stones and arrows. Two other boats were on loan or hired from a Muslim ship-owner called Ibrahim which carried the other horses, including those remaining of the present for the King of China. Ibn Battuta went aboard one powered by 50 oarsmen and carrying 50 Abyssinian fighters. Sailing smoothly from port to port down the coast, the party arrived to drum and trumpet fanfare at the great harbour of Calicut which attracted merchants from east and west. Thirteen Chinese vessels were anchored at that moment. Ibn Battuta comments, '*Everyone of us was lodged in a house, and we stayed there three months as guests of the infidel Sultan awaiting the season of voyage to China which can be done only on Chinese ships.*' There were three kinds of vessel, the largest called *junk*, a middle-sized type called *zaw* and the smallest called *kakam*. The junk is described as a craft with sail and oar power, with a minimum of ten men required to handle each oar from a standing position; among the four decks it carried 600 sailors and 400 armed fighters. Wealthy merchants could enjoy the luxury of privacy in suites with lock and key comprising several rooms and a latrine. While at sea, each junk was accompanied by three other smaller vessels. These were used to tow the junk by oar power if the larger craft became becalmed at sea. Ibn Battuta witnessed their use in practice on his voyage from Java to China.

Ibn Battuta faced unforeseen annoyances in his preparation for embarkation. No suitable accommodation was available on a junk. Chinese merchants had booked all the suites in advance of their departure on their outward voyage from China. He then arranged a set of rooms for himself, his effects and his male and female slaves on a *kakam*, and space was found for the king's gift on a junk. Then tragedy struck. The two vessels stood well out in the roadstead while Ibn Battuta remained ashore for Friday prayers, planning to board the next morning. That night a violent storm whipped the sea into a frenzy and the junk was destroyed, killing all aboard. The *kakam*'s captain seized upon a moment of relative calm to set sail, taking all of Ibn Battuta's belongings with him and leaving Ibn Battuta stranded ashore, his royal mission effectively at an end.

Over the next weeks and months, Ibn Battuta wandered up and down the Malabar coast, hoping for news of the *kakam*. For diversion he joined a military expedition launched by the Sultan of Hinawr against the infidel Sultan of Goa. From there he returned to Calicut, where he learned the fate of his slaves and companions, none of whom he was ever likely to see again. He had to face a decision of what to do and where to go next.

China bound

Despite the abrupt termination of his mission, China did not thereby cease
to hold an attraction for Ibn Battuta. There were simply other attractions
to visit on the way. Two months after receiving the news of the scattered survivors of the ill-fated China venture he boarded a ship for the
ten days' crossing from Calicut to the Muslim inhabited islands of Dhibat
al-Mahal, better known today as the Maldives.

> *These islands are one of the wonders of the world. They number about two
> thousand in all. Each hundred or less of them form a circular cluster resembling
> a ring having one entrance like a gateway, and only through this entrance can
> ships reach the islands. When a vessel arrives at any one of them it requires one
> of the inhabitants to pilot it to the other islands. They are so close set that on
> leaving one island the tops of the palms on another are visible. If a ship loses its
> course it is unable to enter and is carried by the wind to the Indian coast or to
> Ceylon.*

In the event, Ibn Battuta decided he was in no hurry to see China and
remained in the Maldives for 18 months, although it has been argued that
his stay may have been as little as eight months. He was appointed religious judge (*qadi*), a position he had held in Delhi, married several times
and left rather abruptly after becoming embroiled in the islands' politics.
He set sail for the south eastern Indian Coromandel coast, a distance of
normally three days, but, owing to the inexperience of the pilot and after
nine days at sea, the ship landed instead on the island of Ceylon! The
major attraction here was the mountain of Sarandib on the summit of
which was the imprint of the foot of Adam indicating where, according
to Muslim lore, he had landed on earth after his expulsion from paradise.
Ibn Battuta dutifully made the pilgrimage to the site and after returning
to port set sail for the eastern Indian Maabar coast, a day and a night's
journey away.

The decision to return to the mainland was not a happy one. During
the crossing a storm nearly dashed the ship upon rocks although it ran
aground a few miles from shore. '*We were face to face with death*,' wrote Ibn
Battuta dramatically. The sailors made a raft from ship's parts, and Ibn

Battuta's companions and slave girls bearing his valuables reached safety with a favourable wind. Ibn Battuta remained behind, perched on the ship's poop all night until a rescue party of infidels arrived in the morning to bring him ashore.

Next to befall him was a severe attack of fever, grave enough for him to imagine his end was near. After treatment he recovered sufficiently to leave from the port of Fattan on a ship bound for the Yemen. It stopped over in Kawlam on the Malabar coast and Ibn Battuta disembarked to remain there for three months to recover fully. He then determined to visit his former friend-at-arms, the Sultan of Hinawr. Before reaching Hinawr by sea, their ship was attacked by infidel pirates and captured. '*They took everything everybody had and set us down on the shore,*' he lamented, and he returned to Calicut wearing only the trousers the pirates had allowed him to keep. Repairing to a mosque he was sent adequate clothing by a *qadi* and a merchant. The pirate attack deeply affected Ibn Battuta, as the event is later mentioned several times in the course of his travel narrative.

Doubtless anxious by now to put India behind him, Ibn Battuta pondered a return to the Maldives despite the ill will some still felt towards him. A wife he left behind pregnant had borne a son he had just learned about and whom he wished to see. The visit was short, as Ibn Battuta acknowledged it best to leave the child with his Maldivian family. He sought permission to leave and the next sea stage of his travels is laconically expressed thus: '*I left and we were at sea for forty-three days and then reached the country of Bengal.*'

Bengal detained him long enough to make a one-month trip into the mountains of Assam to meet a famous holy man, Jalal al-Din al-Tabrizi. Upon his return down river to the port city of Sunarkawan (Sonargaon), he found a junk bound for Sumatra (*al-Jawa*) and embarked upon it for a voyage of 40 days. The Sultan of Sumatra received Ibn Battuta warmly. Two weeks later he arranged for a well-provisioned junk to take his guest and company on a three-week voyage to the port of Qaqula in Java (*Mul Jawa*), the centre of a Hindu empire. The infidel sultan welcomed his guests with hospitality for three days and then they were off again. From Java until he reached the China coast, Ibn Battuta's narrative minimally traces a voyage of 88 days before arrival first at a mysterious land that scholars have not yet satisfactorily identified:

We set sail and after thirty-four days reached the Tranquil Sea … it has no wind, no waves, and no movement in spite of its extent. We sailed on this sea for thirty-seven days. … Then we reached the country of Tawalisi. … When we left the country of Tawalisi and after seventeen days of sailing very rapidly and comfortably with a favourable wind we reached the country of China.

On this occasion, the accompanying smaller tow-boats were put into action to row the large junk over the Tranquil Sea, assisted by gigantic oars kept on the junk which each required 30 men to manipulate.

Ibn Batutta set foot on Chinese soil at the port city of Zaitun, a name he found amusing, since, as he states, there were no olives (*zaitun*) to be found in the entire country. He judged it to be the largest harbour in the world, accommodating about 100 large junks and countless smaller ones. The country as a whole, he claimed, was the safest anywhere for the traveller, allowing one to journey for months carrying considerable wealth without fear. Whether Ibn Battuta actually visited all the places he describes is still debated by experts. Possibly he reached Canton, but could not have done so entirely by river as he states; it seems unlikely he made it to Khan Baliq (Peking), the capital of the Sultan of China. Nonetheless, rebellion and the ensuing political turmoil were perhaps the immediate causes of his leaving China, setting out on the long journey home to Morocco.

Homeward bound

The return voyage is told in much the same bland manner as the eastward run from south India, save for one curiously understated incident. As they approached Tawalisi the wind changed, the sky darkened and it rained heavily. 'Then,' says Ibn Battuta, '*we entered an unknown sea, the crew of the junk were frightened and wanted to return to China but that was impossible. We spent forty-two days without knowing in which sea we were.*' The difficulties with Ibn Battuta's chronology have already been noted. When he reached Kawlam in south India, it was the season of the Ramadan fast which he celebrated there. From Kawlam he went to Calicut and boarded a ship to cross the Arabian Sea, landing 28 days later, for the second time, in Zafar on the south Arabian coast. It was the first month, Muharram, of the year 748AH (April 1347CE), 14 years after his arrival in the Indus valley.

By January 1348, he was in Baghdad, from which, moving north along the Euphrates, he turned west and, passing through Tadmor (Palmyra), fabled city of the prophet Solomon, he headed towards Damascus. There, he learned of the deaths of his father, 15 years earlier, and that of a son a dozen years before; his mother was still alive.

Ibn Battuta set out on his final pilgrimage and reached Mecca in mid-November 1348; he fasted through Ramadan and performed the pilgrimage rites in late February 1349. Two months later he was aboard a small boat (*qurqura*) sailing westwards along the southern Mediterranean coast from Alexandria. The thought of homecoming stirred in him a sense of '*affection for my people and friends, and love for my country which for me is better than all others*'. A stopover in Tunis was followed by a short run to Sardinia aboard a Catalan Christian-owned ship, and another vessel brought him back to the North African coast. On the road to Fez, so close to his birthplace, Tangier, Ibn Battuta heard the sad news of his mother's death from the plague. In early November 1349, he reached the Marinid capital.

At this point there is a sudden shift of tone in Ibn Battuta's narrative. Both the traveller and his editor indulge for a dozen pages in a eulogy of the Sultan of Fez, the Marinid sovereign, Abu Inan Faris. Every aspect of his person and rule are fulsomely praised, each characteristic compared to that of other Muslim rulers – to their detriment. To all appearances, this grand flourish of praise should have signalled a conclusion and brought the work to an end. But no, for the narrative just as abruptly comes back to earth and Ibn Battuta says '*Let us return to the narrative of our travels.*' These referred to a trip to nearby al-Andalus, where he visited the cities of Marbella, Malaga, Ronda and Granada, familiar to every modern tourist to Spanish Andalucia; his last journey was undertaken to the Land of the Blacks (*Bilad al-Sudan*), covering areas of the modern countries of Mauritania, Mali and Niger.

Ibn Battuta's first duty after paying due respects to his sovereign was to visit his mother's grave in Tangier. Illness then detained him in Ceuta for several months. His motive for crossing the straits of Gibraltar – in a galley (*shatti*) – was, he said, that as God had cured him, he '*wanted to take part in the holy war and the frontier fighting*'. The Nasrid kingdom of Granada, founded in 1232, survived the long Christian re-conquest of the peninsula until 1492. By time of Ibn Battuta's visit in 1350, Gibraltar had recently been rescued from siege by Christian Spanish forces, although the kingdom's land and sea frontiers remained insecure. Ibn Battuta's presence was symbolic rather than practical, as he noted that '*recompense is treasured up for those who stay or travel there*'.

He returned to Morocco and moved about from place to place in Marinid domains for some months. From Fez, Ibn Battuta travelled to Sijilmasa, where he purchased camels and four months' supply of fodder, and in February 1352 he joined a merchant caravan with the object of crossing the Sahara desert to Iwalatan on the edge of the Land of the Blacks. The two-month journey passed without incident if not without hazard. Becoming separated from the caravan and lost in the desert was one danger, the scarcity of water another. At a three-day stop part way, water supplies were replenished from underground sources. From this point onwards, tribal guides (*takhsif*) were sent ahead with letters from caravan members to contacts in Iwalatan requesting that lodging be arranged and for them to meet the caravan with water four days out from the city. Ibn Battuta graphically describes the dangers all encounter:

> *Sometimes the* takhshif *perishes in this desert and the people of Iwalatan know nothing of the caravan, and its people or most of them perish too. There are many demons in that desert. If the* takhshif *is alone they play tricks on him and delude him till he loses his way and perishes. There is no road to be seen in the desert and no track, only sand blown about by the wind. You see mountains of sand in one place and then you see they have moved to another.*

Ibn Battuta remained in Iwalatan for 50 days and then set off for the kingdom of Mali. The journey was covered in 24 days with only a guide and three companions, for the road was safe and shaded by large baobab trees. In this region, he says, '*The traveller does not carry food or condiments or dinars or dirhams, but only pieces of salt, glass trinkets and some articles of perfume*', the objects carried used in exchange for goods and services in a basically barter economy. Ibn Battuta and company reached a large river he believed was the Nile, a commonly held mistake for the Niger River until the nineteenth century. By fording one of its nearby tributaries, they entered the Mali capital. It was the end of June 1352 and he remained there for the next eight months, although two months of that period he spent recovering from a severe case of food poisoning from which one of his companions died. He set off on an indirect return journey home in February 1353, riding a camel, as horses were very expensive. When the animal died, he hired two young men to fetch a replacement for him. At first, he followed the Niger valley for a considerable distance and then continued eastwards overland in the company of a caravan towards Takadda (Azelik); he fell ill again from the extreme heat. At Takadda he received a message from the sultan, Abu Inan, ordering him to return to Fez. For the long journey back two riding camels and provisions for 70 days were purchased for his personal use and he travelled in the protection of a large caravan, leaving Takadda in mid-September 1353. They arrived in Sijilmasa where they rested for two weeks and then set off again at the end of December. Ibn Battuta's last comment on his travels was to describe their crossing a defile in the Atlas Mountains south of Fez: *'It was a time of intense cold and a great deal of snow had settled on the road. I have seen difficult roads and much snow in Bukhara, Samarqand, Khurasan and the country of the Turks, but I never saw one more difficult than this.'*

Here ends Ibn Battuta's *'Gift to those who contemplate the wonders of cities and the marvels of travelling'*, completed, he states, on the 3rd of Dhu-l Hijja of the year 756AH, that is, 13 December 1355CE. He adds, *'Praise be to God and peace upon those of his servants whom he has chosen.'*

But it is Ibn Juzayy who has the very last word. *'The copying of this work was completed in Safar of the year seven hundred and fifty-seven* [February 1356CE]. *God reward him who copied it.'*

Afterword

Ibn Battuta's snow-bound homecoming may have seemed a cold and frosty welcome to his final journey. His legacy is the story of his odyssey, but not quite his alone. His only known work, *The Travels*, was commissioned by Sultan Abu Inan who, in a modest way, shares in the traveller's fame, being immortalized by the lavish attention given him in the work by Ibn Battuta and his editor, Ibn Juzayy. The latter's memory is assured in the occasional poetic interjection and comment he made in *The Travels*; we cannot judge how different the work may have been had Ibn Battuta written it by himself. Nothing certain is known of the last decade of his life except that he outlived his patron and collaborator who both died shortly after the book's completion. Presumably he spent the remaining years in Morocco, possibly as a judge in some town or city, with or without a family around him, but certainly with company to whom he could recount his myriad tales.

One other person merits mention again as representative of the many who shared his role, that of travel companion. Ibn Battuta had departed Tangier alone, accompanied only by his long-held desire to visit the Holy Cities. Soon he had joined with others from the natural need of companionship and security along the way. Thereafter he seems always to have been in the company of others in caravans or had become responsible for others who travelled with him. He rarely discloses their names or numbers or gender and the very few named individuals who travelled with him were slaves, male and female. When he arrived in Delhi, his entourage had increased from the ten with him in Anatolia to 40 persons, of which ten (all males) were called companions, the remainder servants and slave boys. We are not told how long any had been with him. Except for one man. Ibn Battuta had met him in Cairo, and his name was al-Hajj Abdallah b. Abu Bakr b. al-Farhan al-Tuzari, whom we have met briefly before. He said of al-Tuzari that '*he continued to accompany me for many years, until we quitted the land of India, when he died at Sandabur* [Goa] *as we shall relate in due course*'. Ibn Battuta failed to mention his death as promised. He is probably the same person whom he called his companion (*rafiq*), one Afif al-Din al-Tuzari, for whom he purchased a small wagon for their journey to meet the Sultan of the Golden Horde. Ibn Battuta had purchased a larger conveyance for himself and a slave girl. Al-Tuzari, as his longest-serving companion on the road, was perhaps also the subject of tales told to eager listeners in the twilight years of his life.

❧ ❧

CHAPTER 3

Tales of Food and Hospitality

A part from Ibn Battuta's apparently all-consuming passion for travel, modern commentators have remarked upon other of his major interests. One was enjoying the pleasures of the table. Janssens discreetly qualified this judgement, saying that the Tangerine was more a gourmand than gourmet. That is to say, he delighted in eating well and heartily rather than being a connoisseur of fine food and drink. Beckingham, on the other hand, pointed to his fondness for food together with an attraction to women. In its own terms, each comment may be judged as valid. But each also overlooks an important link which the traveller himself often explicitly expresses, that food or nourishment in the broadest sense had both sacred and worldly dimensions. Each aspect is alluded to during the very first stage of his journey in 1325. While still in Tunis, Ibn Battuta celebrated the Feast of the Breaking of the Fast (*Id al-Fitr*). This marked the end of the month of fasting, Ramadan, during which abstinence from all food and drink and sexual intercourse between the hours of sunrise and sunset was a religious obligation. Some ten weeks later, while on the road, the caravan observed the major Feast of Sacrifice (*Id al-Adha*), which occurred at the end of the annual pilgrimage rites in Mecca. There, as elsewhere in Muslim domains, animals like sheep or camels and other cattle were sacrificed and most of the meat distributed for pious purposes. Following upon these religious festivals, Ibn Battuta celebrated his second marriage by throwing a wedding party (*walima*) for the whole caravan.

The rigours of fasting and the pleasures of feasting or simply eating to live rather than living to eat concerned everyone from both mundane and religious motives. Members of the cultured urban elite during the heyday of the Abbasid caliphate (750–900) expressed and accessed these interests in a variety of literary genres. The religious interest, of course, was embedded in Islam's sacred sources. These were God's own words expressed in the Quran and in the traditions (*hadith*) relating to God's Prophet and Messenger, Muhammad. Thus the Quran broadly enjoined that one should 'eat of what your Lord has given you and render thanks to Him' (Q 34:15; 2:57). The natural world was, collectively, one of God's 'signs':

> it is He who spread out the earth, placed firm mountains and rivers on it and made two of every kind of fruit. ... There are in the land, neighbouring plots, gardens of vineyards, cornfields, palm trees in clusters or otherwise, all watered with the same water, yet We make some of them better for eating than others: these truly are signs (*ayat*) for people who (reflect) and reason (Q 13:3–4).

The function of these signs was a reminder of the Creator's majesty and mercy and to elicit humankind's response of worshipful gratitude.

Alluding to food taboos, scripture stated that one should 'eat of what is lawful and wholesome on the earth and do not walk in Satan's footsteps for he is your inveterate foe' (Q 2:168). Specific classes of prohibited foods are mentioned, for '(God) has only forbidden you carrion, blood, pig's meat and animals over which any name other than God's has been invoked' (Q 2:173). The last category is further explained as 'anything strangled, victim of a violent blow, gored or savaged by a beast of prey' (Q 5:3), that is, not slaughtered in the legal manner by cutting its throat while uttering 'in the name of God'. An animal sacrificed on a pagan altar, therefore, is also forbidden to a Muslim. In all, the taboos are few and less complicated than those mentioned in the classification system of Leviticus in the Hebrew Bible. The pig taboo illustrates the different positions of Jews and Muslims. Leviticus 11:7–8 reads, 'the pig, because it has a parted foot and a cloven hoof *but does not chew the cud*; you shall regard it as unclean. You shall not eat their flesh or even touch their dead bodies; you shall regard them as unclean.' The pig is unclean as it does not belong to the category of 'pure' ungulates which are cloven footed *and* cud chewing. In the Quran, by contrast, swine is forbidden without further explanation. The animal in itself bore the value of impurity and its consumption consequently was forbidden.

By the ninth century, major multi-volume collections of Prophetic traditions (*hadith*) were being compiled. The works of al-Bukhari (d. 870)

– whose grave Ibn Battuta would visit in Bukhara – and that of Muslim (d. 875) both contained chapters, among a wide range of topics, on food and drink. These two collections, together with four others collected soon afterwards, achieved canonical status among Muslims. By Ibn Battuta's day, popular abridgements of the 'canonical six' and other collections were made. One of these was by Wali al-Din al-Tabrizi, completed in 1336, entitled *Mishkat al-Masabih* (*Light of Lights*).[1] In the tradition literature the reported sayings and actions of the Prophet take centre stage and their guidance was used by scholars to elucidate, interpret or extend the sense of Quran passages. Taboos on food not mentioned in the Quran are included. The Prophet explicitly prohibited the flesh of the domestic ass although he partook of the flesh of a wild ass. On another occasion he accepted from a companion the hind quarters of a hare he knew had been ritually slaughtered. Although the animal is not mentioned in scripture, the legal method of slaughter was assurance of its cleanliness for consumption. The Prophet was further reported to have declared, 'I neither eat nor prohibit the eating of lizards', leaving individual believers to make their own decisions. Ibn Battuta is uninformative as to the fare he provided for the caravan company at his wedding feast. Had he followed the Prophet's precedent, expressed in several anecdotes, he may have offered a sheep, or bread and meat or, more sparingly, just dates, dried curd and clarified butter.

Later still, a chapter on the etiquette of eating is found in the great classic of religious thought and practice, the *Ihya Ulum al-Din* (*Revival of the Religious Sciences*) by al-Ghazali (d. 1111). The fourteenth-century Maliki scholar Ibn al-Hajj likewise included a chapter on the same theme in his *Kitab al-Madkhal* (*Book of Basics*). These works, too, are based upon sayings of the Prophet and other well-known figures of the early community. Although the specific chapters deal chiefly with manners at the table and with hospitality, an occasional insight into foodways is found; an incidental observation in one anecdote suggests that the simple fare of barley bread and coarse ground salt would be enhanced by mixing thyme with the salt. The list of authors and books in which the subject of nourishment is treated may easily be lengthened. It suffices to indicate that food and drink touched the vital core of Islamic ethics. In part, believers worshipped God through prescribed rituals (*ibadat*) of prayer, fasting, pilgrimage and charity and by obeying scriptural prohibitions and following injunctions to acknowledge one's gratitude to the Creator for his favours to humankind. God is described metaphorically as One who 'gives nourishment (to all) and yet is nourished by no one' (Q 6:14). In part, too, as just noted, food and drink illustrate the sphere of social relationships (*muamalat*), as the faithful are enjoined to give of their own means, however much cherished, to care for parents and kindred, orphans, the needy, the wayfarer, the weak, and to liberate those in bondage (Q 2:177).

Turning to more secular literature, the urban and urbane population's interest in food lore was reflected in lengthy sections in two encyclopaedic works, the *Uyun al-akhbar* (*Choice Histories*) of Ibn Qutayba (d. 889) and the *Iqd al-farid* (*Unique Necklace*) of Ibn Abd Rabbihi (d. 940). Further, the earliest extant cookbook in Arabic, most likely compiled in the late tenth century, is attributed to one Ibn Sayyar al-Warraq and mirrors culinary developments under the early Abbasid caliphs and the emerging bourgeoisie of Baghdad. Later cookbooks illustrate rich culinary traditions of the Middle East down to Ibn Battuta's own time which spanned regions from Iraq and Persia in the East to Morocco and al-Andalus in the West. The cookbooks often suggest how food hygiene and a knowledge of the nature of foodstuffs contribute to sustaining a healthy life. The introductory chapters of Ibn al-Warraq's cookbook discuss the importance of cleanliness in the kitchen and the effects upon the body of foods viewed from the prevailing medical perspective of humoral pathology. Thus lentils are described as cold and dry, producing blood high in black bile, that dry up the body and curb coitus, while mung beans, also cold and dry, are lighter than lentils but less nourishing. And so on.

A second, anonymous, cookbook, *Kanz al-fawaid* for short (*The Treasury of Benefits*), was perhaps compiled in Egypt during the fourteenth century. One chapter entitled 'Concerning a sick person's being nourished by vegetable dishes called *muzawwarat*' offers a dish designated for those suffering from a bilious fever. For their part, physicians working within the same humoral paradigm composed another category of work dealing specifically with nourishment. The famous Abu Bakr al-Razi (d. 923), known in Europe as Rhazes, wrote one such treatise, the purpose of which is neatly expressed in its title, *The Book of Nourishment's Benefits and the Warding Off of its Harmful Effects*. Other early works were written by the Christian Hunayn Ibn Ishaq (d. 856) and al-Razi's Jewish contemporary Ishaq Ibn Sulayman al-Israili (d. *c.* 935). Finally, mention should be made of a consciously religious expression of these medical works of a type known as Medicine of the Prophet or, among Shia Muslims, Medicine of the Imams, imams being the religious leaders of this minority Muslim community. One of the very first works of its kind, compiled by the Andalusi scholar Abd al-Malik b. Habib (d. 853), resulted from his travels to countries of the Muslim east and Mecca where he gathered material of a more popular nature, some magical, on the cure of illnesses and conservation of health. A later much larger work was written by the theologian and physician Ibn Qayyim al-Jawziyya (d. 1350), Ibn Battuta's contemporary, who lived in Syria and Egypt. He divided medical ailments into two kinds, sickness of the heart and sickness of the body. Both are alluded to in the Quran, although he considered the former more important.

Gifted with a natural sense of curiosity, Ibn Battuta's own interest in matters of nourishment had been, therefore, further fed by these literary traditions both sacred and profane. His English translator, H.A.R. Gibb, famously styled him a 'geographer in spite of himself'. And in one way, he seemed to emulate the practice of earlier Arab geographers who included data on food products in their descriptions of settled areas. The tenth-century geographer al-Muqaddasi (d. *c.* 990) described Egypt's capital – the old city, al-Fustat, combined with its adjacent new city, al-Qahira, or Cairo – in glowing terms as 'the market place for all mankind'. Its markets were stocked with wholesome food: 'victuals here are most appetising, their savouries superb. Confectioneries are cheap, bananas plentiful, as are fresh dates; vegetables and firewood are abundant.'[2] He mentions a scattering of other towns and briefly their food resources such as the date palms and vineyards of Aswan and Akhmim in Upper Egypt and the fine rice fields of the Fayyum. Further data on food items is provided in the chapter's final section, a 'Summary account of the conditions of Egypt'. Al-Muqaddasi's objective was to compose a systematic, factually exhaustive account of each region of the Muslim domains suitable, he believed, for the use of travellers, merchants, commoner and elite. He eschewed any wish to entertain and chided his geographer predecessor Ibn al-Faqih with frivolity – for exciting tears at one point and provoking laughter at another. Ibn Battuta's approach, at once more rambling yet engaging, aimed to entertain as well as inform. The contrast between the two authors and their books was that the geographer was a cataloguer of facts while the traveller was a collector of people.

Ibn Batutta's text has been examined for its contribution to 'ethnography' and in one respect found wanting. Chelhod criticized the abundant use of stereotyped cliché in the descriptions of towns or cities which invariably make reference to food resources.[3] A case in point occurs on his travels through the Yemen. He writes. *'We came to Jubla, a small and pretty town with palms, fruit trees and streams.'* Again, the city of Aqsara in Anatolia is described as *'surrounded by flowing streams and gardens on every side'*. And Oman was *'fertile, with streams, trees, orchards, palm groves and abundant fruit of various kinds'*. Examples could be multiplied for other regions. Is the criticism, however, entirely warranted? First, repetitive detail of places that strike the traveller as verdant and fertile may be an inevitable feature of a travel narrative which mentions several hundred locations visited. Moreover, not every town or city does receive the same treatment. The large city of Aden, on the south Arabian coast, is described bluntly as having no crops, no trees and no water; only during the rainy season was water collected in reservoirs situated at some distance from the city, making them vulnerable to interference from Bedouins. Description of the island of Sawakin, off the African coast of the Red Sea, begins in similar fashion, for it also was without water, trees or cereal crops (except a coarse-grained type of millet called *jurjur*). Water was transported to it in boats, and cisterns on the island captured rain water. Yet its inhabitants enjoyed the flesh of ostriches, gazelles and wild asses, while goats provided milk products and ghee that were exported to Mecca along with the millet. Finally, there are similar descriptions of the markets of two coastal cities, Zaila and Zafar, each dismissed as filthy and stinking, the stench attributed chiefly to the large quantities of fish sold, and additionally either to the blood of slaughtered camels staining the street or to rotting fruit. So, although repetitive description occurs, Ibn Battuta's account in fact offers quite rich material on such matters as food resources.

Food phases

The data on foodstuffs and foodways is scattered throughout the travel narrative in a way that makes systematic arrangement difficult. The different processes of the medieval food system, as proposed by Goody for example, include the phases of production, distribution, preparation and consumption of food. Some data on the first three phases can be collated, although they occur chiefly in the travels through Egypt and Syria and to a lesser extent in Arabia. It is apparent, however, that Ibn Battuta's attention was most fully engaged with food consumption, to which preparation was implicitly joined if only infrequently described. The focus on consumption is understandable since it was intimately related to the notion of hospitality that formed an important aspect of Muslim religious ethics. This joint theme of consumption-hospitality commences in the first part of this chapter, particularly during his journeys into southern Persia and Iraq prior to his second pilgrimage and his sojourn in Mecca for nearly three years. Further coverage of Arabia itself includes his trip through the Yemen and subsequent journey by boat along the southern Arabian coast. Description of the food customs of East Africa are of interest, as they anticipate his later journey to India. The second part of the chapter develops Ibn Battuta's comments on hospitality in his travels through Anatolia and next during his stay among the Turks of the Golden Horde and then his sojourn in India. The geographical sequence of the travels detailed in the previous chapter is therefore followed in the present one.

Egypt, Syria and Arabia

Ibn Battuta visited Egypt nearly four centuries later than al-Muqaddasi, journeying from Alexandria to the capital, now a vast metropolis which he called Misr, the contemporary name for the country as a whole. He was struck by a singular feature of the land of Egypt, the mighty River Nile, which he claimed surpassed all other rivers on earth, its basin being the most heavily cultivated of any river anywhere. From his own viewpoint,

> *There is no need for a traveller on the Nile to take any provision with him, because whenever he wishes to descend on the bank he may do so for ablutions, prayers, purchasing provisions, or any other purpose. There is a continuous series of markets from the city of Alexandra to Cairo and from Cairo to the city of Aswan in Upper Egypt.*

In the Delta region between Alexandra and Cairo, he briefly notes the town of Fawwa as full of orchards, of al-Nahrariya as possessing fine markets, and the district of Burlus as rich in date palms and fruit trees. Some of these products would have found their way to Cairene markets just as pomegranates (*rumman*) were exported from a town appropriately called Ashmun al-Rumman and bananas from Damietta.

In Damietta, situated on the bank of the Nile, large quantities of very plump sea fowl were sold, where buffalo milk unequalled for its delicate sweetness was available and fish called *buri*, a species of grey mullet, were caught and also transported to Cairo, or even further afield to Syria and Anatolia. The extent of this distribution suggests a commodity of some popularity, even delicacy, to which we shall return below. While passing through Upper Egypt, Ibn Battuta visited the small town of Manlawi where, he reports, 11 sugar presses functioned. What captured his interest was the owners' practice of allowing poor people to bring chunks of fresh bread, dip them into a cooking vat and consume the richly sugar-coated pieces. Without having to say so, he believed the practice confirmed a charitable religious impulse to care for the needy. Finally, the Red Sea port of Aydhab is described as a large town well supplied with fish and milk, while dates and grain were imported from Upper Egypt; the majority of its inhabitants appeared to be of the semi-nomadic African Beja tribe whose main food was milk of the camels they used for transport.

Ibn Battuta's account acknowledges the adage that Egypt was the gift of the Nile. Cairo, capital of the Mamluk dynasty then led by Sultan Malik al-Nasir (reigned 1293–1341), was the political and economic magnet that attracted goods and produce from the areas in the Nile valley under the sultan's effective rule. He notes, '*The reason why the revenues of the land of Egypt are so large is that all the landed estates belong to the Treasury.*' Only Aydhab, where, as Ibn Battuta remarks, two-thirds of the city belonged to the Beja king, was in current conflict with the sultan, whose troops had been driven out. Notably, the city was able to draw its grain supplies from other areas in Upper Egypt.

Ibn Battuta's journeys through Syria, which included modern-day Palestine and Lebanon, occupied chiefly the areas lying between the Jordan and Orontes rivers and the Mediterranean coast. Like the Nile Delta, it was a fertile region. From our traveller's viewpoint the heart of the region was Jabal Lubnan, '*one of the most fertile mountain ranges in the world for in it are found all manner of fruits and water fountains*'. Yet to the north and south of the mountain there were also several cities famous for their fruit culture: Sidon was rich in figs, raisins and olive oil for export to Egypt; al-Maarra was famous for its orchards of figs and pistachios and nearby Sarmin was another olive-growing area; Hamah produced great quantities of fruit, the choicest among them being the almond apricot (*al-mishmish al-lawzi*), or 'white apricot', whose kernel was like a sweet almond. (When visiting Isfahan in Persia, Ibn Battuta reported a similar apricot with an almond-like kernel; the fruit was called *qamar al-din* and was dried and preserved.) Nablus was like Sidon but more so, richer in olives and its oil for export. Its melons were judged of excellent quality. The jewel of the Mount Lebanon range was the ancient city of Baalbakk, nestled in the valley and '*surrounded by glorious orchards and superb gardens with flowing streams traversing its land and rivalling Damascus in its boundless amenities*'. A superabundance of cherries was grown and the famous sweet paste, *dibs*, was made there.

In stark contrast to both Egypt and Syria, Ibn Battuta makes only the briefest mention of fertile areas in Arabia lying between Medina and Mecca, the most proximate locations supplying Mecca with some of its fruit and vegetables. The thirteenth-century Arabian traveller Ibn al-Mujawir specifically lists melons, varieties of cucumber, egg plants and leeks supplied to Mecca from its immediate hinterland. Ibn Jubayr, who performed the pilgrimage in 1183, adds a number of other fine products to this list: fruits such as figs, grapes and quince, and vegetables such as the pumpkin, carrot and cauliflower. Until his arrival in the Holy Land, he states, he had thought his native al-Andalus (Iberian peninsula) was especially favoured above all other regions. Yet the Meccan watermelon, he acknowledged, had a fragrance and sweetness that could not be captured in words. More soberly, Ibn Jubayr observed that the commercial high point of the Meccan year was the pilgrimage season, when markets overflowed with every kind of product. Clearly, he adds, this was a blessing and miracle wrought by God especially for Mecca.

Caravan travel within Arabia itself is also noted by Ibn Battuta in a sketchy fashion. He underlined the constant attention to water supplies as the first priority. Upon departing from Mecca for Kufa after completing his first pilgrimage, he observed that the caravan included water-carrying camels to supply poorer pilgrims who travelled on foot (*abna al-sabil*). Other camels bore provisions for use as charity gifts as well as medicines, potions and sugar for anyone who fell ill. Caravans were like small towns on the move, and food provisions available on the caravan's departure were supplemented by goods acquired en route, such as sheep, clarified butter and curdled milk. These were brought to the caravan by local Bedouin who exchanged them for goods that met their own needs such as coarse cotton cloth.

Passages in the travels that relate to the preparation of food are sparse as well and refer in the main to products of the commercial sector and rarely to dishes prepared in the domestic kitchen. Detailed description of these latter dishes can be found in the contemporary Arabic culinary manuals. Let us take the example of the fish called *buri*, caught at Damietta in the Egyptian Delta. The cookbook *Kanz al-fawaid* (*The Treasury of Benefits*) contains a number of recipes for fish. They are generally of unspecified type, almost always fresh but sometimes salted, among which is one for grey mullet, or *buri*.[4] First, onion is chopped fine, fried in sweet oil and set aside. Then a mixture prepared with saffron, a blend of aromatic spices, hazelnuts, ginger, mint, rue, a selection of vegetables and raisins is placed in a quantity of wine vinegar and cooked together. The *buri*, which has already been fried, is covered with the mixture (plus the onions) and left to steep overnight for consumption the following day. The compiler's comment at the end of the recipe describes the result simply as 'extraordinary'; in today's gastronomic jargon, one imagines it would be 'divine'.

Ibn Battuta's Moroccan readers would have been familiar with *buri*, as one grey mullet species was common from the Black Sea through to the Mediterranean. The cookbook recipe described above belonged to the urban bourgeois culinary culture of Cairo or Damascus. Like recipes of other substantial dishes with meat or fowl, it was but one of several methods of preparation. There is a recipe for *buri* in the cookbook of Ibn Razin al-Tujibi, a mid-thirteenth-century work representing North African-Iberian culinary practices.[5] In some details the ingredients and method are similar to the 'Egyptian' dish given here, the major difference is its being more elaborately spiced than the al-Tujibi version.

Ibn Battuta's interest, therefore, lay in reporting commercial food preparations that would be less familiar to his readers than homemade dishes. In the Upper Egyptian town of Manfalut, for example, he describes a kind of 'honey' product called *naida*[6] that was made from wheat by soaking it for several days, then drying and crushing it; the resulting sweet also found its way to the Cairo markets. In Nablus, Syria, the carob sweet made there had achieved a reputation that reached well beyond the city walls. Ibn Battuta notes the preparation: '*The carobs* (kharub) *are cooked and then pressed, the juice that is expressed from them is gathered and a sweet produced from it. The juice itself is also exported to Egypt and other parts of Syria.'* Sweet ripe carob pods from an evergreen tree of great longevity have been valued for their sweetness since ancient times. As the pods are also known as locust beans, some have held that John the Baptist, who, during his sojourn in the desert lived on locusts and honey, may have actually consumed the plant food rather than the insect.

Another well-known commercial product was *dibs* which Ibn Battuta describes as a thick fruit juice made from grapes to which is added a kind of powder (*turba* or 'clay'!) so that it thickens or even solidifies. Thus when the paste is placed in a jar, it can be broken, leaving the substance in one piece. *'From this dibs is manufactured a sweetmeat into which pistachios and almonds are put, called al-mulabban.'* *Dibs* was also made from dates, which were pressed to extract the juice or else boiled in water until the dates disintegrated. The resulting mixture was strained and placed in large containers in the sun to thicken, or else boiled down to the consistency required. Purchased from the market and used in the domestic kitchen, *dibs* was an ingredient in the preparation of various kinds of condiment. In one recipe from the anonymous cookbook, the sweetness of *dibs* is used to balance the acidity of vinegar. In a complicated preparation for a type of pickled lemon, *dibs* is suggested as an alternative sweetening agent for sugar or honey – again to offset the presence of vinegar. A very short recipe in *The Treasury of Benefits* recommends making a sweet from *al-mulabban* which, with the addition of sesame oil and (more!) sugar produces a delicacy akin to another more complicated sweet preparation called *sabuniyya*. The compiler's enthusiastic comment on the result was, approximately, 'divinely delicious'.[7]

Finally, returning to the world of the pilgrim caravans venturing along the arduous routes of Arabia, food was prepared in large brass cauldrons called *dasts* from which poor pilgrims and those without provisions of their own were fed.

Hospitality

The consumption of food was discussed by religious scholars such as al-Ghazali within the wider conduct of hospitality. A sequence that began with the invitation to a meal and its acceptance, was followed by one's attendance, the serving of food, eating, and ended with taking leave of one's host. Ibn Battuta reports on hospitality in various cultural contexts but not with an explicit awareness of this order of partaking in a meal. Scholars' views were intended as guidance rather than as precise norms to which every Muslim must strictly adhere, although the Prophet's practice or *sunna* was held to be an exemplary guide. There was a funda-mental ethical thrust underpinning matters of food and the body which Muslims, especially those living in urban environments, were urged to contemplate seriously. First of all, al-Ghazali observed that the 'greatest moral peril into which mankind may fall is the desire of the stomach'.[8] Even sexual desire ranked second to the stomach as a source of temptation and error. According to al-Ghazali, repletion (*shaba*) following a meal was a perilous innovation, a practice introduced after the Prophet's death that contravened his own *sunna*. The danger of repletion was arousal of the passions and the stimulation of ailments in the body. Thus, secondly, proper knowledge of God's guidance and the deeds performed in light of it could be acquired only by means of a healthy body; and a healthy body was achieved only through food in necessary quantities over time. Moreover, if eating were a part of faith, eating in the company of others was more desirable than eating alone. The Prophet's custom had not been to eat by himself and he was remembered as saying 'The best food is that over which there are many hands.' This dictum expressed the ethos of hospitality that Ibn Battuta conveys in his narrative, and he experienced other enriching aspects that we shall encounter in due course.

Ibn Battuta's first mention of hospitality accorded to him personally occurs in the anecdote of a pious Egyptian *shaykh*, tales of whom he had picked up in Alexandria. This holy man, al-Murshidi, was believed to possess great powers, being able to bestow gifts from the 'divine store' and to experience visions of the unseen world. He was said to live alone in an isolated hospice (*zawiya*) outside the town of Fawwa in the Nile Delta, in retreat from the world, having with him neither servant nor companion. Yet his company was sought daily by men of all walks of life, high and low. All who visited him were offered food: *'Every man of them would express his desire for a particular dish, or fruit or sweetmeat and to everyone he would bring what his guest desired, though that was often out of season.'* When Ibn Battuta visited the hospice, the *shaykh* rose to embrace him and invited him to eat, but nothing is said of what he was offered. Upon departure the following day, the *shaykh* gave him travel provisions of '*small cakes* [kuaykat, sing. kaak] *and a few silver coins*'. The episode is important in the overall narrative as it was this same *shaykh* who had uncannily disclosed and interpreted his guest's dream of being borne afar on the wings of a giant bird, foretelling his future travels and lengthy sojourn in India. Ibn Battuta expressed his gratitude for having acquired the holy man's blessings (*barakat*) to guide and guard him on the pilgrimage and throughout his adventures beyond. More crucially for the present discussion, the story employs food as a metaphor for the *shaykh*'s real gift of hospitality, providing his guests with spiritual sustenance. The small cakes given to each guest setting out on the road would have been made from coarsely milled, unleavened barley. This is confirmed by Ibn Battuta's visits not long after his first pilgrimage to two other holy men, each of whom also made an impression upon him. One he met in a hermitage (*rabita*) perched on top of Mount Sinjar in northern Iraq. He, too, was endowed with miraculous powers and could fast for 40 days at a stretch, only breaking the fast with half a flat barley bread (*qars*). Like the *kaak*, these may have resembled rusks which required softening in water, broth or ghee before eating and were well adapted to the traveller's requirements. They may, indeed, be relatives of the traditional Greek biscuit Paximadia. The second encounter was with a famous ascetic in the Yemen who occupied a tiny, bare cell beside a mosque and offered his visitors pieces of dried barley bread with salt and thyme. Once again, by contrast, the urban bourgeois version of the cake (*kaak*), for example, might typically be made from the finest wheat flour, clarified butter and sesame oil scented with musk and rosewater and ground nuts sprinkled on top.

Food was in fact provided in many types of religious house that Ibn Battuta either heard about or visited himself. He describes one of the numerous 'monasteries' (*khanqa*) in Cairo, this one inhabited mainly by educated Persians, who were celibate and adepts of the Sufi path. When the company gathered for meals twice a day, each was given bread and broth in his own dish, none sharing with another, and sugar sweets every Thursday evening. In Syria, he mentions two hospices, one in Antakiya, the other on the outskirts of Sahyun, both of which offered food to all comers; interestingly, beside each hospice was situated the tomb of a holy man of repute locally or more widely. In the environs of al-Ladhiqiya there was a Christian monastery (*dayr*), the largest in Syria and Egypt, inhabited by monks. Christians from all over visited it, while '*Every Muslim who stops there is entertained by the Christians; their food is bread, cheese, olives, vinegar and capers*.' The fare was always modest although here apparently somewhat more substantially provided than elsewhere in this Christian monastery. There is an interesting parallel concerning al-Ghazali's argument for the spiritual merits of hunger and the beatitude from Jesus' Sermon on the Mount: 'Blessed are those who hunger and thirst for righteousness, for they shall be filled.' Among several of the Prophet's sayings related to the subject, al-Ghazali cites this: 'The most exalted amongst you in God's sight on the Day of Judgement shall be those who hungered and meditated the longest for His sake.'[9] He also cites a saying attributed to Jesus and one allegedly found in the Torah.

Before we come to Ibn Battuta's narrative on Arabia, we can round out the story thus far by following his footsteps during the months between his first and second pilgrimage, as he travelled first from Mecca to Kufa, Wasit and Basra in southern Iraq and then into south west Persia. While his caravan remained camped for three days outside Wasit, he set out for a village a day's journey from the city, intending to visit the tomb of the famed founder of the Rifaiyya Sufi order. An enormous hermitage (*ribat*) there housed '*thousands of poor brethren*'. After a ritual display of drumming and dancing by the brethren, the sunset prayers were said and a meal was presented consisting of rice bread, fish, milk and dates, followed by a ritual *dhikr* recitation. The mention of rice immediately catches our attention.[10] Rice cultivation generally required good water supplies; river valleys that flooded naturally or land that was irrigated from them were ideal. The districts around Wasit, the lower Euphrates and the canals that connected it to the Tigris had all witnessed the ancient crop's diffusion during the first centuries of the Islamic era. As in the present context, rice was often associated with fish consumption in Iraq and Persia. Moreover, rice bread – if not rice itself – was judged by some to be the poor man's ordinary fare, one view stating that it was a famine food. Stories circulated of misers in Basra who offered rice bread and little or nothing else to their guests, but that simply indicated that rice was inexpensive and even suited a skinflint's style of hospitality. The physician al-Razi's opinion was that rice bread was generally more difficult to digest and evacuate than wheat bread and hence people from experience would eat it only if accompanied by salty or very fatty dishes, or with milk or garlic. Ibn Sayyar al-Warraq discussed the merits of different grains in his cookbook. He classified wheat as the most suitable for human consumption. Rice was deemed very nourishing and cooking it with lots of fat facilitated digestion, while cooking it with milk and sugar produced a wonderfully healthy dish. Ibn Qayyim al-Jawziyya (d. 1350) in his *Tibb al-nabawi* (*Medicine of the Prophet*) noted that rice was the most nourishing grain after wheat and that Indian physicians claimed it was the most excellent of foodstuffs when cooked with cow's milk. The anonymous cookbook *The Treasury of Benefits* contains recipes for rice dishes showing the rice as an integral part of the dish and not an accompaniment to a main dish. *Rukhamiyya*, for example, was a dish of rice cooked in fresh milk and richly spiced. These were not dishes enjoyed by our poor brethren in the hermitage, but their simple fare nonetheless appeared to approximate to the physician's recommendation for at least one healthy daily meal.

Ibn Battuta praised the people of Basra for their generosity and hospitality, saying that no stranger felt lonely amongst them. The city's most notable feature was its vast number of palm groves. The city's religious judge sent him a huge basket of dates that the porter could scarcely carry. Another scholar invited him to table and gave him clothes and money, while a third also fed him and provided him with (more) dates, money and a 'date honey' called *sayalan*. This appears to be a local name for *dibs* where the syrup was extracted from the dates by applying the pressure of weights. Ibn Battuta does not explain to what use the 'honey' was put. Some months later, however, while on board ship sailing along the south Arabian coast, he mentions a meal prepared by an Omani merchant the like of which he claimed never to have eaten before or since: cooked unground millet with *sayalan* poured over what must otherwise have been an unappetizing gruel.

In Basra someone had recommended that Ibn Battuta travel through southern Persia (Iraq al-Ajam) before continuing his journey through Iraq al-Arab to Baghdad and the north. The route from Basra to Tustar and thence to Isfahan offered larger, more organized and possibly better-provisioned hospices for wayfarers than in all his previous experience. He says: *At the end of each stage of this journey was a hospice at which every travel-ler was supplied with bread, meat and sweetmeats. Their sweetmeats are made with grape-syrup mixed with flour and ghee. In each hospice there is a shaykh, a prayer-leader, a muezzin, and a servitor for the poor brethren, together with*

slaves and servants who cook the food.' In Tustar itself, Ibn Battuta lodged
in a religious college (*madrasa*) run by an eminent *shaykh* and descendant
of the famous ascetic Sahl b. Abdallah. He also managed the neighbouring hospice with the assistance of servitors, two of whom administered its
endowments and daily expenditure; another pair divided between them
the tasks of table management and food distribution for visitors and super-
vising the cooks, water carriers and domestics. The establishment accom-
modated the Tangerine for 16 days with hospitality he had not previously
enjoyed. He claimed that his food was sufficient for four persons: rice
mufalfal cooked in ghee, fried chicken, bread, meat and sweetmeats.
According to one recipe in *The Treasury of Benefits*, the rice dish was made
with meat, plenty of fat and houmus, the rice seasoned with the aromatic
resin mastic and cinnamon.

From Tustar heading towards Isfahan, Ibn Battuta travelled through
mountainous areas, lodging in hospices which in this region he noted
were called 'colleges' (*madrasa*), all handsomely endowed by the regional
king, or *atabek*. He made a passing observation that the mountains were
heavily forested with oak trees, and from the acorn – evidently a sweet,
palatable variety – bread was baked. He says nothing of his daily fare in
Isfahan where he lodged for two weeks in a hospice, but recalls that its
pious and devotee *shaykh* sent him food upon arrival and a local speci-
ality, watermelon of green rind and very sweet red pulp. They were, he
says, preserved, as were dried figs in his native Maghrib. As he was not
accustomed to eating them, his first attempt produced a strong 'relaxation'
of the bowels that took a few days to set right. For the rest of his travels
through southern Persia and Iraq he reveals little of food interest: a cheese
of remarkable flavour made in the town of Yazdukhas and the fare of the
hospice at Kazuran, where they offered *harisa* made from meat, wheat and
ghee accompanied by loaves of thin flat bread. This appears to be a simpli-
fied version of the *harisa* recipe in *The Treasury of Benefits*, in which beef
and husked wheat are cooked together with mastic, cinnamon, cheese and
dill.

Although Ibn Battuta seems consciously to have preferred the hospitality of a variety of religious institutions – indeed his travels seem very
cost effective from today's tourists' perspective – he does report also on
the generosity of merchants. His visit to Sarja in the Yemen introduced
him to a group of generous men famed for feeding wayfarers and pilgrims,

supplying them with provisions and transport. Good deeds received their own reward for '*God multiplied their wealth and gave them increase in His bounty and aided them in their good works.*' A merchant in Aden with whom he lodged entertained each night a company of merchants who were all '*men of piety, humility, uprightness and generosity, doing good to the stranger, giving freely to the poor brother, and paying God's dues in charity* [zakat] *as obliged by the sacred law*'.

We may now rejoin Ibn Battuta on the final stage of his first pilgrimage to Mecca. He relates an anecdote about the Prophet in connection with a particular location on the route just to the north of Mecca. As his caravan approached the pool of Khulays that lay in an open plain of numerous palm groves, it had to pass through a very sandy defile called Sawiq. The significance of the place he then explains to his reader. Once, when Muhammad and some companions passed through this narrow, sandy pass they realized that none of them was carrying rations. According to the famous *hadith* of this incident, the Prophet gathered some sand in his hands and offered it to the group which they 'supped', discovering the sand had miraculously transformed into a kind of gruel called *sawiq*. This episode was subsequently re-enacted annually by many pilgrims who would bring *sawiq* with them and consume it at this same site. Alternatively, caravan organizers provided the basic material and, says Ibn Battuta, '*It is served to people to sup mixed with sugar, and the caravan amirs fill water containers with it and serve the people from them.*'

Ibn Battuta's readers would have been familiar with the incident and with the food mentioned. *Sawiq* was made from grain such as wheat, but more popularly barley, the grain being lightly washed and soaked overnight; it was then drained and washed a second time, next toasted and, when cooled, ground fine, sifted and stored away for later use. It was, therefore, a very convenient form of nourishment for travellers to carry with them. When required, the toasted, ground flour was reconstituted with water, and sugar was added to taste; in other versions, *sawiq* flour could be moistened with either clarified butter or sheep's tail fat. Recipes for *sawiq* were known in the urban cuisine from at least the tenth century, including one version calling for a mixture of prepared wheat grain and dried pomegranate seeds together with fine sugar. Another up-market preparation combined equal parts of ground almonds and prepared wheat grain, without fat but with the aromatics musk, saffron and camphor.

Of *sawiq*, an anonymous poet appropriately said that mixed with water, 'It satisfies one's hunger and cools the heart after scorching heat'.[11] Ibn Battuta's account could be de-mystified, since *sawiq*, in the absence of water, was also eaten dry by licking a quantity of it from the palm of the hand. One could imagine, therefore, that what the Prophet offered his companions appeared to be 'sand', which they discovered was simply dried *sawiq* flour. Seen in this light, however, the story would not conform to the belief in the Prophet's wondrous powers.

Ibn Battuta observed that the inhabitants of Mecca ate but once a day, after the afternoon prayer, abstaining from further food until the same time the next day. Ibn al-Mujawir notes laconically that Meccans ate meat, ghee and bread.[12] Dried dates alone were consumed if anyone wished to eat at another time, and it was this food, in Ibn Battuta's opinion, that kept people healthy, with few diseases and infirmities found among them. Our traveller's view was seconded by his contemporary Ibn Qayyim al-Jawz-iyya. He states that dates (*tamr*), being hot and dry in nature, were well suited to inhabitants of hot countries, whose own temperaments tended to be cold. 'For this reason, people of Hijaz, Yemen and Taif and neighbour-ing countries [like Mecca] … eat a great deal of hot food which others find difficult, such as dates and honey.'[13] He explains that owing to the Hijaz's particular combination of soil and air and the date's natural prop-erties, it was not only a suitable food but also a beneficial drug to counter bodily ailments.

While residing in the Muzaffariya religious college, Ibn Battuta relates how he came to share in the blessings of the Holy City. One night he dreamed of the Prophet seated in a room in the Muzaffariya beside a window that looked out upon the shrine of the Kaaba. In the dream there appeared also a famous and pious Maliki resident called Khalil, known personally to Ibn Battuta. Dressed in the short white tunic of the Sufis, the man made several vows to the Prophet, among them never to turn a destitute person away from his house. Ibn Battuta recounted the dream to his friend who was deeply moved by it. From that day Khalil's servants baked bread and prepared cooked food that was brought to Ibn Battuta each day following the afternoon prayer.

This tale closely reflects certain features of another told to Ibn Battuta by a 'trustworthy' source during his first visit to Alexandria. In the city there lived a certain pious Maliki scholar and holy man. He was renowned for miracles (sing. *karama*) attributed to him, specifically in receiving ecstatic revelations in his sleep. One night the Prophet Muhammad spoke to him in a dream requesting that he visit Medina. The man humbly obeyed and when, at journey's end, he entered the Prophet's mosque and saluted the Messenger's tomb, he then sat on the floor against a pillar, his head resting on his knees in a posture commonly adopted by Sufis. After a time he raised his head to find loaves of bread, jugs of milk and a plate of dates set before him! He and his companions shared these provisions and then set out on the return trip to Alexandria.

The two dreams differ inasmuch as Ibn Battuta saw in his the Prophet seated silently by a window while in the other he addressed the holy man. Visions of the Prophet in dreams were nonetheless a widespread phenomenon in Muslim piety. They were always considered true, for, according to several versions of a well-known tradition, the Prophet said, 'He who sees me in a dream has seen me, for the devil does not appear in my form.'[14] In another version, a good vision (*ruya*) comes from God while a dream of the *hulm* type is from the devil. Variations on the story of the holy man's dream and his visit to the Prophet's tomb as his guest in Medina are found in other sources. Ibn Battuta's dream seems more idiosyncratic. It was popularly believed that stories of the legends and miracles of Muhammad helped establish a personal relationship between believers and their Prophet; the telling of, the listening to or the composing of such tales brought blessings upon all involved. Seeing the Prophet in a dream held the prospect of even greater *baraka*. When Khalil was told of it, the Prophet's blessing was cast upon both himself and Ibn Battuta. Then we recall that in Mecca Ibn Battutta was recovering from a serious illness while residing in the Muzaffariya college. Visions of the Prophet were believed to have a healing effect, among others. As Ibn Battuta attributed his recovery to God, he is clearly referring to the dream and the subsequent nourishment provided him by his pious friend's charity.

East Africa and south Arabian coast

During his voyage to the East African coast, Ibn Battuta's first recorded stop was Mogadishu. This was a large town of merchants established in the tenth century by Arabs from the Persian Gulf. As he was not of the merchant fraternity, but a jurist or 'man of religion', Ibn Battuta was obliged by local custom to await the sultan's pleasure. The traveller was housed in a residence for students of religion and food brought from the sultan's nearby residence. His description is worth quoting in full:

> *Their food is rice cooked with ghee and placed in a large wooden platter. On top of this they set platters of* kushan. *This is the seasoning made of chicken, meat, fish and vegetables. They cook unripe bananas in fresh milk and put this in one dish, while in another dish they put curdled milk on which they place pieces of pickled lemon, bunches of pickled pepper steeped in vinegar and salted, green ginger and mangoes. These resemble apples but have a stone; when ripe they are exceedingly sweet and are eaten like other fruit, but before ripening they are acid like lemons, and they pickle them in vinegar. When they take a mouthful of rice, they eat some of these salted and vinegar conserves after it. A single person of Mogadishu eats as much as a whole company of us would eat, as a matter of habit, and they are corpulent and fat in the extreme.*

Food was brought to him three times a day although he does not say in what quantities. In any event, Ibn Battuta enjoyed the sultan's favour for the customary three days, after which he doubtless found another agreeable host. Ibn Battuta uses the term *kushan* again while relating a story of the mausoleum in Shiraz of a famous *shaykh* who had spent time in Ceylon. Digressing on his own visit to Ceylon, Ibn Battuta notes how infidels had cooked food for himself and his party. '*They would bring banana leaves and put rice on them – this is their regular food – and they would pour over it* kushan, *which is a meat sauce.*' Here the term *kushan* is glossed as 'meat sauce' and above as 'seasoning', the same Arabic word *idam* employed in both contexts. In one sense *idam* could refer to 'any savoury food', but more particularly it meant a 'condiment' or 'seasoning' to accompany bread. In its widest sense, *idam* was anything that added relish – appreciation or pleasure – to one's food; hence, the classical adage that 'The best *idam* is hunger.'

Ibn Battuta next briefly visited the island of Mombasa before sailing further south to the African mainland city of Kulwa, from where his return journey to Zafar on the south Arabian coast commenced. He says of the Mombasa populace, '*Their food consists mostly of bananas and fish.*' They planted no grain but had to bring it from the African mainland. The island's main trees were the banana, lemon and the citron and there was a fruit the people called *jammun*, resembling an olive except that it was very sweet with an olive-like stone inside.

Mention of this fruit highlights interesting observations on food in Ibn Battuta's narrative of his voyage to East Africa and the south Arabian coast. *Jammun* (or *jumun*) is, according to the famous Anglo-Indian dictionary *Hobson-Jobson*, 'a poor fruit common in many parts of India' and often confused with the rose apple.[15] Ibn Battuta does not explain how this fruit came to Mombasa but in several passages he alludes to or makes explicit reference to trade in certain commodities native to India, like the *jammun*, from where they were shipped to south Arabia or to East Africa. Reciprocal trade involved at least one well-known Arabian commodity transported to India and that was thoroughbred horses. Ibn Battuta records that the voyage between Zafar (in modern Oman) and India with a favourable wind would take a month. Therefore the rice he had enjoyed in Mogadishu may have been imported from India, and was also exported to the south Arabian coastal cities of Zafar and Qalhat (also in modern Oman). One of the cereals consumed in Zafar was millet grown on land irrigated from deep wells. They also harvested a grain called *alas*, a species of barley. But their main food, says Ibn Battuta, was rice imported from India. In Qalhat, too, he enjoyed fish unparalleled in flavour so that he ate nothing else: '*They broil it on leaves of trees, place it on rice and eat it; the rice is brought to them from India.*' For Mogadishu, however, a more likely possibility was that rice was a cultivated crop. Across the continent in West Africa, cultivated species had developed from indigenous wild rice plants which were still found and gathered. Ibn Battuta's contemporary, the geographer al-Umari (d. 1349), recorded that rice was an important food in the state of Kanem bordering on Lake Chad. When he visited the large city of Kaukau (Goa) on the River Niger in 1352, Ibn Battuta stated that it was well provisioned with food including rice (*arruz*). But Arab authors, including Ibn Battuta, rarely specified whether they referred to the cultivated or wild variety. Nonetheless, as he travelled through villages in the kingdom of Mali, there was food aplenty for purchase, as well as rice, about which he notably remarked that '*it was detrimental to the health of white men*'. It is likely in this case that he had been offered wild rice which appealed neither to his taste nor his stomach, which the rice in Mogadishu, by contrast, evidently did.

At earlier moments during the dictation of his adventures to Ibn Juzayy, future episodes that had an Indian context seemed ever present in

Ibn Battuta's mind. Two anecdotes, one related in his account of Damascus, the other in stories about Mecca, occur as digressions with an Indian connection. And in each there is a common link with the journey to East Africa and south Arabia: reference to the betel leaf. In Mogadishu betel leaves (*tunbul*) and areca nuts (*fufal*) had been served to him and his companions while awaiting the ruler's instructions on their lodgings.[16] Together, these two plant products featured traditionally as an important symbol of hospitality in India, the custom now having been translated to Africa. It is unclear exactly when, where and in what manner, these plants – including the coconut – had been introduced. For example, Ibn al-Mujawir's description of al-Mansura on the south Arabian coast in the early thirteenth century mentions the different regions it imported food from, such as Iraq, Egypt, the Hijaz and Sind. The areca nut and the coconut, he says, were brought from India, and no mention is made of the betel leaf. Ibn Battuta claimed a century later that the betel leaf (and the coconut, *narjil*) were found only in India and in the city of Zafar owing to '*its similarity and proximity*' by sea to the sub-continent, implying that both had been brought from India and grown in Zafar. Likewise in Qalhat Ibn Battuta stated '*there is also betel but it is small leafed*', conveying the impression that another species was grown there. Exceptionally, he adds, there were some coconut trees growing in the Sultan of Zabid's gardens. Ibn Battuta's younger contemporary, the Rasulid Sultan of the Yemen and acknowledged scholar, al-Malik al-Afdal al-Abbas, dated the introduction of the coconut in Zabid to 1330. In 1366 a delegation had brought plants to him from Sind, among which may have been the areca tree which he included among the cultivated tree crops and fruits treated in his agricultural almanac. In short, therefore, the Indian-style hospitality Ibn Battuta received in Mogadishu was likely made with imported leaves and nuts.

He describes the ritual in the following way: '*The Indians attach immense importance to betel. … The gift of betel is for them a far greater matter and more indicative of esteem than the gift of silver and gold.*' Before eating, an areca nut (*fufal*) was crushed into small pieces and then placed in the mouth and chewed. Then betel leaves with a little 'chalk' (*nura*, lime) added were masticated along with the areca. '*Their specific property is that they sweeten the breath, remove foul odours of the mouth, aid digestion and prevent the injurious effect of drinking water on an empty stomach. Eating them gives a sense of exhilaration and promotes sexual intercourse.'*

In the two digressions already mentioned dealing with his travels in the Arab world Ibn Battuta describes first Indian funeral ceremonies, which he judged superior to those he saw in Damascus. As a mark of respect the family of a deceased person ate no betel until the funeral. The religious judge (*qadi*) or whoever performed the ceremonies offered betel leaves to the deceased's heir who ate them, thus concluding the ritual. In the second he adds further benefits of betel leaves and areca nuts already noted, that they '*make one's face and gums redder and act as a preventative of jaundice'*. Other references to betel consumption will be dealt with below in the discussion on nourishment habits in India.

The betel leaf, however, was fairly widely known in other contexts than the honouring of guests. The leaf was used in the Arabic culinary tradition as one ingredient in a well-known aromatic spice mixture (*atraf al-tib*), the actual ingredients of which – up to a dozen – and proportions of each could vary according to a cook's requirements.[17] Otherwise, betel was frequently used together with spikenard (*sunbul*) and other seasonings in many kitchen preparations. Spikenard was also used in medicinal recipes. The areca nut, too, appears as an ingredient in medicinal preparations such as a stomachic and an ointment for hot tumours.[18]

Fish was standard in the diets of the southern Arabian coastal populace. It was the only means of livelihood for the inhabitants of the port of Hasik who caught a fish called *lukham*. This resembled a dogfish and when cut open and sun dried it was used as food. On board boats sailing along the coast, Ibn Battuta's daily fare was dried dates and fish. Another species caught was called *shir mahi* and resembled the fish he knew in his own Berber tongue as *tazart*.

As to the coconut (*narjil*), featured at length alongside the description of the betel leaf, he provides first a physical description of the nut and then, among its properties, of the sweet liquid sipped from its inside that produced a wonderful aphrodisiac action.[19] The pulp, which tasted like a soft boiled egg, he says, sustained him for the 18 months he later spent in the Maldive Islands. The coconut was famous for another marvel, namely that oil, milk and honey could be made from it. The honey was derived from a sap extracted from the fruit stalk and then cooked '*in the same way that grape-juice is cooked when* rubb *is made from it'*. Recipes for *rubb*s, or concentrated juices, are found in both cookbooks and dispensatories detailing medicinal preparations, reflecting the interface between the medieval culinary and medical traditions.[20] The technique of preparation was similar in each, boiling the pressed juice down to a quarter of its original quantity and then straining it for storage. A *rubb* of quince juice, for example, was deemed effective against diarrhoea, vomiting and excessive heat. The concentrated coconut 'honey' was exported from India to the Yemen and China, says Ibn Battuta, from which sweetmeats were made. Coconut milk was prepared in the home by mashing the pulp and steeping it in water so that it assumed the colour and consistency of milk and then used as a sauce. The process of extracting the pulp illustrates this domestic preparation: '*There is in every house a kind of chair upon which a woman sits, having in her hand a stick with a protruding ferrule at one end of it. A hole is made in the nut just large enough to admit that ferrule and mash its contents and all that comes out is gathered on a plate until nothing is left inside the nut.*' For the oil, ripe coconuts were peeled, cut up, sun dried and cooked in cauldrons to extract the substance. It was used for quite different purposes, for lighting, as a sauce and for women's hair. Other sources claimed that the oil was used to improve memory and cure haemorrhoids. And coconut was said to be a component in concoctions that aided intercourse and increased semen. During his sojourn in the Maldive Islands, Ibn Battuta noted that the majority of trees were coco palms, one of the chief sources of the Maldivians' food along with fish. These received his enthusiastic endorsement because '*all these products of the coco-palm and the fish which they live on have an amazing and unparalleled effect in sexual intercourse and the people of these islands perform wonders in this respect*'. Understandably, one of his favourite dishes was the root of a plant that was ground into flour, from which vermicelli was made and cooked in coconut milk. Nowhere else on his travels does he record a place where one could live on a diet of aphrodisiacs.

Anatolian hospitality

If there is a single theme that distinguishes the Anatolian narrative, it is expressed in the author's opening passage describing *Bilad al-Rum*, the land that had once belonged to and been ruled over by Byzantine Greeks from the capital Constantinople. These Christians, still present in significant numbers, were now under the protection of Muslims known as Turkmen. Ibn Battuta perceived the essential quality of this politically and culturally dominant Muslim population as kindliness, where people asked after travellers' needs and treated them as though they were kin. The point was illustrated by describing the men's custom of bringing them fresh bread and accompanying condiment (*idam*) as a special favour with the entreaty, '*The women have sent this to you and beg of you a prayer.*' The theme is hospitality.

As we have seen in the previous chapter, the religious association of the *akhi*s had deeply impressed Ibn Battuta, and his praise for their welcoming spirit towards strangers provided the main, if not exclusive, focus of the hospitality theme. Naturally, as elsewhere on his travels, many other individuals had also received him and his party kindly, such as a local judge (*qadi*), a preacher (*khatib*), head of a religious college (*madrasa*) or even one of its occupants; in this last instance a learned professor and pilgrim who resided in the *madrasa* in Akridur, '*received us with the utmost generosity and lavishly supplied our needs*', he says with grateful satisfaction. Even the commander of the castle at Tawas sent them a hospitality gift (*diyafa*) and other provisions while they lodged in a hospice outside its walls.

The Anatolian experience was enriched by the hospitality of local rulers, or sultans. Ibn Battuta was in Akridur during Ramadan. For most of the month, the sultan of the city invited them to break the daily fast at sunset with him and his other guests. Exceptionally in this section of the travels, he mentions a specific prepared dish, *tharid*. He says, '*the first dish with which the fast was broken was* tharid *served in a small platter and topped with lentils soaked in butter and sugar*' and explains that owing to the Prophet's preference for the dish above all others, it was appropriate to break the fast with it. The reference is to the well-known tradition from the Prophet in which he declared that 'The excellence of Aisha [widely held to have been his favourite wife] over other women is as the excellence of *tharid* over all other food.' The dish was a thick soup based on bread and meat. In his *Medicine of the Prophet*, Ibn Qayyim al-Jawziyya describes it thus and states that as bread was the best of foods and meat the king of condiments, their combination produced the most excellent of dishes.[21]

Al-Warraq's cookbook contains two recipes for *tharid*, one attributed to the Abbasid caliph al-Mamun, the son and successor of the legendary Harun al-Rashid (d. 833). In the court version, chickpeas were first soaked in water until softened. Then two plump pullets, cut into pieces, were placed in a clean pot together with the water and half the soaked chickpeas and seasoned with cumin and salt. The meat was placed over the fire until half cooked and then small whole onions and old, sharp cheese were added and cooked until both meat and onions were done. At this point black pepper was added and eggs broken over the pot, leaving them to set sunny side up. In a second serving dish, white bread was broken into pieces and the broth poured over it, to which were added the meat and onions – but not the chickpeas because they caused flatulence – then a cup of sweet olive oil was poured on top and finally garnished with the poached eggs. Ibn Battuta's abbreviated description suggests that over a thick soupy concoction of bread and meat, the lentils soaked in butter and sugar were added.

Tharid was only the first of several dishes indulged in each evening. In either preparation, the Prophet's favourite dish was suitably commemorated, although one imagines it had been a more austere version of *tharid* that once incited the Prophet's enthusiasm. The feast ending Ramadan was celebrated in another city, Ladhiq, at the residence of its sultan and no one, rich or poor, was turned away from the sultan's door on that day.

The sultans of some other cities extended hospitality to the traveller, although Ibn Battuta explicitly mentions only one other dish he was offered. The Sultan of Laranda, for example, sent him '*quantities of food, fruit and sweetmeats in silver platters*' while he visited the city. The Sultan of Birgi invited him to share his table at his retreat in the hills. He provided Ibn Battuta and his companions with a mobile Turkmen tent and also sent them '*presents of rice, flour and butter in sheep's stomachs, this being the practice of the Turks*'. Once, while visiting him in turn, the sultan noticed that the servants, who were cooking out of doors, had no spices or vegetables for the pot and therefore he ordered supplies brought for them while chastising his store-keeper for neglecting the guests. Later, in the sultan's city residence, the party was served bowls of refreshing diluted *jullab* into which lemon juice had been squeezed and small pieces of biscuit added. Undiluted *jullab* (from which the English word 'julep' derives) was a very sweet, thick syrupy paste made from sugar, water and rose water heated together; it was used in both culinary and medicinal recipes. Ibn Battuta's legal eye was quick to catch the detail that the *jullab* was served in two types of container, in gold and silver bowls with matching spoons, and also in porcelain bowls with wooden spoons. Those who, for pious reasons, wished to abstain from using gold or silver objects reproved by the Prophet, could still enjoy the refreshment from the other bowls.

Returning now to the receptive behaviour of the *akhi* associations, Ibn Battuta's party discovered on one occasion that ignorance of the Turkish language and of *akhi* customs caused them great alarm at what proved to be a wholly innocent, albeit rowdy, encounter. In Ladhiq, as elsewhere, rival associations of *akhis* lived and competed for the attention of passing strangers. In the Ladhiq market place, one group of young men (*fityan*) emerged suddenly and seized their horses' bridles while another group challenged them, apparently threatening a major altercation. Each party of *fityan*, amidst a scuffle, clamoured to offer lodging and food to their guests. Fortunately an Arabic-speaking Turk intervened and the matter was resolved by drawing lots for which side would be first to serve them. '*We marvelled at their natural generosity (fa-ajabna min karam nufusihim)*,' Ibn Battuta remarked in retrospect. The first group, led by the *akhi* Sinan, conducted the travellers to his hospice where they were served '*with several dishes*'. They were then taken to the bath house, each personally attended by a young man. Thereafter they were presented with a '*great banquet with sweetmeats and quantities of fruits*'. The second group of *akhi*, led by Tuman, repeated their rival's invitation in the matter of lodging and food but '*went one better inasmuch as they gave us a good sprinkling of rose water when we came out of the bath*'.

Throughout his Anatolian travels, Ibn Battuta was welcomed in at least two dozen *akhi* hospices. His recollection of their hospitality conveys the impression that he experienced greater generosity with each new hospice he lodged at. Certainly his gratitude was most patently expressed while enduring the rigours of the Anatolian winter. When his party arrived at an *akhi* hospice in Buli, he commented on their custom of keeping a fire alight during the weeks of bitter cold. After changing his clothes and warming himself by the fire he exclaimed effusively, '*the* akhi *not only brought food and fruit but lavished them. What an excellent body of men these are … how unselfish … how kindly affectionate to the visitor, how magnanimous in their solicitude for him! The coming of a stranger to them is exactly as if he were coming to the dearest of his own kin.*' Their behaviour he compared to that of the people of Shiraz and Isfahan, but the *akhis* were in their way '*more affectionate to the wayfarer and show him more honour and kindness*'.

The travellers' last stop in Anatolia was Sanub (Sinope), a charming fortified city on the southern shore of the Black Sea. Most of the fruits grown there were figs and grapes. The party lodged in a hospice and visited the beautiful congregational mosque, the likely scene of the following anecdote. The local populace, as throughout Anatolia, belonged to the Hanafi school of law, while Ibn Battuta's allegiance was to the Maliki school. The locals noticed their visitors prayed with their arms hanging by their sides, instead of bending them upwards at the elbow in the Hanafi fashion. Suspicions were raised that they might be Shia Rafidi 'heretics' and they remained unconvinced by Ibn Battuta's attempt to explain that Malikis did pray that way. To test their doubts, the sultan's deputy presented them with a live hare, and a witness was instructed to report what they did with it. '*We slaughtered it ritually, cooked it and ate it,*' says Ibn Battuta, and suspicions were at once allayed, as it was known that Rafidis, by their own religious norms, were prohibited from eating hare! As an instance of how food taboos could be used to detect and expose a heretic, a similar tactic was used by the conquering Christian authorities in al-Andalus against Jews and Muslims to test their professed 'conversion' to the true faith by catching them out *refusing* to eat pork.

The Golden Horde

Once he had crossed the Black Sea into the Crimea and the extensive steppes beyond, Ibn Battuta entered the domains of the Golden Horde, one of the successor states to the empire of Genghis Khan. Its present ruler was Sultan Muhammad Uzbek. The traveller's first description of the people's lives was their means of transport by horse-drawn (or oxen- or camel-drawn) four-wheeled wagon, described in the previous chapter. His second impression was of their food customs, which commenced:

> *These Turks do not eat bread nor any solid food, but they prepare a dish from something like millet in their country which they call* dugi. *They put water in a pot over the fire and when it has boiled they pour into it some of this* dugi *and if there is any meat they cut it in small pieces and cook it along with the* dugi. *Then every man is given his portion in a bowl and they pour over it curdled milk to drink; sometimes they drink it with mare's milk they call* qimizz [qumiss]. *They are powerful and hardy men with sound constitutions.*

He then declared that '*they regard the eating of sweetmeats as a disgrace*'.

This passage is puzzling. Ibn Battuta claims that these Turks did not eat bread and were averse to sweetmeats. Some 90 years earlier, the elderly Franciscan John of Plano Carpini had travelled through Golden Horde territory on his way to the great Mongol assembly held near Kara-korum in Central Asia. In his account of the Tartars, or Mongols, he expressed his loathing for their food and eating habits and noted: 'They have neither bread nor herbs nor vegetables nor anything else, nothing but meat of which, however, they eat so little that other people would scarcely be able to live on it.'[22] He mentions, too, their preparation of millet and their consumption of milk from various animals. These observations, however, refer to Central Asian Mongol culture and not to that of the Golden Horde. Recent research, moreover, has shown that Turki-cization of the areas later conquered by the Mongols of Genghis Khan had been most pronounced and rapid among the Golden Horde. From early eleventh-century Arabic and Persian commentaries on the Turks it is evident that settled and nomadic Turkish peoples used a variety of grain products in addition to their traditional dairy and animal foods. These grain dishes included porridge, noodles, pancakes and breads of different kinds. By the thirteenth century Islamized Turks had not only absorbed much of Middle Eastern food customs but had begun to make their own contributions, among them possibly the prototype of the sweet-meat baklava, although its parentage is contested.[23] As we have seen in the previous section on Anatolia, Ibn Battuta had been entertained by his Turkish hosts with both bread and sweetmeats. In the same passage cited above, he observes that Muhammad Uzbek's governor of Qirim had invited Ibn Battuta's party to his hospice outside the city and prepared for them '*a great banquet, including bread*'. Here, curiously, bread appears to be mentioned incidentally as an exception. Yet, in an example noted below, bread was provided for them by one of the sultan's wives. Why then, the supposed difference between food habits of the Anatolian Turks and those of the Golden Horde? At this remove in time it is difficult to fathom Ibn Battuta's intention, and its execution by Ibn Juzayy has left an unwitting error unattended until the present.

Ibn Battuta returns to firmer ground in noting the beverage of mare's milk or *qumiss*, widely known among all the nomadic peoples of Central Asia, but he does not describe its preparation. For this we fortunately possess the account by another Franciscan, Friar William of Rubruck, who also reported on Mongol life in the mid-thirteenth century. Both he and Ibn Battuta were well aware of the economic importance of the large flocks of sheep and herds of horses to the steppe inhabitants. The latter provides details of the lucrative horse trade with India, while William observed that the flesh of a dead horse alone was used in different ways: cut into strips, dried in the sun and wind and kept for future consumption; and sausages made from the intestines, eaten fresh, were deemed by him to be better than the pork variety. The mare, too, was a valuable source of milk. For the preparation of *qumiss*, a large quantity of the milk was poured into a skin bag and churning begun with a 'stick which is as big as a man's head at its lower end and hollowed out; and when they beat it quickly it begins to bubble like new wine and to turn sour and ferment, and they churn it until they can extract the butter'. The remaining, fairly pungent liquid, says the good friar, 'greatly delights the inner man'.[24] The butter, completely boiled down, was stored unsalted in containers made of sheep's bellies, and kept for use in winter; here Rubruck describes the very gift, mentioned above, sent to Ibn Battuta by the Sultan of Birgi.

Two other dishes are described by Ibn Battuta which appear to be similar in that each was made from dough and taken with milk. In *burkhani*, the dough was cut into small pieces with a hole in each, cooked, and supped with curdled milk. *Rishta* was a preparation of thin noodles made from fresh dough (rather than the sun-dried variety called *itriya*) cooked and supped with fresh milk. A beverage colloquially called *buza* was fermented millet to which Ibn Battuta assigned the label *nabidh*, or wine, forbidden by the majority of Muslim schools of law. He helpfully adds, however, that as these Turks adhered to the Hanafi school, *nabidh* was *'permissible according to their doctrine'*. Together these items underlined the importance of grains and dairy products to the diet of this Turkish herding community.

Ibn Battuta's principal objective in travelling through the lands of the Golden Horde was to visit the sultan's court. It will be remembered that Muhammad Uzbek was listed in the travel account as one of the seven mighty kings in the world. His capital was the city of New Sarai on the River Volga, but being a prudent ruler, he moved his government and court about to make his presence felt everywhere and keep a close eye on his realm. Ibn Battuta, therefore, was obliged to inquire after his current location. That was reportedly at Bish Dagh, or Five Mountains, but he arrived only to find the sultan's residence (*urdu*) had moved on again. Finally they came upon the vast mobile city '*with its inhabitants, with mosques and bazaars in it, the smoke of the kitchens rising in the air (for they cook while on the march), and horse-drawn wagons transporting the people*'. The sultan and his retinue, comprising armed slaves and officers of state, travelled in its own camp (*mahalla*), while each of his wives travelled separately, accompanied by companions, servants and guards. Amidst the multitude of thousands, the traveller from Tangier had placed his modest wagon tents on a nearby hilltop. Passing by chance, one of the sultan's wives noticed the flag of the newcomer flying in front of his shelter. She inquired after its owner and Ibn Battuta reciprocated by sending her a small gift, a gesture that resulted in her issuing orders that he should encamp near her quarters and that of the sultan's son. The Tangerine had indeed arrived!

At this point the Golden Horde narrative is set apart from the Anatolian. Whereas the latter had focused upon religiously inspired hospitality within the *akhi* hospices, the narrator's main concern here is the ruling institution's lavish pomp and ceremony. Hospitality was not forsaken, of course, but expressed in a different manner; as Ibn Battuta remarks, '*these Turks do not know the practice of giving hospitable lodging to the visitor and providing him with maintenance. What they do is send him sheep and horses and skins of qumiss, and this is their way of honourable treatment*'. Shortly after his arrival, Ibn Battuta prayed in the sultan's company and joined him in the meal afterwards. '*They brought in dishes of various soups, like that made from* dugi, *then roasted flesh meat, both of sheep and of horses*'. Subsequent references to food are made in the context of the sultan's court ceremonial and in meeting each of his four wives. The principal wife, Taitughli, served the company *qumiss* in wooden bowls and offered one to the traveller personally with her own hands. This was '*the highest of honours in their estimation*', he cooed. But, as this was his first experience of *qumiss* and he found it disagreeable, he passed the bowl to a companion. Another wife, Bayalun, sent the company after their visit '*food, a great quantity of bread (!), ghee, sheep, money, a fine robe, three horses of good breed and ten of ordinary stock*'. The fourth wife they visited, Urduja by name, '*ordered food to be served, then when we had eaten in her presence she called for* qumiss, *and our companions drank*'. These passages are ambiguous inasmuch as Ibn

Battuta declared his dislike of *qumiss* for its taste, not that he realized it might be alcoholic, while his companions indulged apparently untouched by religious scruples, or else tacitly adopting the Hanafi approach.

There follows a long description of the ceremonies accompanying the festival of breaking the Ramadan fast. An enormous, richly appointed tent had been erected for the royal household, male and female, army commanders of high and lower rank, and possibly government officials as well. Food was brought in on tables of gold and silver borne by at least four men. A meat carver (*bawarji*) was assigned to each table to cut the joints of boiled horse meat and mutton. Elegantly attired in silken robes and apron, a set of sheathed knives slung from his belt, the carver sliced the meat into small pieces and placed them in a small silver or gold dish in which salt had been dissolved in water. The meat was artfully cut up on the bone as '*the Turks do not eat any meat unless the bones are mixed with it*'. The favoured brew on these occasions was fermented honey (*nabidh asal*), a Turkish-style mead, also served in gold and silver vessels; the alcoholic content of the liquor again was excused by the escape clause in Hanafi law. Amid an elaborate hierarchical ritual that accompanied the drinking, songs and chants were performed by a chorus. A second pavilion had been set up for religious personnel, judges, preachers, jurists and *shaykhs*, including Ibn Battuta, and food was brought to them in the same manner. Some legists present abstained for religious reasons from eating off gold and silver tables. The climax of festivities witnessed the distribution of wagon loads of *qumiss* among the guests; Ibn Battuta gave his cart load to a doubtless grateful Turkish neighbour.

A note of distress touches Ibn Battuta's account of the Golden Horde and it concerned the consumption of alcohol. He twice explained Turkish habits to his readers by the Hanafis' lenient position on drinking. Yet, for him, there remained a specific problem. Following the Ramadan feast, the pavilion guests withdrew to the mosque for Friday prayers. It was mooted among the waiting worshippers whether the sultan would be in a fit state to attend. In the event he arrived well past the appointed time of prayer and was distinctly unsteady on his feet. 'Teetering' is how his condition was expressed. The sultan's drinking bout resumed after prayers and continued into the night, punctuated only by later summons to worship. Ibn Battuta had already met two men related by marriage to Sultan Uzbek who suffered from an ailment affecting their legs. One was unable to walk or ride a horse and had to be carried by servants into the sultan's audience hall. Later he visited the sultan's governor of Khwarizm who suffered in the same way. The disease he identified as gout (*niqris*), '*a malady very common among the Turks*'. A suggested relief for the condition was a poultice made with chicory. A second recommendation, based on a Prophetic tradition, was to eat figs, although Ibn Qayyim al-Jawziyya was not convinced, saying, 'There is room for speculation as to the validity of this.'[25] Although Ibn Battuta did not relate the condition to a particular cause, his repeated mention of it probably expressed his concern for the sultan's own health and future well being. Rather than condemning the sultan's behaviour from a religious viewpoint, he chose to highlight its potential or perhaps inevitable consequences. On the other hand, judging overall his experience among the Golden Horde, the sense of distress was in a measure relieved by his fascination at meeting the sultan's wives and daughter and receiving their generous hospitality.

Between his departure from Muhammad Uzbek's capital of New Sarai until his arrival at the Indian frontier of the Indus River valley, Ibn Battuta has little more to add on matters of food. On the second, 30-day stage of their arduous trek to the city of Khwarizm, the short halts were enough to cook quickly, in '*a single boiling*', millet (*duqi*), to which were added pieces of dried meat and sour milk poured on top. Then everyone ate (and slept) while the wagon was on the move. In Khwarizm, the governor's warm reception, despite his gouty condition, involved a lengthy chat with the traveller about his recent experiences, and then food was served: '*roasted fowls, cranes, young pigeons, bread baked with butter, which they call* kulija, *biscuits and sweetmeats … followed by seeded pomegranates, grapes and wonderful melons*'. The melons became the topic of a lengthy note extolling them as equal to those of Isfahan and Bukhara. Cut into strips, sun dried, packed in baskets and exported to distant parts, they were acknowledged as second to none for their sweetness. After their session with the governor, he sent to their lodgings a gift of rice, flour, sheep, butter, spices and loads of firewood to use for cooking and heating for the journey ahead.

India now beckoned, and Ibn Battuta the traveller would for nearly a decade revert to the role of sojourner in Delhi, imperial capital of Sultan Muhammad b. Tughluq.

The sultanate of Delhi

Readers of the second volume of the travels would have been struck by
some of Ibn Battuta's first impressions of India: the close border super-
vision by the sultan's intelligence officers and their meticulous reports
on travellers; a hint of the empire's vast extent given the 50-day march
to the capital Delhi from his crossing point on the Indus; strange and
dangerous beasts like the rhinoceros that attacked their party as it passed
through a reed forest; and finally, a people in the town of Janani, Hindus
long established in Sind who prohibited exogamous marriage and forbade
commensality with anyone outside their community. This was the Moroccan's introduction to another continent, another people and their ancient
civilization that pre-dated the rise of Islam, a people who in so many
respects were alien to it except in their shared humanity.

India was not Anatolia, nor even the domains of the Golden Horde.
Each of these latter territories was slowly absorbed into the *Dar al-Islam*
(the Abode of Islam) through conquest and conversion. By contrast,
India was the Abode of Islam for the politically dominant minority while
remaining surrounded by the Abode of War (*Dar al-Harb*) of the overwhelming Hindu majority. The Muslim political presence in India proper
began towards the end of the twelfth century with the capture of Delhi
from Hindu Rajput rule. When Muhammad b. Tughluq succeeded to his
father's title as sultan, by the prior arrangement of his 'accidental' death,
Ibn Battuta was fortunately on hand to furnish posterity with a picture of
court life and Tughluq's rule between 1333 and about 1342, which in historian Peter Jackson's judgement is unmatched anywhere in its vividness.
He adds:

> In describing Muslim and Hindu territories as geographically separated,
> Ibn Battuta was pointing to a feature of the Sultanate that marked it
> out from other Muslim polities. Elsewhere in the Islamic world it made
> sense to talk of the Dar al-Islam and the Dar al-Harb; but not India. ...
> [Nothing was so clear cut] ... Obeisance, like tribute, was intermittent.
> ... The open countryside, the forests, the hills, these were the domain of
> the infidel. ... The Muslim population of the Sultanate largely resided in
> its fortified towns and cities, and even there they were not unusually a
> minority.[26]

Ibn Battuta said of the great fortress of Gwalior that it was '*an isolated and inaccessible castle, in the midst of the infidel Hindus, and that the generality of its inhabitants were infidels as well*'.

The demographic mosaic translated into culinary terms meant that commensal relations between Hindu and Muslim were off limits, except possibly at court. Even then, the Hindu veneration of the cow and the Muslim taboo against pork were religious barriers involving concepts of impurity and contamination, which neither tradition could challenge. Ibn Battuta found, too, that he had to explain Indian food customs to his readers of Arabic in terms that would make the strange familiar to them. This involved another linguistic layer, Persian, which had become a lingua franca among Muslims in India. The first reference to foodstuffs related to the large town of Siwasitan where melons were grown by the side of the Indus. The inhabitants fed modestly upon sorghum and peas called *mush-unk*, from which bread was baked, evidently a loaf of inferior quality from our traveller's viewpoint. There was a plentiful supply of fish and buffalo milk, but Ibn Battuta recoiled from people's habit of eating skink (*saqan-qur*). This, he explained, was a small animal resembling a lizard caught by digging it out of the sand. He next described its preparation: '*they slit open its stomach, discard the contents and stuff it with turmeric* (kurkum). *This is what they call* zard shubah, *meaning yellow stick, and takes the place of saffron with them. When I saw this small animal and them eating it, I deemed it impure and would not eat it.*' The Persian words in this passage, therefore, required explanation in order to make his observations intelligible.

Yet a further linguistic obstacle required surmounting. The mango (*anbah*), for example, was '*a tree which resembles orange trees but is larger and more leafy ... and its fruit is of the size of a large pear*'. According to *Hobson-Jobson*, the north Indian names for mango were *Am* and *Amba*, and Ibn Battuta's European contemporary Friar Jordanus (*c.* 1328) had used the word *aniba* to describe it in his book of wonders of India. Ibn Battuta continued, explaining its use by employing comparison with practices in Morocco: '*When the fruit is green and not yet fully ripe the people gather those that fall, put salt on them and pickle them as limes and lemons are pickled in our country.*' The ripened fruit was eaten like apples, either cut with a knife or sucked. Indians also pickled green ginger and peppers '*which they eat with meat dishes, taking after each mouthful a little of these pickled fruits*'. As the notion of pickled fruit was familiar to Moroccans, its extension to other food items and their use at table with meat were additional details of Indian foodways Ibn Battuta conveyed to his readers.

The passage continues with the fruit described as the best in India, the *shaki* and the *barki*, known in English as jack fruit.[27] The fruit grows directly from the tree trunk on a short stem and, according to a modern account, can occasionally weigh up to 40kg. Ibn Battuta assigns the name to the fruit that grows next to the ground *barki*, and *shaki* to the one higher up. '*The former are sweeter and better flavoured; the latter resemble large gourds and have a skin like oxhide.*' Inside each fruit, he says, there may be up to 200 pods, resembling cucumbers, each pod with a kernel like a large bean. A modern account describes the kernels as being like chestnuts and when boiled to remove any bitterness they can be made into flour or candied. Ibn Battuta also noted that the kernels could be roasted or boiled and tasted like beans for current consumption, or they could be stored in earth until the following year. He describes several other fruits, each time drawing comparisons for his readers' appreciation: the fruit of the ebony tree was '*about the size and colour of an apricot and very sweet*' and another fruit, when sun-dried, tasted like figs; he ate it as a substitute for them, since figs were not found in India.

A passage on cereals grown for food in India mentions a variety of millet as the most common grain. Another type of millet (*qal*) resembled what, in Ibn Battuta's own Berber tongue, he called *anli*. *Shamakh* was a wild grain that provided food for '*devotees and ascetics, the poor and needy*'. It was gathered by beating the husk with a stick so that it fell into the collector's basket. After drying in the sun the husk was separated from the pith by pounding in a wooden mortar. The dried white pith could be baked as bread or cooked with buffalo milk to make gruel, his own preference which he frequently enjoyed. A dish made with a kind of pea was cooked with rice and eaten with ghee; it was called *kishri* and consumed every day for breakfast in the same way *harira* was the breakfast food of Moroccans. What Ibn Battuta omitted to say is that *kishri* was a traditional favourite among Hindus and readily adopted by Muslims. Much later, it became the breakfast fare known as kedgeree (from the Hindi *khichri*) popular among the British during the Indian Raj and in Victorian England. Ibn Battuta concluded his digression on Indian food grains and fruits with the remark that '*their land is generous and of good heart*'.

The objective of scholars and adventurers from western Muslim lands who travelled to Delhi was to secure an appointment at the sultan's court, *'to gain riches and return home'*, as Ibn Battuta put it succinctly. Muhammad b. Tughluq was known abroad for the favours he granted 'foreigners', or 'distinguished strangers', in welcoming them to his administration. On our traveller's arrival in Delhi the sultan was absent and his officials, acting upon their master's orders, took immediate care of the newcomers. Furnished accommodation was provided for Ibn Battuta and his companions, servants and slaves – about 40 persons in all – and an initial subvention of some 5,000 silver dinars which was accompanied by the sultan's hospitality gift of food supplies: 1,000 pounds of flour, one-third fine, two-thirds coarsely ground; 1,000 pounds of flesh meat, Indian restorative plants (*salif*), sugar, and areca nuts with 1,000 betel leaves. The sultan's mother sent further supplies which fed the entire party plus aiding some of the local poor with leftovers of bread-cakes, sweetmeats and candy that lasted several days. He was then assigned the revenue of several villages to produce an annual income of 5,000 dinars. At last he was introduced into the sultan's presence to be informed by a presiding high official, "'Do homage to the Master of the World, for he has appointed you religious judge for the royal city of Delhi and has fixed your stipend at twelve thousand dinars a year.'"

Despite his new domestic responsibilities, someone apparently imagined Ibn Battuta would now make his formal social debut and offer others his hospitality, what with his new administrative post and a ready supply of areca nuts and betel leaves. If he did entertain, we are not told about the occasions. Ibn Battuta was, above all, fascinated by the intricate, hierarchical ceremonial ways of the court. Although he claimed to have attended numerous small private gatherings with the sultan, he describes nothing of the fare provided. The food offered at the sultan's public meals, which he also attended, is described simply as, *'thin rounds of bread, round cakes in portions and filled with sweet confections, rice, chickens and* samusak'. The meal was preceded by cups of candy water and finished with mugs of barley water. The final symbolic touch was the presentation to each guest of *'a spoonful of powdered areca with fifteen leaves of betel tied in a bunch with a red silk thread'*.

The public meal appears, however, closely patterned on a large repast which the sultan had arranged each evening for an important religious dignitary from Tirmidh and his family as they were travelling, like Ibn

Battuta, the long road from Multan to Delhi. On one occasion he was invited to join the *qadi*'s company at dinner prepared by 20 cooks. The passage is worth quoting in full, noting again Ibn Battuta's use of comparison to explain the meal for his readers.

> *They would serve bread (consisting of thin round cakes like those we call* jardaqa*); they cut up the roasted meat into large pieces of a size such that one sheep makes four to six pieces, and they put one piece before each man. They served also round dough cakes made with ghee, resembling the bread called* mushrak *in our country, which they stuff with a sweet called* sabuniyya, *and on top of each dough cake they put a sweet cake which they call* khisti *(which means 'brick shaped'), made of flour, sugar and ghee. They then serve in large porcelain bowls meat cooked with ghee, onions and green ginger. After that they serve something they call* samusak *made of meat hashed and cooked with almonds, walnuts, pistachios, onions and spices, put inside a piece of thin bread fried in ghee. They put five (or four) of these before each person. Next they serve rice cooked in ghee with chickens on top and follow this with* luqaymat al-qadi *which they call* hashimi, *and then set down the* qahiriyya. *When they sit down to eat at the beginning vessels of gold, silver and glass are brought filled with sugared water, that is to say syrup* (jullab) *diluted with water. They call that* shurba *(sherbet) and drink it before eating. When they finish eating they are given jugs of barley water* (fuqqaa). *Finally they are given betel leaves* (tunbul) *and areca nut* (fulfal).[28]

Ibn Battuta does not note whether the barley water was, in this case, an alcoholic beverage or not. An interesting detail of this and the previous description of the public meal is our traveller's observation that a portion of every dish was placed before each guest which he ate from his own plate rather than the more familiar Middle Eastern custom of eating with other persons from the same larger 'communal' plate.

Ibn Battuta's account of India is essentially the story of Muhammad b. Tughluq, whose dominant quality was generosity. The tale of Indian foodways recounted here is the story, too, of generosity that reflected the hierarchical order of the ruling institution and the power exercised by the sultan at its centre. Moreover, as already stated, guests would eat separately from their individual plates. Ibn Battuta had noted a similar practice of ranking guests at the court feasts of Sultan Uzbek of the Golden Horde. In both cases, however, the ethos of the hospitality differed from the spiritual intimacy he had experienced among the hospices of Anatolia especially, but in other religious institutions as well, notably in southern Persia and Mecca and in the private quarters of *qadis*, jurists and pious devotees. In Anatolia, that intimacy was expressed on the numerous occasions, whether at the invitation of a sultan or of an *akhi* hospice, when a meal was followed by Quran recitation and the readers' voices '*worked upon men's souls ... at which hearts are humbled*', the evening ending with spiritual singing and dancing.

The last intimate meals Ibn Battuta describes occurred after he had left Delhi during a stay at the court of the Sultan of Hinawr (Honavar) on the Malabar coast. He was Sultan Jamal al-Din, '*one of the best and most powerful*' of rulers who was feared along the coast owing to the strength of his sea power and army; yet he was, remarkably, under the suzerainty of an infidel ruler called Haryab. Ibn Battuta and three colleagues were invited daily to break their fast with Sultan Jamal al-Din. The meal was served by a beautiful slave girl wearing a fine silk garment and the order of the meal centred upon her ladling out a large spoonful of rice with each course: the first comprised rice with salted peppers, green ginger, salted lemons and mangoes; then rice with various kinds of fowl; next, rice with fish; then rice with vegetables; and finally milk dishes with rice. Ibn Battuta's remark on this period in south India, the Maldives and Ceylon was that during the whole time he never had bread to eat and so after '*three years eating nothing but rice, I could not swallow it except by taking it with water*'.

Finally, despite this period of gastronomic discomfort and his several recorded bouts of illness, he seems to have suffered, shortly after leaving Delhi, only one serious spell of hunger and thirst throughout his travels where his life was imperilled. In that episode he was rescued by none other than a saint. But that is a tale for the following chapter.

CHAPTER 4

Tales of Sacred Places, Saints, Miracles and Marvels

Arguably the most striking feature of *The Travels* is Ibn Battuta's presentation of an international cast of often colourful characters. This is unsurprising when we recall Ibn Juzayy's introduction to *The Travels* and his notice to the reader that, in addition to the cities visited and events experienced, Ibn Battuta's account would describe the rulers, distinguished men of learning (*ulama al-akhyar*) and pious saints (*awliya al-abrar*) he had met. Scores of others are mentioned as well, some long deceased, some alive but whose acquaintance he had not enjoyed. These he had learned about from 'reliable informants'. In Ibn Battuta's day there was seldom as clear a division between scholars and saints as there had once been. An expert in one or several of the many Islamic branches of knowledge could also have possessed strong ascetic or mystical leanings, but this matter will occupy our attention later.

As for the category of sovereigns, Ibn Battuta had met many lesser or greater individuals whom he invariably designated as 'sultan', one who held power over a greater or lesser piece of territory, from a small city state to an empire. The label acknowledged only a person's actual possession of temporal authority, with none of the more grandiose pretensions to religious authority possessed by a caliph. We recall that he had divided the world among seven great rulers, five of whom he had met in person. Of the seven, however, only two he considered of real importance and for quite different reasons. First, there was the Sultan of Delhi, Muhammad b. Tughluq, to whom he devoted two entire chapters of his narrative and a third to his own experiences in Delhi, much of which related to that sovereign as well. Ibn Battuta's summary description of him is concise and balanced:

*This sovereign is, of all men, the most addicted to the giving of gifts and the
shedding of blood. His gate is never without some poor man enriched or some
living being executed. Stories circulate among the people of his generosity and
courage and of his cruelty and violence towards criminals.*

Ibn Battuta added that he strictly enforced religious ritual and was severe
towards those who neglected prayer. He was modest, judged affairs equi-
tably and was immensely successful as a ruler. Overall his dominant quality was that of generosity.

The other sovereign of note was, in fact, first on Ibn Battuta's list of
great sovereigns. This was Abu Inan Faris, the ruler of Morocco, who,
from his capital Fez, governed between 1348 and 1358. He was scion of
the Marinid founder who had established the dynasty in 1268. Both Ibn
Battuta and Ibn Juzayy claim more for Abu Inan than mere lordship of
a North African dynasty. In his introduction to *The Travels*, Ibn Juzayy
wrote:

> We pray God Most High for our master, the Caliph-Imam, the
> Commander of the Faithful, who places his trust in God Lord of the
> Universe ... Abu Inan Faris, the descendant of our masters the rightly
> guided Imams and orthodox Caliphs ... who is indeed the Shadow of
> God which is extended over mankind.

Ibn Battuta added that he had commenced his travels during the reign of
Abu Inan's grandfather, Abu Said (reigned 1310–31). The importance of
these passages was that the Marinid dynasty was trumpeted as the legitimate successor to the Abbasid caliphs, whose rule had been effectively
extinguished by the Mongol invasion and the destruction of Baghdad in
1258. A member of the Abbasid house escaped from Baghdad to Cairo
where the Mamluk ruler of Egypt and Syria, Baybars (reigned 1260–77),
set him up as a puppet caliph and feigned obedience to him to enhance
his own legitimacy. Ibn Battuta and Ibn Juzayy ignored this fiction and
concurred with popular Marinid sentiment and the official claim that Abu
Inan was the only contemporary Muslim ruler who fulfilled the legal and
traditional qualifications for leadership of the universal Sunni caliphate.
Both employed all of the traditional titles of the Abbasid caliphs in these
flattering passages. Just how feeble a fiction all such claims were in reality
Ibn Battuta illustrated by reporting Muhammad b. Tughluq's successful

effort to secure Sunni legitimacy for his own reign through investiture by the Abbasid shadow caliph from Cairo.

Ibn Battuta's return to Morocco from his world tour commenced at the city of Taza, where he learned the sad news of his mother's death from the plague. His next stop was Fez and his first meeting with Abu Inan. In his later reflection on the encounter he listed each of Abu Inan's qualities compared to the same virtue in some other ruler he had known. One comparison was with Muhammad b. Tughluq, that Abu Inan's *'beauty made me forget that of the King of India'*. The passage is a prelude to an encomium of more than a dozen pages in which both the traveller and his editor, Ibn Juzayy, joined thoughts in their estimation of the Marinid ruler. The virtues of justice, clemency and courage are listed with accompanying examples. Abu Inan dispensed alms to the poor, built hospices for the distribution of food to wayfarers to an extent that no other ruler Ibn Battuta had known matched. Moreover, he was active in defence of the shrinking Muslim frontier in al-Andalus, and combated the constant pressure from Christian forces dedicated to the re-conquest of the Iberian peninsula. Ibn Battuta claimed he had witnessed examples of all these qualities and that Abu Inan excelled in every matter beyond the attainment of any ruler or scholar one could imagine. All this was due to Abu Inan's total trust in God and God's unswerving support in return.

It would be easy to dismiss these pages of praise for what they are, obsequious flattery from two subjects utterly dependent upon their ruler's beneficence. More important is that the one-dimensional, monochrome portrayal of the Moroccan ruler stands in total contrast with the more nuanced, warts-and-all characterization of the sovereign of India. Ibn Battuta knew the strengths and weaknesses of Muhammad b. Tughluq, whom he had served for nearly a decade, compared with a man he had never met until his return to Morocco from years abroad.

Nonetheless, one detail merits attention. This concerned Abu Inan's reported interest in religious knowledge. Each day after the dawn prayer, there gathered in his palace mosque leading jurists and distinguished students to read aloud commentaries on the Quran, traditions (*hadith*) of the Prophet, the teachings of Maliki legal thought and practice which were dominant in North Africa and al-Andalus and, finally, books of the mystics known as Sufis. Ibn Juzayy added his opinion that Abu Inan grasped the meanings of Sufi symbolism and had been influenced in his humble behaviour by Sufi example, despite his elevated status as sovereign.

Ibn Battuta's observation that the Marinid court was a centre for the exposition of Maliki legal thought and of Sufi values is confirmed by modern scholarship. In Moroccan Islam under the Marinids a middle ground of 'juridical Sufism' existed as the most representative expression of religious thought and practice, a mid-point between the extremes of legal literalism and metaphysical mysticism.[1] Throughout the Marinid era, the rulers had sought legitimacy by promoting a popular form of piety as well as piety among the elite of religious scholars. This manifestation of Sufism remained subservient to the religious law (*sharia*) rather than being a potential threat to it. Suffice it to say here that Ibn Battuta, trained in Maliki jurisprudence, had, in addition, grown up within the prevailing climate of Moroccan Sufism that had then influenced his own thought and manner during his years abroad. He was sensitive to the nature of piety in both its legal and inner personal dimensions. The discussion at this point now requires a brief outline of the development of piety and Sufism within Islam.

Piety and Sufism

The mystical dimension of Islam, Sufism, emerged in the eastern Muslim heartlands of Iraq and Persia as early as the mid-eighth century. In Morocco it arrived later, appearing at about the beginning of the eleventh century. The name is widely accepted to have derived from the Arabic word *suf*, 'wool', after the woollen garment worn by ascetics. As the religious law evolved, it assumed an entire social system by outlining a privileged relationship between God and the entire Muslim community (*umma*). It embraced, on the one hand, the worship of God through the rituals of prayer, fasting, charity, pilgrimage and the emblematic declaration that 'There is no god but Allah, and Muhammad is his Prophet'. Added to ritual was the doctrinal belief in God's angels, His books of revelation, His prophets and messengers and the Day of Judgement. On the other hand, the law stressed the importance of social relationships and the proper behaviour essential to maintaining community cohesion in God's eyes. Adherence to the letter of the law and doctrine was upheld by traditionalist jurists and theologians. Most believers conformed to the 'external' meaning required by their religious texts, the Quran and the sayings and actions of the Prophet preserved in the *hadith*; this was deemed sufficient fulfilment of God's will in preparation for salvation and the afterlife.

Some, however, read the sacred texts in a more personal manner. For example, God seemed to communicate the prospect of an inward, spiritual path leading to a nearness and friendship with God: 'Your Lord is well aware of what is in your hearts, if you are righteous (sing. *salih*); he is ever forgiving to those who turn in sincere repentance to Him' (Q 17:25). In a famous *hadith*, 'to do good' (*ihsan*) was defined as 'worshipping God as though you see Him, for even if you do not see Him, He sees you'. Of course, all Muslims sought to do 'the good' by sincere belief and performance of the obligatory rituals. Sufis, who focused upon *ihsan*, viewed it as the heart of religion. It was the effort to internalize and intensify ritual practice and faith to a degree that the inner self or soul was transformed, culminating in a sense of seeing God here and now and drawing near to Him in the present life. Simply put, the Sufi responded to God's entreaty to 'Do good to others as God has done good to you' (Q 28:77).

Jurists who enforced the letter of the law condemned as heresy inner or esoteric truths uttered by certain 'drunken' Sufis – ascetics inebriated not from forbidden drink but from outrageous pretension. The episode of al-Hallaj (d. 922) was the most notorious case of all. Al-Hallaj was born in Persia and, after living in seclusion with Sufi masters, set out on his own to preach a form of esoteric asceticism. On one occasion, he was heard to exclaim in an ecstatic trance, 'I am the Real.' The remark was viewed by opponents as blasphemy. He was condemned for claiming to be divine, 'the Real' (*al-haqq*) being a synonym for God. He was ultimately arrested by the Abbasid government in Baghdad, imprisoned for some years and finally cruelly put to death.

The interpretation by 'sober' Sufis of the Quran's message nonetheless stressed the presence and immanence of God rather than the jurists' and theologians' emphasis on God's transcendence. The Quran verse that says 'Wherever you turn there is the face of God' (Q 2:115) was dealt with by literalist theologians to mean that God did possess a face, the true nature of which could not be explained in human terms. Understood by Sufis in a metaphorical sense, the verse implied God's presence in everything or nearness everywhere. Theologians further insisted that believers would not be granted a vision of God until they reached paradise. For their part, Sufis allowed for the natural human desire to encounter God in the present as well in the afterlife. Hence they emphasized *ihsan* as the effort to worship God as if He could be seen.

Conflict between these opposing positions diminished over time although never vanished, for tensions would reappear at irregular intervals in later periods when Sufis were often charged with fostering superstition at the expense of true faith. Contributions towards this improved situation came from prominent Sufis like the contemporaries Abu Bakr al-Kalabadhi (d. 995) and Abu Talib al-Makki (d. 996), each of whom had set forth a 'sober' vision of mystical piety that helped bridge the gap with orthodox law and theology. A further contribution came from the scholar al-Ghazali, whom we met in the last chapter. He had mastered the disciplines of the jurist, theologian, and philosopher, and his most enduring treatise popularized Sufi values. The historian of medieval Islam Marshall Hodgson has noted that by the twelfth century Sufism was acknowledged as a vital part of Muslim religious life. 'Thus gradually Sufism, from being one form of piety among others, and by no means the most accepted one either officially or popularly, came to dominate religious life not only within the Sunni fold, but to a lesser extent even among the Shia.'[2]

The early, informal and individual expression of ascetic mysticism subsequently developed into groups of seekers gathered around a prominent teacher, all living by a system of rituals for spiritual training within an organized communal life. When the original nucleus grew in fame and novices, other groups emerged as satellites linked to it, all adhering to the grand master's teachings and communal rule. The institution was now commonly called a Sufi order, or *tariqa*, meaning a 'way' or 'path'. One of first *tariqas* to achieve a genuinely international outreach was the Qadiriyya founded in Baghdad and named after the famous preacher and Sufi saint or Friend of God, Abd al-Qadir Jilani (d. 1166). He was head (*shaykh*) of a college (*madrasa*) of Hanbalite law, one of the four recognized schools of Sunni Muslim legal practice that included Maliki law. He also supervised a hermitage (*ribat*) for spiritual training of Sufi novices (sing. *murid*). After Abd al-Qadir's death the order was led by family members, several of whom perished during the Mongol destruction of Baghdad in 1258. While the order did subsequently spread to other regions, its headquarters remained in the erstwhile Abbasid capital.

Ibn Battuta and the Sufi *tariqas*

The Mevlevi order

During his travels through Anatolia, Ibn Battuta visited Koyna, where he lodged in the hospice of the local *qadi*. He also visited the mausoleum and enormous hospice of the founder of a major Sufi order which he referred to in the Moroccan fashion as a *taifa*, meaning 'faction' or 'party'. Ibn Battuta called the order the Jalaliyya, named after Jalal al-Din Rumi (d. 1273). He observed also the title of respect, *mawlana* or 'our Master', accorded to Jalal al-Din by his disciples, from which the actual name of the order – in the Turkish language, Mevlevi – was derived. Although Ibn Battuta did not mention the custom of dancing that Jalal al-Din introduced into the ritual of his community, the order of Mevlevis today is celebrated throughout Europe and North America, and is known as the Whirling Dervishes.

Rumi was born in Balkh (present-day Afghanistan) in 1207. His father, Baba Walad, moved the family about, residing for a time in Baghdad, Mecca and Damascus before settling in Konya where he taught in a *madrasa* until his death in 1230. Jalal al-Din, still in his early 20s, inherited his father's position. One day a wandering Persian mystic named Shams al-Din Tabrizi arrived in Konya. The subsequent meeting between the two men exercised a profound influence upon Jalal al-Din's life and he henceforward dedicated himself to the mystical path. His fame spread throughout Anatolia and novices gathered about him to learn his 'way'. In one of his extant writings, he reflected upon the occasion al-Hallaj had made his 'drunken' outburst, and attempted to explain what he had actually intended: 'When al-Hallaj's love for God reached its utmost limit, he became his own enemy and he set himself at naught. He said, "I am the Real", that is, "I have been annihilated; the Real remains, nothing else." This is extreme humility and the utmost limit of servanthood. It means, "He (God) alone *is*."'³ Far from proclaiming his own divinity, al-Hallaj had declared his abject servitude to the One God.

Jalal al-Din's reputation rests to this day upon his Persian mystical poetry. He is acknowledged as its supreme exponent. His principal work, entitled the *Mathnawi*, is a vast poem of about 26,000 verses, a mix of fables, anecdotes, symbols and reflections designed to explain

Sufi doctrines. It has even been referred to as the Quran in Persian. Ibn Battuta offered the following sketch of this famous life.

Jalal al-Din began his professional life in the Konya *madrasa* as a popular teacher of the law (*faqih*). One day, a seller of sweetmeats entered his lecture with a tray of his wares. After presenting a delicate morsel to the *shaykh*, he left the room offering nothing to anyone else. The *shaykh* had accepted and eaten the sweetmeat, then abandoned his students to follow the seller outside. The *shaykh* failed to return, a search was made to find him, but without success. Ibn Battuta continues the story:

> *Subsequently he came back to them, after many years, but he had become deeply distracted and would speak only in Persian rhymed couplets which no one could understand. His disciples used to follow him and write down that poetry as it issued from him, and they collected it into a book called the* Mathnawi. *The inhabitants of Anatolia greatly revere that book, meditate on its contents, teach it and recite it in their hospices on Thursday nights.*

The anecdote appears to be a popular account Ibn Battuta had picked up describing the meeting between the ambulant Sufi, Shams al-Tabrizi (the sweet seller), and Jalal al-Din. The result was that after the latter's mysterious absence and strange behaviour upon his return, he had been vitally transformed from teacher of orthodox religious law into a metaphysical poet of mysticism. For his part, Ibn Battuta nowhere hints at an interest in the issues that Jalal al-Din wrote about so eloquently and, often, obscurely, such as man's metaphysical state of separation from the primeval union with God. He described Jalal al-Din as a 'virtuous leader' (*imam salih*), but of such an elevated status that he was also the 'supreme Saint of his Age' (*qutb*). Only elite Sufis were designated as saints by a social consensus that included judgements of Sufi and jurist alike; and those acknowledged as the apex of a saintly hierarchy or *qutb* were again recognized by an informal consensus of saints.

The Haydariyya order

Another *taifa* mentioned by Ibn Battuta was the Haydariyya, named after Qutb al-Din Haydari, a native of Zawa in Khurasan. They are described as a group of poor brethren (*faqir*, pl. *fuqara*). This was a Persian order associated with groups known as Qalandariyya that wandered about the regions

1. Arabesque, a traditional complex and ornate Islamic ceramic tile design of geometrical figures. This pattern adorns the wall of a fourteenth-century *madrasa* in Fez, Morocco.

2. Photograph of small shops in the old bazaar in Fez, Morocco, the dynastic capital of the Marinid dynasty during Ibn Battuta's lifetime.

3. Sketch by the Scots artist David Roberts (1796–1864) of the interior of Sultan Hasan's mosque in Cairo. Sultan Hasan (reigned 1347–51, 1354–62) was the son of Sultan al-Nasir Muhammad (reigned 1299–1341), himself a great builder and mentioned several times by Ibn Battuta in his *Travels*. The mosque contained four *madrasas*, one for the teaching of each 'school' of Sunni Islamic law.

4. Ibn Battuta listened to storytellers just as he himself related tales of his travels to others. This sketch is a nineteenth-century European artist's imagined storyteller and audience, including a woman with water vessel pausing to listen on the edge of the group.

5. Among other entertainers, Ibn Battuta would have encountered the poet reciting his wares accompanied by a violest. This scene takes place in Cairo.

6. A nineteenth-century European artist's sketch made from a photograph of the mosque of Umar, or the Dome of the Rock, Jerusalem. Built in 691CE, Ibn Battuta describes it as the third holiest shrine in Islam.

7. Sidon (modern Lebanon). Sketch of the biblical town made around 1900. Ibn Battuta only ventured by boat on the Mediterranean during his return journey from Egypt. The type of boat he used was a *qurqura*, possibly similar to the small vessel shown here.

8. The Holy Mosque, Mecca, in the pilgrimage season, depicting the pilgrims' ritual circumambulation of the Kaaba.

9. The Holy Mosque, Mecca, and the Kaaba depicted in a picture of tiles from sixteenth-century Persia.

10. Traditional-style house in Sanaa, Yemen.

11. Erzerum in eastern Anatolia, where Ibn Battuta lodged in the hospice of an aged *akhi* for three days. At this time, the city was a major caravan crossroads, situated amid mountains 2,000 metres in height.

12. During his travels in Anatolia, Ibn Battuta visited the shrine of the great Sufi, Mawlana Jalal al-Din Rumi, in Konya. In this miniature, the saint miraculously rescues a boat from the danger of being submerged in a whirlpool.

13. Here Mawlana Jalal al-Din is seen advising adepts in the bath to purify their hearts rather than attend to their outer appearance.

14. This miniature shows the Mawlana performing a whirling dance.

15. Modern mud-built Friday mosque in Yaama, Niger.

16. Qutb Minar of the Quwwat al-Islam Mosque in Delhi. Some 70 metres in height, it was described by Ibn Battuta as having 'no parallel in the lands of Islam'.

17. The oldest mosque in Beijing, called Niujie ('Oxen Street'), founded, according to tradition, in 997. The building featured in the centre is the minaret built, like the mosque, in the Chinese architectural style.

18. Wood block of a seagoing Chinese junk of the type Ibn Battuta would have travelled on between India and China.

19. *Dhow.* This photograph and the following depict travel by water and land in the Middle East. These beautiful, tranquil images taken at the setting or rising of the sun create a romantic aura far removed from the trials experienced by Ibn Battuta on his 75,000-mile odyssey.

20. Camel caravan.

of eastern Persia and India with no fixed abode. He notes their peculiar feature was the wearing of iron rings in their hands, necks and ears, and sometimes also in their penises so as not to be able to engage in sexual intercourse. Abstinence from sex might well extend to the renunciation of other forms of material comfort or need, yet celibacy was uncommon among Sufi orders and the label 'poor brethren' did not necessarily refer to economic impoverishment. One Sufi saying describes a poor person (*faqir*) in precisely the same terms as another saying describes a Sufi, namely, that each shows contentment during times of scarcity and generosity to others during times of plenty. Qutb al-Din was, in Ibn Battuta's terms, a *shaykh salih*, a phrase that may be rendered as 'virtuous guide', a Sufi who performed acts of piety for the betterment (*islah*) of his own and the wider community. Ibn Battuta encountered another band of Haydariyya near Delhi who passed a night at his camp. After the night prayer they kindled a large fire and once it had been reduced to glowing embers they entered it chanting, dancing and rolling about. The leader asked Ibn Battuta for one of his shirts and was given a garment of fine material. The man slipped it on and rolled about in the hot coals beating them with his arms until they were extinguished. He returned the shirt to Ibn Battuta who was utterly amazed that there was no scorch mark on it!

The Rifaiyya order

The last *taifa* was the Rifaiyya, named after Abu al-Abbas Ahmad al-Rifai who died in 1183 in a village near Wasit in Iraq. Ibn Battuta had made a special detour while in the vicinity of Wasit to visit the grave of this renowned saint, literally a 'Friend of God' (*wali allah*). The grave was located in the village of Umm Ubaiyda, and there Ibn Battuta found a large tent-like structure that he compared to an enormous hermitage (*ribat*) where he found, he stated, thousands of poor brethren gathered. Ibn Battuta witnessed on this occasion a similar exhibition of fire dancing that he reported among the Haydariyya in India. He added that practices of thaumaturgy *'were their regular custom and it is a peculiar characteristic of the Ahmadi brethren. Some of them will take a large snake and bite its head with their teeth until they bite it clean through.'* The occasion of their assembly was the arrival of Abu al-Abbas's grandson, who had journeyed from his home in Anatolia. The Rifaiyya order had spread from its main base in Iraq to Egypt, Syria and Anatolia. A few years later Ibn Battuta stayed in a hospice in Sunusa, Anatolia, where the Rifaiyya order had a branch. Adherents of the order had even spread to the Rif mountain region of northern Morocco by the beginning of the thirteenth century. From there the story emerged of a spiritual link between Abu al-Abbas and the most celebrated Moroccan saint (*wali allah*) of his day, Abu Madyan Shuayb b. al-Husayn (d. 1198). He had founded a *rabita* in the city of Bijaya (modern-day Algeria) for instruction in juridical Sufism that had been influenced by his reading of al-Ghazali's works, among others. Although the historical link is fanciful, Ibn Battuta nonetheless recounts the story of a meeting between Abu Madyan and Abu al-Abbas in Mecca during the annual pilgrimage. Abu Madyan died in Tlemsen, Algeria, and was buried there in a hermitage cemetery. His tomb and splendid adjoining mosque that stands to this day were built much later by a Marinid predecessor of Abu Inan in 1339.

The question 'Was Ibn Battuta a Sufi?' may be posed, to which a second may be raised, did he enter the company of any particular order? The first question is probably unproductive if we heed the view of experts on Sufism that it is no easy task to distinguish a Muslim who was a Sufi from one who was not. The second question raises its own problem. Ibn Battuta conveyed a fascination with one aspect of Sufi ritual, that is, the novice's patched robe or cloak of initiation (*khirqa*), acquired as a symbol of renunciation and subordination to a *shaykh*'s teachings and authority. Among a list of eminent scholars he had met in Jerusalem, Ibn Battuta almost casually mentions a pious and devout *shaykh* from an Anatolian family who was a disciple in the Rifaiyya order we have just discussed. He noted, '*I associated myself with this shaykh and was clothed by his hands in the patched robe of the Sufi life.*' This incident seems to have occurred well before his visit to the tomb of the Rifaiyya master, Abu al-Abbas, in Iraq and so he was, in an ill-defined sense, a 'member' of the order.

Membership of more than one order, however, was not uncommon. Later, Ibn Battuta's visit to Isfahan in Persia had made a deep impression upon him. He resided for two weeks in a hospice with strong historical associations to the 'sober' strand of ascetic Sufism; it was venerated by many from the wider region who sought blessings from their visit to it. The current *shaykh* of the hospice was a pious and scrupulous devotee, Qutb al-Din Husayn, whose father was a renowned Friend of God. Of

Qutb al-Din, Ibn Battuta remarked, *'What I saw of his zeal in religious exercises and his affection for the poor brethren and the distressed and his humility toward them filled me with wonder.'* The admiring guest then related how the good *shaykh*'s grace (*karama*) had befallen him. Qutb al-Din paid Ibn Battuta a visit to his room in the hospice; it happened to overlook the *shaykh*'s garden, which at that moment featured a clothes line bedecked with the *shaykh*'s washed garments. One was a lined white tunic of the Sufi type made of hundreds of patches sewn together. *'I admired it,'* remarked the guest, *'and said to myself, "This is the kind of thing I was wanting."'* When the *shaykh* entered the room, he looked out upon the garden and called one of his servants to fetch the patched robe. When it was brought the *shaykh* cloaked his guest with it. Ibn Battuta expressed his gratitude in suitable manner: *'I threw myself at his feet, kissing them and begged him to clothe me also with the skull-cap from his head, and to give me the same authorisation* (ijaza) *to transmit as he had received from his father and from all previous shaykhs in the order's spiritual chain.'* The original link in that chain was the fourth Rightly Guided Caliph after the Prophet's death, Ali b. Abi Talib (d. 661). So significant was the occasion for Ibn Battuta that he recorded the exact date, 7 May 1337, of his investiture into the Suhrawardiyya Sufi order, founded in Baghdad in the twelfth century and which later spread to Afghanistan and India.

A final occasion of investiture took place in the city of Uch in the province of Sind in northern India before his arrival in Delhi. There Ibn Battuta had met a devout, ascetic *shaykh* and great saint, Sharif Qutb al-Din Haydar al-Alawi, who cloaked him with a patched robe, although it is unclear to what order the sharif belonged. The garment was among Ibn Battuta's possessions when, years later, infidel Hindu pirates raided his ship and robbed its passengers of all their goods.

Ibn Battuta evidently placed the greatest importance upon his investiture into the Suhrawardiyya order, despite the brusque initiation procedure he underwent. He subsequently made no mention of any use to which he later put his association with the order, although the connection could have proved helpful in his travels through Afghanistan and India. In any event, as one Sufi master once famously remarked of the initiation cloak, playing upon the similar sound of two Arabic words, 'It is the inner flame (*harka*) which makes the Sufi, not the religious dress (*khirqa*).'

The Shadhiliyya order

In Alexandria, Ibn Battuta met a disciple of another famous saint and Friend of God (*wali allah*), Abu al-Hasan al-Shadhili (d. 1258). He was born in northern Morocco near Ibn Battuta's own native city of Tangier in the last years of the twelfth century. He studied religious sciences in Fez, then left for Iraq in 1218 where he studied with the disciple and successor of Ahmad al-Rifai. He returned to Morocco and stayed with a hermit for several years before moving again eastwards to a town near Tunis and then finally settling in Alexandria, Egypt, around 1244. His fame as a teacher and spiritual leader spread and attracted students from near and far. He performed the pilgrimage many times and died in the course of a journey to the Holy Cities in 1258. Ibn Battuta did not need to mention the fact that a major Sufi order, the Shadhiliyya, had grown around Abu al-Hasan's spiritual teachings and practice and spread throughout Egypt and across North Africa. His readers would have been well aware of the fact, just as many were probably also aware that Abu al-Hasan had been acknowledged in his own lifetime as *qutb* or supreme 'Saint of the Age'. The veneration of saints living or dead was not a heterodox phenomenon but enjoyed the seal of broad community approval. As Vincent Cornell has stated, for living persons to be recognized as saints, their 'public image must conform to consensually validated standards before his or her holiness is acknowledged. Only later is the saint's example typified in terms of Sufi doctrine.'[4]

Ibn Battuta recorded one of Abu al-Hasan's miracles, his last in fact, as it was the foretelling of his own death and place of burial. This was at Humaythira in Upper Egypt where he would normally have passed on his way to the port of Aydhab on the Red Sea opposite Jeddah and thence to Mecca. His servant had been instructed before leaving Cairo to arrange the necessities for his burial, including embalming aromatics to be transported with them. He died after completing the final prostration of his prayers. Ibn Battuta had visited the tomb more than once on different journeys and he noted that its inscription confirmed Abu al-Hasan's claim to be descended from the Prophet through Muhammad's grandson al-Hasan, son of Ali, his cousin and son-in-law.

The most interesting feature of Ibn Battuta's brief notice of Abu al-Hasan al-Shadhili is his quoting the text of the saint's best-known short piece, the *Litany of the Sea*. Abu al-Hasan recited this litany every day while making the Red Sea crossing by boat during his many pilgrimages to Mecca. Replete with verses and catchphrases from and allusions to the Quran, this was a fervent prayer from God's humble petitioner for His mercy, favour, forgiveness and succour. The title of the *Litany* was taken from al-Shadhili's appeal to God, "'*Subject to us every sea that is Thine on earth and in heaven, in the world of sense and in the invisible world, the sea of this life and the sea of the life to come*.'" A central passage captures the spirit of the litany as a whole:

> '*Grant us preservation from sin and wellbeing in our spiritual and material life and in the life to come; verily Thou art disposer of all things* [Q 3:26, passim]. *O God, smooth out for us our affairs* [allusion to Q 22:26]; *give peace to our hearts and our bodies, and grant us health and wellbeing in our spiritual and our material life. Be Thou our companion in our journey, and Guardian in our households in our absence.*'

At the *madrasa* in the town of Hu on the Nile bank in Upper Egypt, Ibn Battuta heard the students daily reciting a section of the Quran and al-Shadhili's *Litany of the Sea*. Despite its title the prayer was not merely a talisman against the perils at sea. Students in the classroom committed the Quran to memory, just as they memorized the *Litany*, each as a daily religious exercise. The Quran, God's own word, was the bedrock of the Muslims' faith and guidance. The *Litany*, composed by a Friend of God, was a commentary on a central theme of the sacred text, the relationship between the servant and Master. Abu al-Hasan's words were intended to strengthen believers' resolve and persuade them that God's mercy was not beyond their reach, either in their inner, spiritual lives or in their material lives, now and in the hereafter.

Ibn Battuta would know the Quran verse, 'It is He Who enables you to travel on the land and the sea' (Q 10:22). He probably carried a copy of the *Litany* with him throughout his travels, unless he had already committed it to memory. Its words would help him through every eventuality of his physical journey on land and sea. It accompanied him, too, on his journey of the spirit.

Ibn Battuta's spiritual journey

And what was this parallel journey of the spirit? The reflective side of Ibn
Battuta's nature may have responded to the anonymous Sufi saying that
'Travel (*SaFaR*) is named by this name because it reveals (*yuSFiR*) the
true character of the traveller.'[5] In this sense the *Rihla* would be a record
of adventures in self-discovery, although Ibn Battuta does not explicitly
claim this. Another Sufi view on journeys, this by al-Qushayri (d. 1072),
proposed that travel could be of two modes, 'travel with your body which
implies moving from one place to another; travel with your heart, which
implies rising from one (spiritual) attribute to another. One sees many
who travel with their bodies, while those who travel with their hearts
are few.' The Sufi journey of the heart, like that of the body, occurred in
stages. The journey of the heart, however, differed from that of the body
inasmuch as it was an 'ascent', with the aid of a spiritual guide, through
many stages or 'stations' (*maqamat*) on the upward path towards God. The
stations were matched by 'states' (*ahwal*) or psychological and spiritual
transformations that the traveller underwent in order to pass from one
station to the next, ever onwards, before becoming fully open to the divine
light. Ibn Battuta did not 'travel' in this sense, although from time to time
he was, by his own admission, drawn towards that path. Al-Qushayri,
moreover, conceded that Sufis held different views as to whether travel
was preferable to remaining in one place. Even those who held the latter
view agreed that a religious obligation such as performing the pilgrimage
would be an exception.

Ibn Battuta in fact had acquired considerable spiritual capital during
the first four years of his travels. He had performed three pilgrimages to
Mecca and had sojourned in the Holy City for about three years. Further
capital was accumulated in these years by his attitude towards *zuhd*, the
act of renunciation by ascetics. A God-conscious piety fostered *zuhd* not
in the medieval Christian sense of extreme repudiation of the flesh but
rather in a disdain for material comfort. Disinterest was not the same as
denial, and economic privation was uncommon among Sufis. Opinion
varied, however, as to what *zuhd* entailed. It was, according to a saying
of Ahmad b. Hanbal (d. 855), the eponymous founder of the orthodox
Hanbali legal school and included in the *Epistle on Sufism* by Abu al-Qasim
al-Qushayri, one of the first spiritual 'stations' on the Sufi way that began

with repentance (*tawba*). It involved three levels of increasingly higher attainment: (1) ordinary believers renounced what the divine law (*sharia*) prohibited, (2) the elect abandoned excess in what was lawful, while (3) the saint abandoned everything that distracted God's servant from God Most High. If this description were applied to Ibn Battuta, he had demonstrated throughout his travels a resolute avoidance of doing anything the law (*sharia*) prohibited. Therefore he belonged to a level higher than that of the ordinary believer. Yet he did not occupy the highest level of saint, as the rigours of travel did not permit the wholehearted dedication to devotional exercises required. He did, nonetheless, comfortably occupy the middle level of ascetic renunciation practised by elite believers who had abandoned excesses in performing what was lawful according to the *sharia*.

The goal of the spiritual side of Ibn Battuta's travels could be described by a story related by the famous ascetic Malik b. Dinar (d. *c.* 747). He had visited Malik's grave during a visit to Basra where he also passed a night at the *ribat* built in Malik's name. Malik recounted the advice God had given to the prophet Moses: 'Take a pair of iron sandals and an iron staff. Then travel the earth, seeking wise traditions and admonitions until the sandals are worn and the staff is broken.' As advice to a prophet this was fine, but the recommended iron travel gear was beyond Ibn Battuta's modest ambitions. God's word to Moses that he should collect edifying stories of the pious and wise and disseminate them for the benefit of others was not alien to Ibn Battuta's notion of *instructing* while informing and entertaining his readers about his earthly adventures. The task he set himself was to track down present traces of past saints, Sufis and the pious, that is, their graves and mausoleums, their disciples and tales that circulated about their lives and feats. In addition, there was the desire to meet pious scholars, holy men and pious women of his day. The quest was to acquire spiritual enrichment in the form of God's blessing or favour (*baraka*) obtained from proximity to a saint's tomb or nearness to those who had been touched in life by God's blessings.

On the other hand, there can be little doubt that Ibn Battuta's interest in Sufi piety was conditioned in part by his upbringing in Morocco and also from personal predilection. His travels over land and sea were complemented by the journey to record Muslim piety wherever he found it, whether or not he was directly involved. Better, therefore, to assume that Ibn Battuta was fully aware of the long-established, publicly recognized reputation of each of the saints whose tombs he had visited, as discussed above. Of course, as we shall see, he sought out not only the tombs of the Muslim pious but also those from a more distant past which also resonated in any pious Muslim's present, namely, the great figures of the patriarchs and prophets of the Torah and the Gospels. These were all familiar from the Quran, and cherished as links in the divine chain of prophethood that God had bestowed upon various nations of his creation from the days of Adam down to the time that marked the end or seal of prophecy in the life of His chosen Muhammad.

Visitation of graves and other blessed places

Egypt: Cairo

There is an epitaph on the grave of Khadija, 'one of God's humble servants', who died in Cairo in 1295, aged about 48.[6] It briefly noted that she had performed the pilgrimage to Mecca on 15 occasions, all but two of them on foot and that she had been able to recite the Quran according to the seven accepted ways of reading the text. The epitaph concluded with the plea, 'O Lord, have mercy on whosoever asks for mercy on her behalf.' It was a common refrain. Another epitaph expressed the wish, 'And make Abdallah's grave a garden for him among the gardens of Paradise and for all men and women who believe.' It ended with the words, 'May God have mercy on whomsoever reads this and prays for mercy on his behalf.' The graves of Khadija and Abdallah were not those of saints but of two humble, virtuous believers.

The practice of visiting graves (*ziyara al-qubur*), which the epitaphs publicly anticipated in their inscriptions, included visits to the graves of relatives, friends or teachers. Their graves, too, were places where the blessing of God was available to those who prayed for it. Visits had been a long-standing practice, but not without raising controversy among legal scholars. The subject was dealt with in the books of Prophetic traditions (*hadith*). It is told that the Prophet wept when he visited his mother's grave. His advice to his community was that visiting a grave was permitted, as it made the visitor mindful of death. Once, when he passed by some graves in Medina, the Prophet faced them and said, 'Peace be upon you, inhabitants of the graves. May God forgive you and us. You have gone before, and we shall come after.'⁷ Often in the case of a tradition reported on the Prophet's authority, an exception to it will be found in another tradition. The famous transmitter of traditions Abu Hurayra reported that the Prophet had cursed women who visited graves. The learned jurists then became divided in their views. Some claimed men and women alike were allowed to visit graves; opponents declared that women were excluded owing to their lack of self-control and their tendency to become greatly upset. A Maliki scholar and contemporary of Ibn Battuta, Ibn al-Hajj, lent his weight to the opponents' case, fuelling it with further charges:

> And among numerous scandalous acts, women walk at night with men during the *ziyara* of the tombs, among all the secluded places there and the many easily accessible buildings. And they expose their faces, and other parts of their bodies, as if they were with their husbands in the privacy of their own homes. And added to this, they have conversations with strange men, and women jest and play around, and there is much laughter and singing in this place of humility.⁸

Ibn al-Hajj, who lived in Cairo, probably had in mind activities in the famous cemetery of al-Qarafa. Ibn Battuta was also familiar with al-Qarafa, although he was either unaware of the view of his fellow Maliki or simply disagreed with it. He described al-Qarafa as a place of enormous repute for blessed power (*taBaRRuK*). He noted its mention in a *hadith* that God had promised that al-Qarafa would be one of the Gardens of Paradise. People had built within its precincts '*beautiful domed structures surrounded by walls so they look like houses with rooms built inside where the services of Quran readers are hired who recite night and day in beautiful voices*'. Others had constructed a hospice or religious college by the side of a mausoleum built for a famous deceased person. And then, he added, '*people go out every Thursday evening to spend the night there with their children and womenfolk and make a circuit of the famous sanctuaries*'. On special occasions merchants took varieties of foods to sell to the crowds of visitors.

Ibn Battuta added to this description some of the notable sanctuaries (pl. *mashahid*) found in al-Qarafa. One was that of the Lady (Sayyida) Nafisa, descendant of the Prophet's cousin and son-in-law, Ali, the fourth ruler after Muhammad over the young Muslim community. Ibn Battuta described her as a woman whose prayers were answered and one zealous in her devoted worship of God. Beside the mausoleum was a *ribat* for religious education and Sufi training. Another mausoleum was that of the founder of one of the four Sunni schools of legal thought, Muhammad b. Idris al-Shafii (d. 820); beside it, too, was a large *ribat*. In addition, there were innumerable graves of eminent men of religious learning (sing. *alim*) and saints (sing. *salih*) as well as those of many Companions of the Prophet. Apart, therefore, from its being a vibrant space for social interaction enjoyed by the Cairo public, the cemetery of al-Qarafa was a powerhouse of spiritual energy.

Organized visits to the tombs of the saints were conducted by individual scholars or mystics of minor status who were familiar with the saints' lives and miracles associated with them.[9] The guides specialized in either day- or night-time weekly visits. Amidst the haphazard layout of the enormous cemetery, they also had to know the precise location of the graves included in the tour. Special days were devoted annually to celebrations for the most notable saints. These were popular, festive occasions organized by Sufi orders that involved dancing, Quran recitation and the repeated invocation of God's name, all involving large gatherings of people at the saint's tomb. And Ibn al-Hajj had another occasion to rant against the evil mixing of the sexes!

The author of the earliest extant guidebook on visiting graves was popularly known simply as Ibn Uthman (d. 1218). Books like his reflected the faith of the vast majority of people who visited graves in medieval Egypt and elsewhere. The guidebooks did address issues of proper conduct and were not entirely uncritical. Rather, they were more balanced than the views of obsessive jurists like Ibn al-Hajj, who saw it as his duty to highlight abuses that had come to his attention. Ibn Uthman stressed the fundamental importance of the visitor's 'pure intention' in wishing to enter the graveyard, the same attitude any sincere believer adopted before prayer, fasting or other ritual. The intention was to visit solely for the sake of God and to eliminate corruption from the believer's heart. The graveyard guidebooks encouraged visitors to reflect upon the lives of the dead, especially relatives of the Prophet and his Companions, or the pious saints, as a way of cultivating piety in themselves and experiencing God's mercy and blessing (*baraka*) from the visit. Also permitted was offering supplication (*dua*) to God for a favour, or a petition on the visitor's behalf or on behalf of the deceased, but any demonstration of excessive anguish must be countered with patience and restraint. In these contexts, albeit not in others, Ibn Battuta would appear to have been in closer touch with the religiosity of the common man and woman than his Maliki contemporary Ibn al-Hajj.

Syria: Damascus

Al-Qarafa was the first major cemetery Ibn Battuta had encountered together with its lively graveyard culture. In Ibn Battuta's description of Damascus and its surroundings, there was a cemetery situated between two of the city gates where a number of the Prophet's Companions were buried along with unnamed martyrs (*shuhada*). In the city's verdant environs important sanctuaries and mosques were located, each type known for its power of blessing (*baraka*). These places drew their *baraka* from a very different source, sites with close association to one or more of the prophets and patriarchs of Jewish and Christian traditions which Islam had inherited and embraced, albeit in somewhat different Quranic versions of the biblical stories. One site was known as the Mosque of the Footprints, situated two miles to the south of the city. The footprints, impressed upon a rock there, were said to be those of Moses, one of a number of locations in central Syria and Palestine that claimed the honour of his final resting place. Salihiyya was situated to the north of the city at the foot of a mountain called Qasiyun, said to be the place where the prophets ascended to heaven. Ibn Battuta claimed that a cave in the hillside over which a large mosque had been built was the birth place of Abraham; yet he knew of a village in Iraq, near Baghdad, that also claimed to be Abraham's birthplace. Another sanctuary near Abraham's cave was the Cave of Blood. Traces of Abel's life force could be seen at the spot where his brother Cain had slain him and dragged his body into the cave. God had caused the evidence to remain fresh. This cave was specially endowed with blessings of the biblical patriarchs, Abraham, Moses, Jesus, Job and Lot, all of whom are mentioned in the Quran. This was the place where each had prayed and was commemorated in Ibn Battuta's time by a large mosque. The mosque could accommodate visitors who came for the twice weekly occasions when the cave was candlelit. Better still was the mountain-top cavern named after the prophet Adam, just below which was the Cave of Hunger. There 70 unnamed prophets had died of hunger after taking refuge in it with only one loaf between them, each one preferring not to partake but passing it to his neighbour until they all perished. Indeed the entire area between the Damascus walls and Salihiyya was said to be where 700 or 70,000 prophets and saints were buried, a truly magnificent expanse of blessed real estate.

At the far western end of the mountain was Rabwa, the place where Jesus and his mother Mary had sought refuge. Ibn Battuta was deeply struck by its overall aspect.

> *It is one of the most beautiful sights in the world and most pleasant in its resorts, lofty palaces, noble buildings and magnificent gardens. Blessed Rabwa is a cave, the size of a small room, and opposite it is a one-roomed structure where al-Khidr is said to have prayed. People crowd around it eager to pray in his hut.*

Al-Khidr is not explicitly mentioned in the Quran, although commentators believed he was alluded to as the mysterious character whom Moses met on his allegorical journey (Q 18:60–82). Commentators disagreed over his genealogy, and debated whether he was a prophet, how long he lived and whether he was alive in the Prophet Muhammad's day or even after him. The name *al-khidr*, or 'green', is explained by his sitting upon a white fur, symbolic of dry earth that turned green underneath him. Among popular folktales told of the ancient prophets, which were widespread in the days of Ibn Battuta, al-Khidr was one to whom God had disclosed the wisdom He had withheld from Moses. Once, Moses sought and was granted his Lord's permission to meet al-Khidr, who lived on an island in some distant sea. Moses finally tracked him down and asked al-Khidr to teach him all he knew. The response was not encouraging, for al-Khidr warned his visitor, 'You will not be able to bear with me' (Q 18:67), since al-Khidr's wisdom derived from the inner meaning of things while Moses' experience was only of their external nature. Al-Khidr is, according to another version of this popular folktale of Moses, replaced by the prophet Ilyas or Elijah of the Bible whom God made at once a heavenly and earthly, human and angelic being. Their association explains the names of two hermitages Ibn Battuta visited, one in southern Iraq, the other in Anatolia, both called al-Khidr-Ilyas after these two exceptional personages.[10]

Palestine

The region where figures from the biblical past resonated most in Muslim memories was the southern region of Syria, or Palestine. In Hebron Ibn Battuta had visited the mosque built over a cave possessed of great blessings that was reputed to contain the tombs of Abraham, Isaac and Jacob opposite three other tombs of their wives. The passageway to the tombs Ibn Battuta reported as blocked off, but to reassure his readers of their existence he consulted an aged, pious and saintly man, Burhan al-Din al-Jabari (d. *c.* 1332), who confirmed the tradition. It was an important association, since in the earliest surviving account of the Prophet Muhammad's life the famous story is related of his journey overnight from Mecca to Jerusalem in the company of the angel Gabriel. In Ibn Battuta's version, the angel took Muhammad first to Hebron and instructed him to pray at the tomb of 'thy father' Abraham, then on to Bethlehem to pray at the tomb of 'thy brother' Jesus before arriving in Jerusalem at the mosque of the Dome of the Rock. In the ancient rendering of the tale by Ibn Ishaq (d. 768), the prophets of old appeared free to wander and were not confined to their tombs since we read that:

> The apostle Muhammad and Gabriel went their way from Mecca and arrived at the Dome of the Rock in Jerusalem. There they found Abraham, Moses and Jesus among a company of the prophets. The apostle acted as their leader and they prayed together. Then he was brought two vessels, one with milk and the other wine. The apostle took the milk and drank it, leaving the wine. Gabriel said: 'You have been rightly guided and so will your people, Muhammad. Wine is forbidden to you.'[11]

Ibn Ishaq reported that when Muhammad's hard-nosed, pagan, merchant, Meccan townsmen heard the story the next day they dismissed it as absurd since everyone knew it took a camel caravan one month to travel from Mecca to Jerusalem and a month to return. Even some of Muhammad's followers lost their faith. Ibn Ishaq explained that the event had surely been a test from God for all Meccans, and whether it was a physical or spiritual journey 'it was all true and actually happened'.

Ibn Battuta also visited the birthplace of Jesus in Bethlehem where he noted, recalling the version of Jesus' birth in the Quran (Q 19:22–3), that a trace of the palm tree that had provided shade for Mary during her difficult labour was still visible in the chapel of the Church of the Nativity. He said that the church was venerated by Christians and arranged hospitality for all who arrived at its doors. One building in Jerusalem, he noted, marked the place where Jesus ascended to heaven, in accord with Muslim belief that Jesus had not been crucified but had been raised into God's protective presence and lived on until God would sanction his return to earth to do battle with and defeat the Antichrist before the Day of Judgement was proclaimed. This belief was based in part on the Quranic verse in which God said, 'O Jesus, I am going to take you and raise you to Me and cleanse you of those who do not believe' (Q 3:55). Hence Ibn Battuta's remark that Christians were deceived in their veneration of the Church of the Holy Sepulchre, which they had made an object of pilgrimage, because they believed located therein was the burial place of Jesus. Another popular tale that circulated among Muslims concerned Jesus. It recounted that after his victory over the Antichrist, the Angel Gabriel advised him that as his earthly mission was complete, he would die like all God's creatures. Angels descended to wash and prepare his body for burial and he was then laid to rest beside the tomb of Muhammad.[12]

At Tiberias near the Sea of Galilee there was a building called the Mosque of the Prophets which was said to contain the tombs of the Arab prophet Shuayb and his daughter, the tomb of the wife of Moses, and those of Solomon, Judah and Reuben. Nearby, too, was the well into which Joseph had been cast by his brothers according to the story related, in their different ways, in both Genesis and the Quran. Ibn Battuta saw Joseph's grave in a mosque in Hebron. His story is treated at length in the Quran (Sura 12); indeed, it is the fullest connected narrative in the Muslim scripture.

Mecca and Medina

Abraham is frequently mentioned by Ibn Battuta, and all places associated with him were regarded as blessed. There was the Well of Abraham in Ascalon in southern Palestine, and the northern Syrian city of Aleppo, *Halab* in Arabic, was also known as *Halab Ibrahim*, or 'Abraham's milk'. The popular tale that Ibn Battuta related is that Abraham used to live there raising large flocks of sheep from which he supplied the poor and destitute so that such unfortunates would gather and ask for the milk of Abraham. Known in the Islamic tradition as Ibrahim, he was given the special honorific of *al-Khalil* or Friend of God. For Muslims, however, Abraham's particular connection was with Mecca, Muhammad's birthplace. Mecca and Medina, together with their surrounding areas, were each considered as sacred territory (*haram*). But it was Mecca that enjoyed the extra Abrahamic glow. Upon entering the city, Ibn Battuta immediately repaired to God's sanctuary, the sacred mosque, that he called the abode of Abraham, God's Friend and the mission home of Muhammad, God's Chosen One. In the middle of the large mosque plaza stands the cube-shaped Kaaba, around which Muslims perform the ritual of a sevenfold circumambulation during the annual pilgrimage. In Muslim legend the structure is attributed to its founder, Abraham/Ibrahim, and his son Ismail, as alluded to in the Quran (Q 2:127). When the building had risen to some height, Ibrahim stood on a stone nearby to survey his work. The stone, said to bear the imprint of his feet, is today covered by a small domed building, called the 'place of Ibrahim's standing' (*maqam Ibrahim*). Ibn Battuta offered a short prayer of thanks upon entering the sacred area, saying, *'Praise be to God, Who has honoured us by visitation to this holy House and has caused us to be numbered amongst those included in the prayer of (His Friend) al-Khalil.'* This is a reference to Abraham's prayer found in the Quran: 'Our Lord, accept this (Kaaba) from us. ... Our Lord, make us surrender (*muslim*) to You, and from our seed a community (*umma muslima*) that will surrender to You' (Q 2:127–8).

The cemetery outside one of the city gates, blessed terrain to be sure, is described by Ibn Battuta as *'a vast throng of the Prophet's companions and their immediate successors, of the learned, the pious, and the saintly, but their tombs have become effaced, and the knowledge of them has been lost among the inhabitants of Mecca, so that none but a few of them are now known'*. Notably, one of these was the grave of Muhammad's first wife, Khadija, mother of all his children save one, an infant who did not survive, also named Ibrahim. His tomb, covered by a white cupola, Ibn Battuta found in one of the holy sanctuaries outside Medina. Of the number of sanctuaries Ibn Battuta listed outside Mecca he noted one point, about a mile out, where there was a large flat stone surmounted by another. There, it was said, the Prophet had often sat to rest, so people sought to gain a blessing by kissing it, or leaning against it so that their bodies would gain blessing from contact with the stone.

Medina, of course, where the Prophet established the embryonic Muslim community and spent his last days, was no less sacred than Mecca, notwithstanding the latter's Abrahamic heritage and its being the hub of the annual pilgrimage. As Ibn Battuta entered the Prophet's mosque through the Gate of Peace, he joined those at prayer in the area between Muhammad's tomb and the pulpit (*minbar*). That area, according to a Prophetic tradition, was said to be like one of the Gardens of Paradise. The Prophet's tomb was shared with two of his oldest Companions, Abu Bakr and Umar, the first caliphs of the Muslim community who ruled successively after Muhammad's death. As with his description of Mecca, Ibn Battuta lists the sanctuaries on the outskirts of the city and places of special significance to Muslims that recalled events in the Prophet's life. A prayer niche in the wall of a mosque marked the spot where Muhammad had bowed in prayer upon his first entry into the city after his forced escape from Mecca. The spot where his camel had knelt down after that long journey now witnessed those who sought blessings by performing the prayer. As he belonged to the Maliki school of juristic practice, Ibn Battuta could not but have noticed two memorials to the school's founder, Abu Abdallah Malik b. Anas (d. 795): his house, situated to the east of the Prophet's mosque, and his tomb which was surmounted by a small and unpretentious dome. Ibn Battuta spent four days in Medina passing each night engaged in spiritual exercises: some worshippers formed circles in the courtyard in candlelight and recited from the Quran; others intoned hymns of praise to God; others sat in silent contemplation of the Prophet's tomb while all around eulogies were chanted in praise of the Prophet.

Iraq: Kufa and Basra

In many instances, Ibn Battuta's comments on specific graves or tombs add interesting contemporary detail to the practice of visiting them. One grave was almost off limits, but not for religious reasons. About six miles from the southern Iraqi city of Basra was located the grave of Anas b. Malik, sometime servant to Muhammad and a famous transmitter of Prophetic traditions. Ibn Battuta noted that the site could only be visited in large groups owing to its isolated location and danger from wild animals, but he does not explicitly say whether he himself had been able to visit the tomb.

Another grave that was easily accessible stirred deep, hostile passions from inhabitants of nearby Kufa. Ibn Battuta had observed a dark blackened patch of ground in a field to the west of the cemetery of Kufa. He was informed that it was the grave site of an accursed man called Ibn Muljam. Each year Kufans brought loads of firewood to the spot and laid a huge fire over it that was constantly stoked and burned for seven days. No question of *baraka* being sought by visitors here! The object of this exercise of civic odium was infamous in the early annals of Islam, reviled as the assassin of the fourth of the so-called Rightly Guided Caliphs who had succeeded to the headship of the Muslim community after the Prophet's death. The victim, Ali b. Abi Talib, who was killed in 661, was Muhammad's cousin and son-in law and therefore a man revered by Sunni Muslims as well as by Shia Muslims who regarded him as their founding leader.

Ibn Battuta had visited the splendid mausoleum of Ali in Najaf lying a few miles west of Kufa. Located just past the perfumers' bazaar in the inner city the mausoleum was surrounded by religious buildings where, Ibn Battuta stated with due caution, '*they claimed*' lay the domed shrine over Ali's tomb. The inhabitants of the city, he asserted, were all Rafidites, supposedly heretical Shia whose word could not be trusted. The *madrasa* adjacent to the tomb he described as populated by '*students and Sufis of the Shia*', employing the more accommodating term 'Shia', suggesting they were more reliable. The fact was that his pious curiosity badly itched and needed scratching. He had heard from them that miracles occurred in the mausoleum, proof that it did indeed contain Ali's tomb. One of these occurred annually on the night of the 27th Rajab, the seventh month, when several dozen crippled persons from near and far arrived and were settled beside the tomb after the last prayer of the day. Onlookers gathered and waited in expectation. When night had advanced into the early morning hours, the entire company arose without a trace of their affliction, repeating the Shia version of the declaration of faith: 'There is no God but Allah; Muhammad is the Messenger of God; Ali is the Friend of God (*wali allah*).' Ibn Battuta remarked in a forthright way, '*This affair is a thing much spoken about among them; I heard it from trustworthy persons, but I was not actually present on any such night.*'

Returning to Kufa, Ibn Battuta remarked that compared to its days of glory, the city's present state was one of advancing ruin. Yet the city could still boast a fine mosque, although it left Ibn Battuta somewhat perplexed owing to an odd collection of sacred relics (*athar karima*) both inside it and in the adjoining area. These comprised: the very spot where Ibn Muljam had murdered Ali, where people continued to pray in the caliph's memory; a prayer niche associated with Abraham; four places associated with Noah, including where the ark was built; a small chamber once used by the biblical Enoch (Arabic, *Idris*); and the chamber where Ali was washed for burial after his murder. Ibn Battuta concluded tersely, '*but God knows best what truth there is in all this*' – indeed, a hopeless confusion of persons, eras and events that God alone would have comprehended.

The large mosque in Basra named after Ali b. Abi Talib had seven minarets, the tallest of which could be seen at a distance from outside the city. If Ibn Battuta had been intrigued by reported miracles associated with Ali's tomb in Najaf, his curiosity was raised again by the story that one of the mosque's minarets trembled whenever the name of Ali b. Abi Talib was mentioned. This time curiosity was complicit with bedevilment; nor did he suggest any miracle was involved, although some Basrans evidently perceived it as a wondrous event. Ibn Battuta climbed the minaret to the topmost balcony accompanied by a local fellow. There they found a wooden hand-grip fitted into the minaret wall. His companion grasped the handle and shook it while he uttered the name of Ali. The whole minaret quivered. Ibn Battuta repeated the ritual but instead of Ali's name, he spoke that of Abu Bakr, the first caliph after the Prophet's death. The whole minaret quivered, much to his companion's astonishment. Ibn Battuta's point was not to belittle the efficacy of Ali's name, but rather to illustrate that he could mention Abu Bakr's name in Basra because its populace adhered to mainstream Sunni Islam, whereas in a location of extreme Rafidites (*rafida ghaliya*), like Najaf, he would have feared for his safety owing to their abhorrence of the caliphs preceding Ali. Ibn Juzayy added his own comment to assure readers that minarets of mosques did waver or, according to him, could be made to quiver if enough people ascended to the top, grasped the sides of the balcony and shook it for all their worth.

Persia: Shiraz

A more tranquil visit took Ibn Battuta to a sanctuary on the edge of the city of Shiraz in southern Persia. There he found the grave of al-Saadi (d.

1292), *'the greatest poet of his time in the Persian language'*. Al-Saadi had built himself a magnificent hospice beside his future burial place with a splendid interior garden near to the source of a large river; this enabled al-Saadi to have constructed small cisterns in marble for washing clothes. People from the city who visited the tomb would be fed at the hospice, wash their clothes and return home. *'I did the same thing at his tomb – May God have mercy upon him'*, Ibn Battuta added. He viewed al-Saadi as a poet, although his literary output did display a familiarity and sympathy with Sufism.[13] As the hospice provided hospitality for all, visitors did engage to that extent with the deceased's memory. There were many sanctuaries in Shiraz, among them the mausoleum of Ahmad b. Musa, a descendant of Ali b. Abi Talib through his son al-Husayn, a sanctuary highly venerated by the populace, *'who visit it to obtain blessing by him and make their petitions to God by his virtue'*.

The miracle (*karama*) of Abu Abdallah b. Khafif (d. 982) occurred in Ceylon and Ibn Battuta referred to it during his own visit to the island. Ibn Khafif was known as the Saint of his Age (*qutb*) and a Friend of God. The founder of 'sober' Sufism in Shiraz, Ibn Khafif, known simply as 'the Shaykh', was buried there and his mausoleum was venerated throughout the entire region of Fars where Shiraz was the principal city. During his stay in Shiraz, Ibn Battuta witnessed special ceremonies at the tomb, which he stated was the object of visitation morning and evening by worshippers who rubbed their hands on it for blessing or kissed it. These included the Sultan of Shiraz's own mother who visited the tomb each Thursday evening.

On the island of Ceylon there was a spectacular conical-shaped mountain known as Adam's Peak. It was so called after a large impression on a black rock which in the Islamic tradition was believed to be the footprint of Adam, on the very spot where it is said he came down to earth after his banishment from the Garden of Eden. It is, in fact, a multi-faith relic, as Buddhists, Hindus and Christians each claim it for their own tradition as well. The ascent to the peak was an object of pilgrimage, one of the two paths being considered a stiff climb. Ibn Khafif, accompanied by some 30 poor brethren, had set out for the mountain but lost their way and were soon feeling the pangs of hunger. The Shaykh was asked if they could kill a young elephant for food, as they were very numerous in that place. The Shaykh forbade this, but the brethren disobeyed him and they caught one, slaughtered it and ate of its flesh. The Shaykh refused to partake. That night, as the entire company slept, elephants gathered from all over, moved among them smelling and killing those who had eaten the flesh. The Shaykh alone was spared as one elephant wrapped its trunk around his body, placed him on its back and took him to a village where it gently placed him upon the ground. The astonished villagers slowly approached the Shaykh, touched his robe for a blessing and then took him off to their king who treated him as an honoured guest. Ibn Battuta commented upon the continued after effect of the Shaykh's miracle following his own visit to Ceylon:

> *Its people still remain in a state of infidelity* (pl. kuffar), *yet they hold the poor brethren of the Muslims in great respect, lodge them in their houses and feed them, and these Muslims will be in their rooms amidst their wives and children, contrary to the practice of all the other infidels of India.*

Central Asia: Bukhara and Balkh

Much further east from Shiraz, on the frontier of Central Asia (in present-day Uzbekistan), Ibn Battuta arrived at Bukhara, a city of one-time splendour that had been destroyed by the armies of Genghis Khan in the early thirteenth century. The great compiler of Prophetic traditions, Muhammad b. Ismail al-Bukhari (d. 870), whose name derived from the city, was also buried there amidst a host of other learned scholars. Ibn Battuta copied many of their tomb inscriptions that contained titles of works each had composed. This material he later lost (in 1346) when Indian pirates attacked his ship at sea and robbed the passengers of all their possessions. During his stay in Bukhara, Ibn Battuta lodged in a large, well-endowed hospice named after the learned and pious ascetic (*alim, abid, zahid*) Sayf al-Din al-Bakharzi (d. 1260), successor to the founder of the Kubrawiya Sufi order that later spread to India where it was known as the Firdawsiya order. His tomb was located in a suburb of the city. Sayf al-Din was also known as one of the great saints, or Friends of God. Ibn Battuta passed 'a most exquisite and delightful evening' in the hospice listening to Quran readers, a sermon, and spiritual songs in Turkish and Persian. South of Bukhara lay the city of Balkh. There Ibn Battuta found the tomb of Ezekiel (*Hizkil*), over which a fine dome had been built. He is mentioned in the

Quran as Dhul-Kifl (Q 21:85; Q 38:48), understood by some commentators to be Ezekiel; as Dhul-Kifl, on the other hand, he was associated with graves in Palestine and Iraq. While in Balkh, Ibn Battuta admitted that he had visited many tombs of saintly persons (pl. *salihin*) but whose names he could not later recall.

Arabesque

While dictating his travels to Ibn Juzayy, Ibn Battuta did not have in mind to create a medieval globetrotter's guide to the cemeteries of the Muslim world, although at times that may have appeared his intention. Of the hundreds of graves, tombs and sanctuaries of individuals he recorded for his audience, the vast majority of them were associated with the Arab Muslim world, that is Egypt, Syria (and Palestine), Arabia and Iraq; and, as we have seen above, these included figures – historical or legendary – from the scriptural pasts of Judaism and Christianity that lived in Muslims' memory from their knowledge of the Islamic sacred texts. Of course, the Muslim past was just as alive for visitors to the graves of deceased family members as it was to graves of famous jurists, judges and rulers. All were sources of blessings (*baraka*) that visitors sought and received from God.

Ibn Battuta's travels were indeed beginning to resemble the creation of ornamental panels widely used to decorate contemporary Moroccan mosques and *madrasas*. This was the art of *zillij*, the arranging of glazed and cut tiles into complex geometric arabesques. A magnificent example can be found on panels on the walls of the Attarin *madrasa* in Fez built around 1325 (see illustration 1). The pattern's central feature is a geometrical rosette with a 12-ray star extending outwards in interlacing bands and intertwined with another rosette and then another and another; the ornamentation's repeated symmetry is not constrained by the surrounding frame but can be extended infinitely in any direction, suggesting that the observer sees just a part of the cosmic whole. This is strongly evocative of the religious idea of omnipresent divine unity. The terrestrial parallel of this idea as described in *The Travels* is the interconnected network of locations and persons that shared God's *baraka*. The overall design in Ibn Battuta's itineraries, therefore, may be said to symbolize the vital piety of the *umma* assured through God's omnipresent grace of *baraka* that Ibn

Battuta seemed determined to explore wherever possible, right to the *umma*'s furthest boundaries.

The divine presence was evident in other phenomena. These are variously referred to as 'acts of grace' or 'miracles'. There are two Arabic terms for 'miracle' in the Islamic tradition. The one that Ibn Battuta used frequently, *karama*, meant a personal distinction granted by God to a saint, living or deceased. Distinct from this was an act of grace described as *mujiza* that was also granted by God. It referred specifically to the probative miracle of a prophet that unequivocally demonstrated the truth of his mission and message. In Islam, although several miracles (pl. *mujizat*) are attributed to the Prophet Muhammad, the most outstanding and widely accepted instance was God's vouchsafing him the revelations of the Quran. The concern here is only with the first type.

Ibn Battuta employed quite a rich vocabulary to describe a person as a saint or someone who displayed 'indications of divine power'. There is no simple one-to-one correspondence between the English term and an Arabic equivalent. Terms that have appeared already include Friend of God (*wali allah*) and Saint of the Age (*qutb*). Another is *salih* (f. *saliha*), roughly meaning a 'virtuous person', a person who embodied the quality of *salah* or socially conscious virtue which Cornell has identified as epitomizing sainthood in the Moroccan tradition.[14] Ibn Battuta used the term *salih* frequently, often in combination with other words, to describe the saints of his own and earlier times who were recipients of God's grace as miracles. We may now examine some of the traveller's tales of such miraculous phenomena.

Miracles: Ibn Battuta

As Ibn Battuta experienced Egypt, which was the region stretching from Alexandria and the Nile Delta to near Luxor on the Upper Nile, it seemed to be a reservoir of sainthood and miracles. No fewer than three 'acts of grace' involved him personally and they all had to do with his worldwide travels before he had even completed the first pilgrimage to the Holy Cities. It was as though the Almighty had arranged Ibn Battuta's global itinerary in advance through His agents on the ground, the pious fraternity of saints.

The first incident occurred in Alexandria. Ibn Battuta was staying with Burhan al-Din al-Araj, 'The Lame', whom he described as a learned, self-denying, pious and humble *imam*, one of the greatest ascetics and a man of singular devotion. Burhan al-Din observed of his guest that, 'I see you are fond of travelling and wandering from land to land.' Ibn Battuta agreed but to himself admitted that he had not at the time considered anything more distant than Mecca. Burhan al-Din continued, 'You must, God willing, visit my brothers Farid al-Din in India, Rukn al-Din in Sind [India] and Burhan al-Din in China, and when you reach them convey my greetings to them.' Ibn Battuta was utterly amazed at this miraculous prediction. He later reflected that once *'the idea of going to these countries had been cast into my mind, my wanderings never ceased until I had met these three that he had named and conveyed his greeting to them'*. The first two he met in India before he arrived at the sultan's capital of Delhi. Farid al-Din was a descendant of the founder of the Chishtiyya Sufi order in Ajodhan and Rukn al-Din (d. 1335) was grandson of the founder of the Suhrawardi-yya order in India.

The final meeting with Burhan al-Din in China involved a confused and bizarre tale of apparent coincidences, resolved of course by the various pieces falling into place by an act of grace (*karama*). Ibn Battuta had set out to meet an aged saint in the mountains of Bengal. His arrival was foretold by the saint who instructed some companions to meet the Moroccan traveller, which they did, two days distant from the saint's retreat. At their first meeting Ibn Battuta was struck by the saint's attire, a goat-hair garment he had worn especially to greet his guest. Reading the covetous look on Ibn Battuta's face, the saint gave him the cloak and his skull cap. Indeed, he had privately informed his companions beforehand that the Moroccan would desire the garment, that an infidel governor would then relieve him of it and, lo! he would give it to Burhan al-Din for whom it was originally intended. Much later, when Ibn Battuta had reached China, he was spotted wearing the goat-hair garment by a government minister who presented him to the local governor. He admired the garment and took it in exchange for ten robes of honour, a fully caparisoned horse and money. The following year Ibn Battuta was in the Chinese capital and sought out Burhan al-Din in his hospice. He found him reading and wearing an identical goat-hair cloak! Ibn Battuta's amazement was doubled when Burhan al-Din showed him a letter from his spiritual brother in Bengal advising him that the garment would reach him by such and such a route, every detail of which occurred precisely as Ibn Battuta had experienced it and was able to verify.

The second living saint Ibn Battuta met in Egypt was Abu Abdallah al-Murshidi (d. 1337) whose reputation had spread far and wide by word of mouth. He even attracted visits from the Mamluk ruler in Cairo, al-Malik al-Nasir. Ibn Battuta set out purposefully from Alexandria to meet him. He described al-Murshidi as a pious, virtuous guide and one of the great saints who enjoyed visions of the unseen world and who possessed the special merit of being able to draw upon divine resources to meet his needs. His miracle (*karama*) was his foreknowledge of a dream of Ibn Battuta's before being informed of it, and his interpretation that it foretold his guest's future globetrotting adventures. Specifically on India, he reported al-Murshidi's words, '*"You will stay there for a long time and you will meet there my brother Dilshad, the Indian, who will rescue you from danger into which you will fall."*' Ibn Battuta said of his meeting, '*His blessed powers have stood me in good stead throughout all my journeys.*'

Some 20 years later, Ibn Battuta had left Delhi charged by Sultan Muhammad b. Tughluq with a mission to China as his ambassador. The most dramatic encounter of Ibn Battuta's travels occurred at this point. In effect, it was the fulfilment of the miracle predicted by al-Murshidi. On the journey from Delhi to a coastal port of embarkation, the large company of court officials and imposing body of troops became distracted from its purpose by news of plunder by hordes of infidel Hindu rebels in nearby villages. It was decided to assist the local Muslim commander to defeat the rebels, but after some initial success Ibn Battuta fell into rebel hands. Expecting to be put to death, he succeeded in talking his way out of his captors' clutches only to find himself wandering about a district where he was an alien and total stranger. On the eighth day, suffering from severe thirst and hunger, there suddenly appeared before him a dark-skinned man carrying a jug, a staff and a knapsack. He greeted Ibn Battuta in the Muslim fashion, 'Peace be upon you!' The greeting was returned in like manner, '*Upon you be peace and the mercies and blessing of God!*' The stranger introduced himself in Arabic as al-Qalb al-Farih ('Joyous Heart') and offered Ibn Battuta food and water. He partook of this simple fare but was still too weak to walk unaided. His new companion insisted on carrying him on his back while urging him to repeat the Quran phrase, 'God is sufficient for us. How excellent a guardian is He' (Q 3:172). Ibn

Battuta reports: '*I repeated this over and over again, but could not keep my eyes open and regained consciousness only on feeling myself fall to the ground. When I came to there was no trace of my rescuer and I was in an inhabited village.*' It was a Hindu village with a Muslim head who took Ibn Battuta into his care. And it was just at that moment he remembered al-Murshidi's words (from years before) that he would be rescued from misfortune in India by his spiritual brother Dilshad. He realized this was the Persian rendering of his rescuer's name 'Joyous Heart'. Ibn Battuta said, '*So I knew that it was he whom the saint had foretold that I should meet, and that he too was one of the saints, but I enjoyed no more of his company than this short space of time.*'

Ibn Battuta's third encounter with a saint in Egypt occurred shortly after meeting al-Murshidi. At the town of Hu on the Upper Nile, he visited Abu Muhammad al-Hasani. He was '*one of the saintliest of men* (min kubar al-salihin)', and the visit was for the sake of acquiring *baraka* by virtue of just seeing and greeting him. Ibn Battuta told al-Hasani of his intention to fulfil his first pilgrimage by way of the Red Sea crossing to Mecca. Al-Hasani warned that Ibn Battuta would not make the crossing on this occasion and would only reach Mecca via the Syrian Road from Damascus. The interesting aspect of this incident is that Ibn Battuta chose to ignore the holy man's caution or advice, but later acknowledged his 'foresight' as a miracle, when he did indeed fail to make the sea crossing from Aydhab to Jeddah and finally reached Mecca only from Damascus.

The British anthropologist Michael Gilsenan undertook fieldwork in Egypt and Lebanon during the mid-1960s and early 1970s and his observations on miracles in the context of an urban Egyptian Sufi order merit attention, too, as a commentary on a medieval document such as Ibn Battuta's travels. The basic principle of miracles was clear:

> Within the world and beneath the surface reality at which men live out their daily existence (the *zahir*) there is the underlying dimension of the hidden reality (the *batin*). From this hidden reality, through the mediation of a holy man or the free gift of blessing by God (*baraka*), flow forces and powers that are witness to the interrelations of God and man and nature.

He likens *karama* to a mini-passion play, a dramatic reminder of the 'real' essence of the universe. In our modern world, given the supreme reign of appearances (the *zahir*), it follows that miracles are never seen, even if they were to happen before our very eyes. For Ibn Battuta (as for the Egyptian Sufis of Gilsenan's study),

> there is a set of shared understanding of the nature of the possibilities within the world, at the centre of which are the notions of *baraka*, *karama* and *mujiza*. Though the miraculous, by definition is extraordinary, it is also incorporated into the potentials of everyday life. It may happen at any time. People expect and look for it. And when it does occur, they are amazed but not surprised![15]

Amazement was precisely Ibn Battuta's reaction to each of the Egyptian saints' predictions of his future meetings with their spiritual brothers in India and China, all of which were realized, albeit many years afterwards.

These miracles taken together might be construed as a conscious narrative device used by Ibn Battuta to convey the impression that his travels were, from beginning to end, especially guided – even determined – by divine favour. There would be a fine line between that judgement and his firm belief in the notion of God's irregular but continuously manifested secret purpose in the form of signs of grace vouchsafed through his saints. Moreover, Ibn Battuta was prepared to seek divine assistance on his own by praying for a sign (*salat al-istikhara*), a common method of determining whether to follow a particular course of action. He employed another method before deciding to take part in a holy war (*jihad*) with the Sultan of Hinawr against the Indian infidel island of Goa. He opened the Quran at random to take an augury and read, 'God helps those who help Him' (Q 22:40); he accepted this as a good omen and joined the expedition.

At the same time, on at least two occasions, Ibn Battuta confessed to being tempted to set aside his wanderlust in exchange for the spiritual peace of full renunciation (*zuhd*). At Abbadan, on the border of southern Iraq with Persia, there was a hermitage named after the prophets al-Khidr and Ilyas alongside a hospice, both run by four poor brethren and their families. From them Ibn Battuta learned of a devotee *shaykh* of great merit who lived alone in the city. A search for the man found him praying in a half-ruined mosque and Ibn Battuta seated himself by his side. The man curtailed his prayer, took his hand and said, "*May God grant you your desire in this world and the next.*" Reflecting upon this moment as he dictated to Ibn Juzayy, Ibn Battuta interjected:

I have indeed – praise be to God – attained my desire in this world, which was to travel through the earth, and I have attained in this respect what no other person has attained to my knowledge. The world to come remains, but my hope is strong in the mercy and clemency of God, and the attainment of my desire to enter the Garden of Paradise.

Returning to the moment in Abbadan, that evening the anonymous devotee sent a fish he had caught with one of the poor brethren to give to Ibn Battuta. The fish was cooked and shared among those in the hospice. Ibn Battuta then claimed that '*For a moment I entertained the idea of spending the rest of my life in the service of this shaykh, but I was dissuaded from it by the pertinacity of my spirit.*'

A second, similar episode occurred later in the city of Hali in the Yemen. The city's beautiful mosque was occupied by a group of poor brethren who dedicated themselves exclusively to religious exercises. One of the company was an Indian saint named Qabula, who had a small bare cell next to the mosque. He was clothed in a patched robe and felt hat. Visitors were offered pieces of dry bread with salt and marjoram. The brethren spent the major part of each day devoted to prayer and performing *dhikr*, rhythmically chanting the divine names or other holy phrases. Ibn Battuta was moved by their devotion and said, '*I should have wished to remain with them for the rest of my life, but my desire was not fulfilled – may God most high compensate us by His benevolence and good fortune.*'

Commentators have overlooked or ignored Ibn Battuta's accounts of his privileged marks of grace concerning the extent of his travels, as well as his reflective desire to end his odyssey. Nevertheless, these moments form an integral part of the narrative of his spiritual journey parallel to the challenges of the physical journey he had undertaken. On the one hand, Ibn Battuta believed he was assured God's blessing to travel anywhere he wished, based upon acts of grace disclosed to him by God's saints. On the other hand, he was sincerely moved by and drawn towards the spiritual lives led by a few he had met in their daily lives which, albeit momentarily, had caused him to pause and consider abandoning any larger travel scheme. Both entailed a spiritual goal but he prayed for God's compensation for what he may have earned by remaining behind. By carrying on he had acquired responsibility for actions that God had created in him.

Miracles, moreover, often gave meaning to seemingly mundane

occurrences in everyday life that, to the modern mind, would be put down to coincidence or chance. For all their apparent predictive value, the stories Ibn Battuta related as acts of grace that involved himself could only be confirmed in retrospect when the miracle 'proved to be true'. That is, the prediction that Ibn Battuta would be assisted by al-Murshidi's brother saint Dilshad in India was fulfilled after his being rescued by someone with a name that signified the same meaning in Arabic and Persian. An everyday example that happened to Ibn Battuta took place in Shiraz. He had entered a mosque to recite the Quran following his midday prayer. The thought occurred to him that he would have preferred to have a copy of the Holy Book before him to recite from. At that moment a young man entered the mosque, thrust a Quran at him saying 'Take!' and abruptly left. Ibn Battuta said he read the entire book that day and waited for the young man's return to restore his property to him. He never saw him again but learned he was from the tribe of Shul who lived in the open country a day's journey from Shiraz. It was only after Ibn Battuta had left Shiraz and camped a night in Shul territory that he realized there lived amongst them a number of saintly devotees (pl. *salihun*). Now confirmed, the miracle (*karama*) was as natural and appropriate as could be for it concerned a matter of religious ritual and the Quran.

In what follows, Ibn Battuta relates tales of contemporaries who played an active role in their societies in different ways as spiritual advisors and around whom stories circulated that sustained, enhanced and spread their reputations as pious persons or saints. Some of these individuals Ibn Battuta met in person, and he was as charmed by their qualities of piety as by the stories told about them.

Shiraz

The tale of Abu Abdallah b. Khafif who was buried in Shiraz has been recounted earlier. The city entranced Ibn Battuta, apart from its physical beauty, for its inhabitants were '*distinguished by piety, sound religion, and purity of manners especially the women*'. He had set out from Isfahan for Shiraz, a distance of ten days' travel, with the sole object of meeting Majd al-Din (d. 1355) whom he fulsomely described as *shaykh, qadi, imam,* the pole of saints (*qutb al-awliya*), and solitaire of the age (*farid al-dahr*) who was noted for his manifest miracles. He resided in a religious college named after him and where Ibn Battuta caught up with him. He was now a man advanced in years and with failing sight. '*When I saluted him, he embraced me and took me by the hand until he came to his prayer mat, then let go my hand and signed me to pray alongside him.*' He continued to deal with people's legal suits and meet city notables on a daily basis. Ibn Battuta noted that the Shirazis never referred to him as just 'the judge' (*qadi*), but as 'Our most venerated master' (*mawlana azam*).

Majd al-Din's fame rested upon an incident of both political and religious import. A descendant of the conquering Mongol leader Genghis Khan, who ruled Persia and Iraq from 1304 to 1316, was called Oljaytu. His brother and predecessor, Ghazan Khan, had converted from his ancestral shamanistic beliefs to Islam, but Oljaytu wavered in his commitment between the majority Sunni Muslim and the rival Shia minority Muslim traditions. During the phase of Shia adherence, around 1310, Oljaytu sent out orders that everyone within his domains must subscribe to Rafidite (as Ibn Battuta called them) doctrines. This inevitably created resistance and in Shiraz, the leader of the opposition was the *qadi* Majd al-Din, then a man much younger in years. He was summoned to Oljaytu's court and as punishment was ordered to be cast to the dogs. Ibn Battuta picks up the thread of the story:

> *These were enormous dogs, with chains on their necks, and trained to eat human beings. When anyone is brought to be delivered to the dogs, he is set at liberty and without chains in a wide plain; those dogs are then loosed on him, so they overtake him, tear him to pieces, and devour his flesh. But when the dogs were loosed on Majd al-Din and reached him, they fawned on him and wagged their tails without attacking him in any way.*

The story is reminiscent of Abu Abdallah b. Khafif's, whose life had been spared by wild elephants. The sequel to Majd al-Din's remarkable display was that when the news reached Oljaytu he confronted the saint '*bare footed and prostrated himself at the qadi's feet, kissing them, and took him by the hand and placed upon him all the garments that he was wearing*'. This was the greatest gesture of honour and distinction a ruler could confer. Moreover, it led to Oljaytu renouncing Rafidi doctrine and joining the followers of the Sunni tradition, much to Ibn Battuta's evident satisfaction.

Khurasan

On the eastern fringes of Persia, in Khurasan, Ibn Battuta's journey took him through several of the major cities of the region. Herat had a large population ruled by a sultan called Husayn. Ibn Battuta described it almost as a model city, that is, one whose inhabitants were *'people of recti-tude, who abstained from unlawful pleasures, were sincere in religion and free of vice'*. A figure who had contributed to Herat's climate of public moral-ity Ibn Battuta described as *'a pious man of eminent virtue and ascetic life'*, Nizam al-Din Mawlana, whom the inhabitants held in deep respect and affection. Nizam al-Din acted as an informal censor of public behaviour and with public support he set out to redress breaches of lawful conduct. Nizam al-Din came into conflict with a leader of Turkish nomads who roamed the open country beyond Herat and the frontier of India but who conducted their affairs according to a pact they had made with Sultan Husayn. At issue here was the Turk's capture of a Muslim woman for whom he had conceived a violent passion. Nizam al-Din succeeded in forcing the Turk to release the woman; however, in consequence Herat suffered punitive raids by the Turks who vowed to desist only when they could lay hands upon Nizam al-Din. At this point a prominent member of the Chishtiya Sufi order, Abu Ahmad al-Jishti (Chishti), intervened. He promised to ensure Nizam al-Din's safety in a meeting with the Turk intended to calm his anger. The meeting ended before it began when the Turk bashed in Nizam al-Din's head with his mace. In the end the matter was resolved by Nizam al-Din's followers, a group of whom ran the Turk through with their swords on the occasion of his ill-judged visit to the city. Ibn Battuta's aim in recounting this story at some length was perhaps his wish to illustrate the pure intention of deeply pious individuals and the often precarious roles they played in other Muslim societies.

From Herat Ibn Battuta went to the smaller city of al-Jam. There he picked up a story of Shihab al-Din Ahmad, a *'self-denying and ascetic saint'*. In his youth, Shihab al-Din had been given to heavy drinking with a large company of friends who would, in turn, hold drinking sessions in their homes. When it came to Shihab al-Din's turn to entertain, he had made a resolution to repent and make his peace with God. As he did not wish to face his companions' immediate censure, he prepared for the day as usual with food and drink. When the wineskins were opened they discovered the liquor was 'sweet', that is, non-intoxicating. Shihab al-Din thereupon confessed his repentance but insisted the wine was no different from what they were accustomed to drinking. At which point the entire company repented, built a hospice and devoted themselves to God's service. Ibn Battuta concluded the story, stating that '*Many miraculous graces* (karamat) *and divinations* (mukashafat) *have been manifested at the hand of this shaykh, Shihab al-Din.*'

From al-Jam Ibn Battuta journeyed next to the large and illustrious city of Tus, noted as the birthplace of the scholar Abu Hamid al-Ghazali (d. 1111), where he visited the tomb of this most famous of scholars. Several stages after Tus, Ibn Battuta arrived at the great Khurasan metropolis of Nishapur. He conceded the exquisite design of its mosque and the four religious colleges inhabited by a great host of students. Nonetheless he asserted that no college anywhere compared with the *madrasa* of singular size and beauty built in Fez by the Marinid ruler Abu Inan, the greatest ruler of all justice-loving caliphs. In the event Nishapur's fame had reached the far western Maghrib, but Ibn Battuta sought to assure his audience that it fell short of the uniqueness of Fez. Nishapur did boast a hospice and a resident scholar, preacher and Saint of the Age (*qutb*) with whom Ibn Battuta lodged and received generous hospitality. Proximity to a saintly figure such as this prompted Ibn Battuta to describe the following personal anecdote as a miracle: '*I had purchased in Nishapur a Turkish slave-boy, and this shaykh, seeing him with me, said to me, "This boy is no good to you; sell him." I said to him, "Very well", and sold the boy the very next day to a merchant.*' Sometime later Ibn Battuta received a letter from a friend in Nishapur. The slave boy had, it was reported, killed another person and had been put to death in retaliation for him, to which Ibn Battuta remarked, '*This is an evident miracle accorded to this shaykh (may God be pleased with him)*', thereby adding his own opinion confirming the saint's acknowledged status.

One is not surprised when a renowned, living saint like Majd al-Din is described as elderly but still as active as his failing faculties permitted. The encounter with another saint sorely tested Ibn Battuta's credulity. Before he reached the Indus valley and the frontier with India, he came upon a hospice in the Panjir valley (modern Afghanistan) where a saintly *shaykh* lived. He was called Ata Awliya, a name combining Turkish and Arabic that meant 'Father of the Saints'. In Persian his name meant 'three hundred', since his followers claimed he was 350 years old. He was well known and popular in the towns and villages round about, with sultans and princesses apparently among his visitors. Ibn Battuta described his appearance as of a man of only about 50 years of age, but was informed by the saint that *'every hundred years there grew on him new hair and teeth'*. For all the warmth of the hospitality offered, Ibn Battuta left Ata Awliya thinking he *'had some doubts about him, and God knows how much truth there was in what he claimed'*. On several later occasions he did meet very elderly men in Anatolia, India and China from whom he secured blessings. They varied in their physical condition but remained mentally sharp and claimed ages between 140 and 200 years.

India: The sultanate of Delhi

The second volume of the travels, as we know, commences with Ibn Battuta's crossing the Indus River into the domains of the Sultan of Delhi, Muhammad b. Tughluq. When he arrived at the walled capital he was struck by its vast size, *'the largest city in India, nay rather the largest of all the cities of Islam in the East'*.

Delhi boasted an enormous congregational mosque. It was constructed after the Muslim conquest in 1192 upon the site of a former Hindu temple of idols. A relic of the Hindu past placed in the centre of the mosque courtyard was the famous iron pillar taken from a fourth-century temple of Vishnu. The red stone minaret, known as the Qutb Minar and which was 70 metres in height, had *'no parallel in the land of Islam'*, according to the awestruck traveller from Morocco.

Before embarking on a historical sketch of Delhi and its sultans, Ibn Battuta remarked briefly on some of the city's 'places of visitation' (*mazarat*) or shrines. One of these was the tomb of the saint Qutb al-Din Bakhtiyar al-Kaaki (d. 1232), a successor in Delhi of the founder of the Chistiyya Sufi order in Ajmer. His tomb *'exuded blessed power and enjoyed great veneration'*. He was famed for aiding debtors and those in need or in poverty. The tomb of the jurist Ala al-Din al-Kirmani was also *'blessed and radiant with light'*. The tombs of many other pious saints were located in the same area, although Ibn Battuta does not single out any more for attention.

Among the pious persons whom Ibn Battuta claimed he had met was one he called Mahmud al-Kubba, who was probably the renowned Chistiyya saint Nasir al-Din Mahmud (d 1356), known as 'the lamp of Delhi' and spiritual successor to the even more famous saint of the Chistiyya, Nizam al-Din Awliya (d. 1325). According to Ibn Battuta, it was Nizam al-Din who, in one of his mystical trances, had predicted the succession of Muhammad b. Tughluq to his father's rule; he died shortly afterward and Ibn Tughluq helped carry his bier at the funeral. Then there was the saintly scholar Sadr al-Din al-Kuhrani, who *'used to fast continually and stand all night in prayer. He renounced the world entirely and rejected all its goods and wore nothing but a woollen cloak.'* When the sultan and government ministers used to visit him he often refused to receive them, and he refused categorically to accept any gifts or money from the sultan even when the funds may have benefited the poor brethren. Given the size and importance of Delhi and the length of time Ibn Battuta spent in the capital (nearly nine years), details of the sanctuaries and living saints are scanty by comparison with some other cities he had visited. After leaving Delhi for good, Ibn Battuta's travels down the west coast of India and in the south brought him into contact with familiar institutions like hospices and holy persons. At the same time, he was more conscious of the mixed religious nature of the population, if not of the degree to which Muslims were a tiny minority within an overwhelming Hindu populace. Meanwhile, Ibn Battuta's attention was focused elsewhere.

Muhammad b. Tughluq

The Sultan of Delhi dominates the Indian narrative of the travels. Ibn Battuta's balanced assessment of him has been cited at the beginning of the chapter. He was essentially generous but displayed a cruel streak in dealing with those he judged his political enemies. With regard to the sultan's generosity, Ibn Battuta found it necessary to anticipate his audience's scepticism and declare, *'I call God and His Angels and His Prophets to witness that all I shall relate of his extraordinary generosity is absolute truth.'* He added that his reports were based upon his eyewitness authority as well as backed by independent sources. He acknowledged, moreover, that he had also benefited from the sultan's open-handed nature. He was granted furnished accommodation, food supplies for himself and his company of around 40 persons and revenue from several villages amounting to 5,000 dinars annually, a sum that was supplemented by a further 12,000 dinars annually. The sultan appointed him as religious judge (*qadi*) of Delhi with a stipend of (another?) 12,000 dinars a year plus a sum of 12,000 dinars in cash to be drawn immediately from the treasury. The total sums involved are confused but they were of an order to impress any reader of the travels back home. To these sums were added gifts from the sultan from time to time and in Ibn Battuta's specific case the settlement of the substantial debts he had incurred. It was generosity of this magnitude that spread the sultan's fame abroad and attracted Arab and Persian scholars and others to his court. He noted that it was part of a deliberate policy to favour foreigners who, in addition, were addressed as *aziz* or 'honourable' so as not to make them feel they were strangers. For their part, Ibn Battuta admitted, foreigners came to Delhi '*to gain riches and return to their countries*', but the downside was that of riches amassed in India '*it is only rarely that anyone gets out of the country with them, and when he does leave it and reaches some other country, God sends upon him some calamity which annihilates all that he possesses*'. Ibn Battuta was perhaps more fortunate than most, as he left India on a mission from the sultan, despite its unfortunate end. He says nothing of his financial condition when he finally arrived home in Morocco.

So, if one basis of Muhammad b. Tughluq's strategy of rule was generosity in order to attract persons loyal to him, cruelty and violence was another used to instil fear in potential rivals. Having discussed examples of the former, Ibn Battuta begins the next section headed: '*This Sultan's murders and reprehensible actions*', and he continued:

> *In spite of all that we have related of his humility, his sense of fairness, his compassion for the needy and his extraordinary liberality, the Sultan was far too free in shedding blood. ... He used to punish small faults and great without respect of persons, whether men of learning or piety or noble descent ... may God deliver us from misfortune.*

He was clearly distressed by the almost daily instances of the sultan's violence. At one point he expressed horror at the sight of mutilated bodies and stuffed skins of executed prisoners exhibited on a city wall, and noted that its purpose was to spread terror among the public. Illustrations of the sultan's darker side dealt chiefly with victims from among the learned (*ulama*) class such as pious Sufi *shaykhs*, jurists, a religious judge, a market inspector and the chief preacher of Delhi. At the end of an account of each victim Ibn Battuta declared a blessing of sympathy, '*May God Most High have mercy upon him.*' In the remaining cases involving the sultan's relatives or notables who had attracted the royal wrath, no blessing was mentioned. This cannot be accidental. As a member himself of the learned class, albeit a foreigner, he was especially sensitive to attacks upon them. His attitude towards the local ruling elite, because he was an outsider, was more aloof.

The case of the Sufi *shaykh* Shihab al-Din was striking. Muhammad b. Tughluq had attempted to bring the respected Sufi, known for his probity and virtue, into his employ, but Shihab al-Din publicly rejected the offer. The sultan then commanded another venerable *shaykh* to pluck out every hair of Shihab al-Din's beard but he refused to do so. So both men had their beards forcibly plucked and were then banished from Delhi for several years. Shihab al-Din was dispatched to Dawlat Abad in the south. Once restored to favour he did accept a government post and rose in rank. Later he secured permission to leave the capital for the nearby hills where he excavated an immense cave to house a workforce that was engaged in cultivating and irrigating the fields. As these were years of dearth, he made a fortune from the produce he sold. The sultan after two or three years summoned him once more to the capital but Shihab al-Din proclaimed he would never again serve an oppressor, citing several instances of his tyrannical conduct. This remark resulted in the *shaykh* being forcibly brought to Delhi in irons and imprisoned. For two weeks he declined any food or drink while fellow *shaykhs* and jurists urged him to recant. He continued to resist and even rejected food sent him by the sultan and declared his readiness to die as the martyrs of old. The sultan then ordered him to be force fed – with human excrement – and when he stubbornly refused to yield, he was finally beheaded. Ibn Battuta ended his tale saying, '*God Most High have mercy upon him!*' He had known the *shaykh* well, having on occasion visited his cave. Their relationship had caused royal suspicion to fall upon Ibn Battuta in turn. Just after Shihab al-Din's arrest, he was detained in the sultan's audience hall watched over by four slaves.

Customarily when the Sultan takes this action with anyone it rarely happens that the person escapes. But God Most High inspired me to recite His words

*'God is sufficient for us, how excellent a protector is He' [Q 3:167]. I recited
these words the first day 33,000 times and passed the night in the audience hall.
I fasted five days on end, reciting the Quran from cover to cover each day, and
tasting nothing but water. After five days I broke my fast and then continued for
another four days on end, and I was released after the execution of the* shaykh,
praise be to God Most High.

As it happened, these traumatic events took place not long before
the end of Ibn Battuta's sojourn in Delhi. They probably contributed
to his decision to leave the sultan's service. And that could have been
a matter of some delicacy – and danger. The situation was resolved by
Ibn Battuta seeking spiritual refuge with a saintly figure called Kamal
al-Din Abdallah, and known as al-Ghari or 'cave man' from a grotto he
inhabited outside Delhi and near the tomb and hospice of the great Chistiyya saint Nizam al-Din al-Awliya. Ibn Battuta described al-Ghari in
lavish language: a learned and saintly *imam* (*al-imam, al-salih, al-alim*), a
godfearing, humble-minded devotee (*al-abid, al-wari, al-khashi*), one of
the Friends of God (*awliya*), outstanding in his time and unique of his age.
Miracles were ascribed to al-Ghari, some of which Ibn Battuta claimed to
have witnessed himself. Then he stated, '*I devoted myself to the service of this
shaykh and gave my possessions to the poor brethren and the needy.*' This was
the first time Ibn Battuta recorded a direct and deep commitment to Sufi
religious exercises. He seems to have attempted to emulate his spiritual
guide who would fast for ten, sometimes 20 days at a time. Quoting a
well-known proverb, al-Ghari advised caution: '*he would check me and bid
me not to overstrain myself in devotional exercise, saying to me "He who breaks
down from exhaustion has neither covered ground nor spared his mount."*' He
felt a continuing obstacle to progress, '*so I rid myself of everything that I
had, little or much, and I gave the clothes off my back to a mendicant and put on
his clothes*'. He remained with al-Ghari for a period of five months as his
disciple.

The sultan in due course learned of Ibn Battuta's retreat and summoned
him. He entered Muhammad b. Tughluq's presence in mendicant's clothing and was treated with great kindness. The sultan sought his return
to court service. Ibn Battuta declined and requested permission to make
the pilgrimage to Mecca which was granted. For the next 40 days, Ibn
Battuta continued his spiritual exercises in a hospice reciting the Quran,

keeping nocturnal vigils and fasting until he could sustain the fast for five consecutive days. At that point the sultan summoned him a second time with the proposition that he undertake a mission to China as his ambassador. With considerable reserve he accepted and arrangements commenced for the long expedition to the East.

One way or another, the events surrounding Shihab al-Din's conflict with the sultan and his brutal execution marked a crucial turning point for Ibn Battuta. For all the material rewards he had received and enjoyed from service to the sultan, he was distressed and perhaps increasingly feared for his vulnerable position as a foreigner faced with Muhammad b. Tughluq's terrible wrath towards opponents. At the sultan's private dinners, to which he was often invited, Ibn Battuta may have met one of the ruler's long-standing confidants, the historian Diya al-Din Barani (d. 1357). The two men differed in background, for Barani was Indian born and his family was well connected to Delhi's ruling circle of indigenous aristocrats, to whose continued political health he primarily dedicated his energies. Barani and Ibn Battuta seemed to share a similar view towards a ruler's political violence. In the affairs of kingship in general, and those of Muhammad b. Tughluq in particular, each recognized that the exercise of the opposite qualities of cruelty and benevolence was essential. Barani elaborated on this view in one of his writings. In what purported to be a conversation with the sultan, he had Muhammad b. Tughluq explain his own view of kingship:

> I inflict capital punishments on the basis of suspicion and presumption of rebellion, disorder and conspiracy. I put people to death for every slight disobedience I see in them, and I will keep inflicting capital punishments in this way till either I perish or the people are set right and give up rebellion and disobedience.

As justification for his attitude he concluded on a note of bitterness, 'I have distributed so much treasure among the people, but no one has become my sincere well wisher.'[16]

One can imagine Ibn Battuta's growing unease at remaining in the sultan's service. The example made of Shihab al-Din and the repercussions for himself must have made him seek spiritual solace and strength with his Sufi companion al-Ghari while imagining ways of leaving Delhi for good. He countered the sultan's first request to return to court service with a petition to leave for the pilgrimage to Mecca, a religious obligation the sultan would find difficult to reject. It allowed Ibn Battuta time to resume his spiritual exercises until departure upon the pilgrim road. The sultan's next proposal to send Ibn Battuta on a mission to China brought him back into court service, but from Ibn Battuta's viewpoint the mission was an opportunity to leave Delhi and India behind.

Journey southwards

The first main objective was to reach a port of embarkation on the south west Indian coast. After his 'miraculous' rescue from thirst and hunger by the saint Dilshad, Ibn Battuta was able to proceed on his mission with what was left of the company that had set out from Delhi. They were now beyond the limits of Delhi province, venturing into the territory of well-fortified cities like Kanauj with a Muslim governor, to towns '*inhabited chiefly by infidels under Muslim control*' to others described as '*belonging to the Muslims but situated in infidel territory*'. He interspersed details of the itinerary with stories of warfare between infidel and Muslim. Gwalior was a fortified town on the summit of a hill, whose governor he had met on a previous occasion. Ibn Battuta recorded that he had once intervened with the governor to spare a Hindu's execution because he had never witnessed a death by beheading; the man was then imprisoned. Much further south some infidel sultans were under Muhammad b. Tughluq's suzerainty and sent him annual gifts; others acted in the same manner while actively plotting rebellion against Delhi.

It was all dangerous territory, but not every threat appeared to come from humans. In the town of Parvan Ibn Battuta heard tales of danger from man-eating tigers – tigers with peculiar habits, such as the one which did not eat its victim's flesh but only drank his blood. Someone explained to the visitor that it was not really a tiger who committed such barbarity, but a man who could appear in the shape of a tiger, a magician of the group known as a *juki* (yogi). '*When I heard of this,*' retorted Ibn Battuta, '*I refused to believe it. But a number of people told me the same thing, so let us give a story or two about these magicians.*'

Among the marvellous things yogis accomplished was to abstain from food and drink for months, some spending the time buried under the earth with only a gap available for breathing. Ibn Battuta claimed that

Muslims also became yogis' disciples to learn the secrets of their arts. He had seen one Muslim yogi in Mangalore seated on top of a high platform without food or drink for nearly a month, although how long he remained there he could not say. Most were vegetarian and, with approval, Ibn Battuta said that it was obvious *'they have so disciplined themselves in ascetic practices that they have no need of any of the goods or vanities of this world'*.

The sultan admitted yogis into his company and once, when Ibn Battuta visited him in his private apartments, he saw the assembled group being entertained by two yogis. The sultan suggested they should demonstrate one of their tricks that his guest would never have seen. *'One of them squatted on the ground and then rose into the air above our heads, still in a sitting posture. I was so astonished and frightened that I fell to the floor in a faint.'* He had to be revived with a potion, all in time to witness the dramatic sequel. The seated man's associate had beaten his sandal furiously on the ground until it, too, rose in the air and assaulted his companion on the neck as he slowly descended to the ground. The sultan remarked that he would have asked the yogis to perform even stranger things had he not been concerned for Ibn Battuta's sanity. He left feeling quite giddy until a strong draught had been administered to bring him round.

A similar but more dramatic exhibition of wizardry Ibn Battuta had witnessed in China. It involved a young man being followed by an older collaborator, each clambering up a rope that vanished into thin air above the courtyard surface. The latter, armed with a knife, then began to toss down various of the young man's severed limbs, head, feet, hands and torso. After descending, the older man attached the limbs together and then kicked the young man who, being dutifully restored, stood up before the assembly, much to Ibn Battuta's horror and amazement. As a potion was brought to calm his palpitating heart, a *qadi* seated at his side said in a soothing voice, 'By God, there was no climbing up or down or cutting off of limbs. It is all legerdemain (*shaawadha*)!'

Yogis were reputed to be able to cure diseases like leprosy and elephantiasis. One was also involved in the demise of an odious Muslim Sultan of Madurai in the territory of Maabar, south India. Ibn Battuta and this sultan, Ghiyath al-Din, had each married daughters of Sultan Sharif Jalal al-Din Ahsan Shah who had revolted in the south against the rule of Delhi. Ghiyath al-Din took a special pleasure in killing Hindu captives, men, women and children. He had once done so in the presence of Ibn

Battuta. When Hindu prisoners were killed by skewering them on stakes, Ibn Battuta expressed his revulsion in the comment, *'This was an abomination which I have not known of any other king. That is why God hastened his death.'* God's instrument was an innocent yogi who, at Ghiyath al-Din's request, had prepared some pills for the octogenarian as an aphrodisiac. The pills contained iron filings and their efficacy was so rewarding that the old man overdosed and died. Ibn Battuta's explanation is ambiguous: it is unclear whether death was caused by the effect of the iron filings or from excessive copulation.

Ibn Battuta's attitude to the yogis was mixed. They performed marvels (*ajaib*) not miracles, and although some were dedicated to a religious discipline others could be quite terrifying. He would not have grasped the differences between various forms of yoga but he did recognize charlatan exhibitionists. There were other intriguing aspects of India, parts of the south in particular, where he noticed and recorded things of religious interest but without adding further comment.

Ibn Battuta arrived by ship at Hili, one of the ports, together with Calicut and Kawlam, that marked the farthest reach by ships from China. The place was visited by Muslims and Hindus alike on account of its congregational mosque. It was venerated, *'for it is of great blessedness and resplendent with radiant light'*. Seafarers made votive offerings to it. Its treasury was well endowed to provide for students of religious science with stipends, and its kitchen attended the needs of all travellers and the poor Muslims of the town. Ibn Battuta almost met his equal in the mosque, a saintly jurist (*faqih salih*) from Mogadishu in Somalia who had studied in Mecca and Medina for nearly 30 years and who had travelled in India and China. The next place of interest was Dahfattan in the territories of the Sultan of Jurfattan, called Kuwail. There, beside the congregational mosque was a *'tender green tree with leaves like fig leaves but smooth and surrounded by a wall'*. The tree was known as the tree of testimony, for in the autumn of each year a single leaf fell from it after first turning yellow, then red, and written upon it *'by the pen of the divine power were the words "There is no god but Allah, Muhammad is the apostle of Allah."'* Muslims and infidels sat under the tree together waiting for the leaf to fall. When it did, half was taken by Muslims and the other half was placed in the Hindu sultan's treasury and used for healing the sick. The tree was the cause for the conversion of Sultan Kuwail's ancestor who had understood the writing on the leaf and built the mosque as a result. Once, the tree had been angrily uprooted by an infidel until no trace of it was left, but it afterwards sprouted and grew again as fine as ever; and the infidel perished quickly for his infamous act.

The next town was Budfattan where the majority of the inhabitants were Brahmans, venerated by the infidel who hated Muslims and hence no Muslim lived among them. There was a mosque outside the town where visiting Muslims worshipped. Ibn Battuta related an anecdote with a moral about the mosque. A Brahman had removed its roof to use for his own house, but it later burst into flames and his family perished and all his goods were destroyed. Henceforward the mosque was left untouched and Brahmans actually served it by providing a water source for all manner of travellers.

Throughout his entire journey southwards, Ibn Battuta displayed a growing awareness of moving from a domain of Islam to an area of contested religious traditions, where in many places there was a total absence of Muslim values. One of Muhammad b. Tughluq's positive qualities, according to Ibn Battuta, had been his strict insistence on Muslims' observance of the rituals of faith, on their acquiring knowledge of religious obligations and on the state upholding religious law (*sharia*). For example, attendance at the congregational prayer on Fridays was obligatory and dereliction of this duty was severely punished. People in general could be questioned on their knowledge of matters binding upon them as Muslims and failure to give correct answers was punished by enforced study sessions. Ibn Battuta's approval of these measures was conditioned in part by his own personal norms and his awareness, too, that Islam was a still a young and shallow-rooted faith in India that required active state support. This accompanied his insight that outside of Delhi proper the populace was overwhelmingly non-Muslim. The sultan's strictures over compliance with Islamic norms, therefore, were probably only effective in areas nearest to the centre of power in Delhi.

Ibn Battuta acutely observed that the contiguous distribution of Muslims and non-Muslims (whom he invariably called 'infidels') applied especially to regions outside the capital of the sultanate:

> *The infidels in the land of India inhabit a territory which is not geographically separated from that of the Muslims, and their lands are contiguous, but though*

the Muslims have the upper hand over them yet the infidels maintain themselves
in inaccessible mountains and rugged places … they live in forests which are for
them as good as city walls … so they cannot be overcome except by strong armies.

Ibn Battuta's description of his journey from Delhi to south India confirmed these words. There was, nonetheless, one further moment of intense religious exercise he experienced. It occurred in the wake of the loss of the ship bearing the Sultan of Delhi's gifts to the Sultan of China, together with many of the mission's personnel and all of Ibn Battuta's belongings. Shortly afterward he joined the Muslim Sultan of Hinawr on the Indian coast and there, as he described it:

I spent most of my time in his mosque and used to read the Quran through every
day, and later twice a day, beginning the first recital after the dawn prayer and
ending it in the early afternoon, then after making fresh ablutions, I would
begin the second recital and end it about sunset. I continued to do this for three
months during which I went into retreat for forty days.

At the time he dictated the Indian narrative to Ibn Juzayy he would already have had an opportunity to reflect upon the vulnerable and delicate situation on another frontier between Muslims and their proximate enemy, the Christian Catholics' campaign of re-conquest of the Iberian peninsula adjacent to the Marinid domains in North Africa. On both these fronts, strong leaders and their armies were essential to defend either a shrinking portion of the *umma*, or to attempt to maintain and expand it in another. In Ibn Battuta's view Abu Inan and Muhammad b. Tughluq were rulers on the front lines. So was Muhammad Uzbek in confronting Byzantium. As Ibn Battuta was not a military strategist he would not have given such matters a passing thought. He would continue to live by his faith that the *umma* would prosper, while conceding all its imperfections, so long as God continued to bestow acts of grace upon enough persons of piety and devotion so as to fill the *umma* with His blessings.

꙳ ꙳

CHAPTER 5

Tales of the 'Other'

I n previous chapters we have explored themes that highlight the narrative of Ibn Battuta's travels. The rather cumbersome title of *The Travels*, we recall, was *Gift to Those Who Contemplate the Wonders of Cities and the Marvels of Travelling*. In the course of relating *where* he travelled, Ibn Battuta at the same time expressed *how* he experienced his journeys, especially over land – he is almost totally silent about the perils of the sea during the extensive voyages he undertook, apart from when he was shipwrecked and attacked by pirates. Given the extent of his voyages, these two singular events, traumatic as they were, suggest he had otherwise enjoyed extraordinary good fortune.

In this, the concluding chapter, we examine a modest refinement to those 'wonders' and 'marvels' that characterize the travels as a whole. It was H.A.R. Gibb who had remarked that Ibn Battuta was a geographer in spite of himself ('le géographe malgré lui'), but who prefaced that observation explaining that his 'interest in places was subordinate to his interest in persons'.[1] Some of what will be discussed here has been anticipated in previous chapters, namely, the way Ibn Battuta remembered 'others' he encountered on his travels and how he represented them in his narrative.

Roxanne Euben explained in her discussion on the techniques of representation employed in *The Travels* that these helped organize what Ibn Battuta saw and, at the same time, constrained how he saw and described it. Recording all that he had judged to be worthwhile implied a flip-side of the coin, that is, the persons or things he failed to see or represent. For example, despite his lengthy sojourn in India, she writes, 'Ibn Battuta registers little awareness either of the distinction between Hindus and Buddhists, or of the existence of the caste system all around him.' On the other hand, even a brief encounter with *juki*s (yogis) and their – to him rather frightening – exhibitions of magic, was enough to allow Ibn

Battuta to recognize that other yogis were engaged in exercises of genuine religious devotion and in acts of healing. It is certainly more broadly true that 'Ibn Battuta scarcely notes the poor, ordinary, and powerless in his narrative, even when it is evident that his own comfort is predicated on their existence, mobility and labour.'[2] The difficulty with an argument from silence – what an author fails to record – is that it can provide only a suggestive but not conclusive explanation for the silence. In the example cited, Ibn Battuta may well have understood his own comfort was predicated on the labour of others, and simply took that state of affairs for granted and therefore not worth mentioning. The object here is to illustrate Ibn Battuta's representation of 'the other' as far as possible from what he says about those he represents without inferring meaning from what he omits to record. In this way, too, it is hoped that what he does say contributes to an emerging picture of him as a person. One of the more interesting categories in *The Travels* is his perception and representation of women in the various societies he engaged with.

Women as the 'other'

We may commence with the women in Ibn Battuta's private life, that is, his wives, of whom ten are mentioned, although there may have been more. He was, as far as he allows us to understand, more of a serial monogamist than polygamist, except for his 18- (or perhaps only eight-) month sojourn in the Maldive Islands where he acquired the legal maximum of four wives at one time and additional concubines. But that is looking many years ahead. The point to note in the tales that follow is that in reading Ibn Battuta's *Travels*,

> one is struck by his relative outspokenness about matters that are usually considered too private or too un-prestigious to write about. ... Medieval Arab authors do not especially eschew the mentioning of women in general. Their reticence is restricted to women that belong to the family circle, those who were ... screened off from the public sphere to which literature by its very nature belongs.[3]

Thus Remke Kruk argued in her article on Ibn Battuta's family life.

Wives

To begin at the beginning, despite an eagerness to perform the pilgrimage, Ibn Battuta left Tangier with a heavy heart. The '*sorrow of separation*' he suffered was for his parents, of whom his mother at least was still relatively young, and for '*loved ones, female and male*'. He contracted his first marriage a few months after departure and that quickly ended in his first divorce, not because the girl was at fault but because Ibn Battuta had quarrelled with her father over some undisclosed matter. His second marriage followed close upon the first and the couple arrived together in Alexandria. Whether they left together on the journey to Cairo and up the Nile valley is not known. Whatever the case, these marriages seem to have met the need to heal the sorrow of leaving home and his confessed loneliness on the road.

Ibn Battuta does not disclose his next conjugal union until near the very end of *The Travels* as he passed through Damascus again on his homeward journey. He had been absent for 20 years, he says, and '*I had left there a pregnant wife. While I was in India I learnt that she had given birth to a male child. I had sent forty Indian gold dinars for his mother to his grandfather who was from Meknes in the Maghrib. When I came to Damascus this time, I had no other concern than to ask after my son.*' He learned that the boy had died a dozen years before his return but he tells us nothing of the mother's fate. Nor do we discover whether his second wife was still with him at the time of the third, Damascus marriage which probably took place in 1326, before he completed his first pilgrimage. Admittedly the duration of his stay in Damascus raises a problem. The marriage apart, Ibn Battuta claimed to have become absorbed in further learning. He studied Prophetic traditions from at least two pious women scholars of *hadith*, each of whom gave him a general licence to teach the works he had read with them. One, named Zaynab, was famed for her extensive travels and had earned the nickname of the 'goal of world's travel'.

Nevertheless a pattern had become established, namely, that Ibn Battuta seldom, if ever, took a wife with him much further than the place where he had contracted the union. There is no mention that he had a wife with him in Mecca on his first pilgrimage or during the period he was in the Holy City as a sojourner (*mujawir*). Remke Kruk has suggested that the decision for a wife to stay behind may have been made by mutual consent.[4] A woman's decision to leave the familiarity and protection of her family would not have been taken lightly. In one case, Ibn Battuta agreed that a wife could release herself from the union if he did not return from abroad after an agreed period. When he sent money from India to the wife who had borne him a child in Damascus, did he regard himself still married to her and, therefore, to an extent still responsible? On the other hand, why would the same wife not accept joining her husband to fulfil the obligation of pilgrimage to Mecca, unless her pregnancy had prevented that choice?

If Ibn Battuta had no conjugal relations during his stay in Mecca, Meccan women, for their part, did make an impression upon him. The local populace in general were elegant and clean in their attire. The women he described were

> *of rare and surpassing beauty, pious and chaste* (afaf). *They too, like the men, make much use of perfumes, to such a degree that a woman will spend the night hungry and buy perfume with the price of her food. They make a practice of performing the circuit of the sacred mosque on the eve of each Friday, and come in their finest apparel, and the sanctuary is saturated with the smell of their perfume. When one of these women goes away, the odour of the perfume clings as an effluvium to the place after she has gone.*

The modern reader may wonder what Ibn Battuta meant by beauty. This description does not refer specifically to the rites of the pilgrimage season, when women would be unveiled and dressed in simple, seamless white garments. Was it, therefore, women's individual qualities he perceived, or was it rather a sense of place, the Holy City itself, that caused him to view Meccan women as essentially beautiful in a spiritual sense? Was the overpowering presence of perfume an imitation of one of the Prophet's known and favoured adornments?

The next reference to a wife occurred, casually enough, in an account about provincial revolts in south India against the Sultan of Delhi. Pestilence had broken out in the sultan's army that claimed many victims and gave rise to a rumour that the sultan himself had succumbed. The son of a rebel governor, whom Ibn Battuta knew as handsome, brave and generous, became ambitious to seize the sultan's throne. Ibn Battuta then interjected the comment, '*I was married to his sister Hurnasab; she was a pious woman, who used to spend part of the night in prayers and to compose prayers for the recollection of God and she bore a daughter by me.'* Ibn Battuta said he did not know what God had done with them both. He used the same expression of his only named son, Ahmad, who he had left behind in Delhi, not with the boy's mother, who may have been the same Hurnasab, but with a prominent male friend.

Maldivian wives

Following the events of the journey from Delhi, including the grave loss of the sultan's gift to the Chinese ruler and the collapse of his ambassadorial mission, Ibn Battuta must have rejoiced to discover the Maldive Islands were near to paradise on earth. The staple diet was based upon fish and the products derived from the coconut which had an *'amazing and unparalleled effect in sexual intercourse, and the people of these islands perform wonders in this respect. I myself had four wives there, and concubines as well, and I used to visit all of them every day and pass the night with the wife whose turn it was'*, and this continued for the whole of the time he was on the islands. Ibn Battuta, now in his early 40s, was not flaunting his sexual prowess with these words but rather emphasizing the equal treatment of his four wives in accordance with the injunction of the Quran (Q 4:3). Whether he had studied the famous work by al-Ghazali, a controversial figure in Morocco, we do not know. A passage from his *Revival of the Religious Sciences* did reflect a contemporary pious attitude towards marriage: 'One should come to his wife every four nights, as is fairest, since the number of wives one may have is four. One may wait this long to do so, certainly, though one should come to her more or less than this, according to the amount she needs to remain chaste (*tahsin*) since it is obligatory for a husband to enable her to keep chaste.'[5] The ladies in question all held a firm position in the Maldive social register. Two government ministers competed to have Ibn Battuta marry their daughters. One he refused as an ill omen, since she had been twice widowed and was still a virgin. The other liaison he agreed to but was stood up on the day of the ceremony, the lady being described as 'her own mistress'. As consolation, the chief minister offered to pay the dowry for his son's mother-in law and Ibn Battuta accepted. Of her he wrote, *'She was one of the best of women, and was so affectionate that when I married her she used to anoint me with perfume and cense my garments, laughing all the while and without showing any displeasure.'* He claimed to be

exceedingly fond of another wife, but his fourth wife, yet another minister's daughter, he declared was his favourite of all. And this, to his jurist's
mind, presumably did not imply his failure to treat each of them equally.
Along with women of rank whom he could marry, Ibn Battuta was offered
by a government minister the gift of slave girls or concubines. Two who
are named were not Maldivian but from India. One was called Anbari.
The other was named Gulistan (Persian for 'rose garden'), who pleased
Ibn Battuta very much because she could converse in Persian with him,
since *'the people of those islands have a language of their own which I did not
understand'*. Presumably he could communicate with his wives who, being
educated to a degree, would have had conversational Arabic or Persian as
did his fathers-in-law.

Alas, paradise on earth was short lived as Ibn Battuta discovered.
Strained relations developed into open rift between him and the father of
his favourite wife. This father-in-law was an important political figure who
had married the current female ruler, Sultana Khadija, after the death of
her first husband. He feared Ibn Battuta was plotting internally to remove
him or was acting as an agent of the Sultan of Delhi to raise a revolt
against him. Ibn Battuta frankly admitted that only after his estrange-
ment from the minister did he consider the prospect of intervening with
the assistance of the sultan of a southern Indian province to whom he was
also related by a previous marriage. His immediate decision was to resign
from his post as religious judge and leave the islands. The problem was
what to do with his wives. Maldivian women were understandably reluc-
tant to leave their island paradise.

His solution was to divorce one wife. For a second who was with child,
he made an agreement to return to her within a period of nine months,
failing which she was her own mistress; however, before he finally left
the Maldives, he had divorced her, too. He heard later that she had borne
him a son. His two other wives accompanied him on the first stage of a
trip through the islands, although when one of them fell ill and wished
to return, the couple divorced. Marina Tolmacheva has written of this
episode that 'Ibn Battuta's compliance with the wife's wish and his concern
over her future comfort are apparently dictated by local custom and political concern. Importantly … divorce is clearly perceived in the narrative as
a deserving deed rather than an act of abandonment.'[6] Together with his
last wife and a slave girl (*jariya*) of whom he was fond and had sent for,

they continued their island tour. He deposited the wife with her family on the beautiful island of Muluk, where he remained more than two months and, inexplicably, twice married again, presumably divorcing them before his final departure. In any event, they are the last marriages Ibn Battuta mentions and, of his total of ten, six were contracted during a relatively short stay in the Maldives. Using his own data, he would have married on average every three months. As he explained:

> It is easy to get married in these islands on account of smallness of the dowries and the pleasure of their women's society. … When ships arrive the crews marry wives and when they want to sail they divorce them; it is really a sort of temporary marriage (nikah mutah), and the women never leave their country. I have never found in the world any women more agreeable to consort with than they are.

And little wonder, for a wife never allowed another person to cater for the husband's needs, fetching the food and removing the remainder of a meal, washing his hands, bringing water for the pre-prayer ablutions, and ensuring his feet were covered in bed. The downside of Maldive marriage from Ibn Battuta's point of view is interesting for the frustration it caused him. Customarily, the woman did not eat with her husband nor was he aware of what she ate. He managed after some effort to cajole one or two to share his table, but he failed utterly to see any of them eating alone. The custom went against his natural sociability.

Children

Family life, as the vast majority of Muslims experienced it, never fitted Ibn Battuta's style of existence. He mentioned begetting five children, all by different wives, three of whom were male. One of these was by the pregnant Maldivian wife he had made a compact with and then divorced. He had heard of the son's birth sometime after his return to India and decided to revisit the islands. The wife complained against the absent father's wish to fetch the child away but the chief minister said he would not prevent it. In the end, Ibn Battuta decided the child's best interests were served by leaving him with his own people.

A touching story of one of his offspring concerned a baby girl born of a relationship with a slave he had acquired, along with many others, during the course of his travels. The girl appears suddenly in the narrative just after Ibn Battuta had left Bukhara. Nearing her term, she was carried in a camel litter and the father wished her to give birth in the fabled city of Samarqand some days distant. Instead, they found the camp of the *'pious and exalted'* Sultan of Transoxania, Ala al-Din Tarmashirin, who, at the moment of their arrival, was absent. The travellers were provided with a traditional Turkish nomad's cupola-shaped tent covered in felt material and that very night the infant was born. Ibn Battuta was informed it was a boy. Only after the naming ceremony a week later was he told by his companions, and confirmed with a degree of embarrassment by female servants, that the baby was a girl. His reaction to the news was that *'This girl was born under a lucky star, and I experienced everything to give me joy and satisfaction from the time of her birth.'*

A few weeks after Ibn Battuta's arrival in Delhi, the baby girl died not having reached her first birthday. The sultan's chief minister (*wazir*) arranged for her to be buried in a hospice close to the tomb of a famous *shaykh* from Anatolia. The sultan, who was absent from the capital on campaign against rebels, acknowledged his *wazir*'s letter concerning the child. Ibn Battuta detailed the customary ceremony held on the third day after a burial, all arranged by the *wazir*. The court chamberlain, the chief *qadi* and a number of the city's principal men all attended to recite the Quran, followed by professional reciters. A political colouring tinted the proceedings as the *qadi* recited an elegy on the dead girl and a panegyric to the absent sultan. Rose water was sprinkled over those in attendance and cups of candy sherbet and betel leaves distributed. Ibn Battuta and his companions were each given a robe of honour. When he returned to his house, he was astonished by the quantities of food sent from the palace by the sultan's blind mother Makhduma Jahan ('Mistress of the World'), whom Ibn Battuta described following a visit to her as *'one of the most virtuous of women and munificent in charity who has founded many hospices and endowed them to supply food to all travellers'.* Surplus food from what she provided was distributed to the poor. Ibn Battuta reciprocated and sent the sultan's mother the gift of a Turkish slave girl he had brought from Anatolia. Some days later a silk curtained litter was brought by eunuchs from the mother's palace to fetch the mother of the deceased child. She remained overnight at the palace and returned laden with money and lavish gifts. The episode ended with Ibn Battuta's distribution of Makhduma Jahan's gifts and money among his companions while paying off merchants to whom he was indebted. He explained his move, *'to protect myself and guard my honour, because intelligence agents were sending reports to the Sultan about everything that concerned me'*. The deceased child's lucky star had lost its sparkle, perhaps, but his feelings towards the child (and to the mother) appeared quite genuine. Remke Kruk judged the story to be remarkable on several counts:

> First, there is the fact that Ibn Battuta does not consider it beneath his dignity to mention his fussing about the pregnant girl; then there is the embarrassment of the women when they have to tell him that the child (apparently expected with much concern) was a girl; and there are Ibn Battuta's subsequent positive remarks about the baby, which imply that his sense of happiness about her existence induced him to connect everything pleasant that happened to him ... with the very fact of her existence.[7]

Slave girls and concubines

At some point in his travels, Ibn Battuta determined that female company was important on the road, and this was with slaves he had purchased or had received as gifts. The term 'slave' was often employed as an equivalent to concubine, although contexts are often unclear. He does not record when or where he adopted the practice, but circumstantial evidence points to Anatolia. The Sultan of Birgi had generously entertained the traveller and his party for two weeks and upon their departure he had bestowed upon Ibn Battuta a handsome gift of gold and silver coins and a Greek slave called Mikhail. Soon after, while passing through the city of Aya Suluq, Ibn Battuta purchased an expensive horse and a Greek slave girl, a virgin, for 40 gold dinars, almost certainly paid for from the Sultan of Birgi's gift. In quick succession, he reported the gift of another male Greek slave called Niqula and his purchase of another Greek slave girl named Marghalita. When Ibn Battuta set out for the camp of Muhammad Uzbek, Sultan of the Golden Horde, he purchased a wagon for himself and a slave girl in which to make the journey. Next, during one stage of the journey into Khurasan, three slave girls accompanied him in his wagon. From there until he reached Delhi, he seems to have enjoyed the constant companionship of at least one slave girl, including the mother of the child he later mourned. If slavery was an institution taken for granted in circum-Mediterranean societies, it is worth recalling Ibn Battuta's censure of certain practices associated with it. The inhabitants of Ladhiq, including the city's *qadi*, were guilty in his eyes of immoral behaviour for buying beautiful Greek slave girls and employing them for prostitution; he was especially moved to fury at their use in the public bath houses where they mixed with men to commit acts of depravity (*fasad*).

Slave status was almost invariably the consequence of a victor's army capturing members of an enemy's population. This was certainly the case with what Ibn Battuta called 'infidel' Indians captured in raids on villages by the Sultan of Delhi's troops. On one occasion he was sent ten girls by the *wazir* for his own use but his reaction was less than enthusiastic:

> *I gave the man who brought them one – he was not at all pleased at that – and my companions took three young ones amongst them; as for the rest I do not know what happened to them. Female captives are very cheap there because they are dirty and do not know civilised ways. Even the educated ones are cheap, so that no one there needs to buy captives.*

They were an expendable human commodity of no value.

In China, Ibn Battuta reported rather different circumstances. There, he said, '*Slave girls are cheap in price, but all the Chinese sell their sons and daughters, and it is not thought shameful among them.*' Parents sought to assure some protection for their children through moral persuasion with a purchaser to treat them properly. If a foreign merchant wished to marry a Chinese girl, he could do so but not simply to pursue a debauched (*fasad*) relationship or take her away against her will. Ibn Battuta cited what he claimed was a general Chinese attitude: '*They say: We do not want it said in the Muslim countries that they lose their money in our country, and that it is a land of debauchery and fleeting pleasure.*'

Ibn Battuta's treatment of another of his slave girls again showed some sensitivity. He was a self-confessed non-swimmer and felt uncomfortable aboard a ship. That probably explained his initial response to his ship's running aground off the Malabar coast on a short voyage from Ceylon. The sailors had managed to construct a raft from salvaged portions of the ship and Ibn Battuta was about to board it when his companions asked him fearfully if he was going to abandon them. He had two slave girls with him, one of whom he professed to love dearly. He quickly placed their safety, and that of two companions, before his own. The second girl who claimed to be a good swimmer clung to a raft rope and swam alongside. Ibn Battuta and others were rescued the following day.

The women of Zabid

The material in *The Travels* that treats of women and matters of family is extensive, as illustrated above. Ibn Battuta also remarked on individual women he met in the course of his travels and commented upon various groups of women, for example his observations on the spiritual beauty of female inhabitants of Mecca cited previously. He was struck, too, by the populace of Zabid, second city of the Yemen. They were courteous, upright and handsome. The women were of

> *exceeding and preeminent beauty … and they are virtuous and generous in character. They have a predilection for the stranger and do not refuse to marry him, as the women of our country do. When he wishes to travel, his wife goes out with him and bids him farewell; and if there should be a child between them, it is she who takes care of it and supplies what is needed for it until its father returns. During his absence she makes no demands on him for maintenance or clothes or anything else, and when he is resident she is content with little for upkeep and clothes. But the women never leave their own town and would not consent to do so even if one of them were offered any sum to her on condition that she should leave her town.*

This is not like the picture of Meccan women's religious nature but rather more a sociological assessment of the pros and cons of Zabidi women from a traveller's perspective. We have no idea whether he was with wife at the time of his visit to Zabid, but as he had already displayed the pattern of leaving spouses behind, there would have been one less problem to cope with had he married one of their women. It is, moreover, difficult to judge whether he was comparing Zabidi women with Tangerines, to the advantage or detriment of the latter in their attitude to marrying strangers.

The women of Shiraz

One other collective of women he depicted in vivid, pious terms. The people of Shiraz in southern Persia were distinguished by their piety, sound religion and uprightness (*affaf*), especially the women.

> *These latter wear short boots, and when out of doors are swathed in mantles and*
> *head-veils, so that no part of them is to be seen, and they are famed for their*
> *charitable alms and their good works. One of their strange customs is that they*
> *meet in the principle mosque every Monday, Thursday and Friday, to listen*
> *to the preacher, sometimes one or two thousand of them, carrying fans in their*
> *hands on account of the great heat. I have never seen in any land an assembly*
> *of women in such numbers.*

His tone of approval for the women's devotion to preaching seemed tempered to a degree by what, for him, was the unusual scene of women gathered in such numbers in a public space, despite its being a mosque. It is interesting to note that the Arabic term for the English rendering 'swathed in mantles' is the verbal root from which the noun *burqa* is derived, a word now familiar to Westerners who would associate *burqa*-clad women with present-day Afghanistan. It would be interesting, too, if we knew how the fourteenth-century Shiraz *burqa* resembled its modern Afghani equivalent. Textile manufacture was the single most important industry in the medieval Mediterranean world, yet so few examples of domestic costume have survived even as fragments. This is understandable, for, unlike the survival rate of ancient dwellings, textiles are inherently prone to decay as the fibres begin to deteriorate from the moment they are made. Verbal pictures, fortunately, survive in literature. Ibn Battuta's description is a good example: a woman appearing in public, even in hot weather, wearing a body garment and head dress where the total effect was to shroud her totally from public gaze.

Ibn Battuta's observations on women's groups in different regions are notable in another sense, namely, that throughout the medieval *umma* there was no uniform fashion of dress for Muslim women (and, by extension, for men as well). This might be stating the obvious except for the current heated debate in some Muslim communities and among certain Muslim groups about what constitutes an 'Islamic dress code' for women and, in some cases, the attempt to impose such a code upon them. The current debate is complex and cannot be reviewed here. Ibn Battuta saw Muslim women in different ethnic, cultural and social contexts. As he reports nothing of what was familiar to him in Moroccan female dress, what he says of other women's appearance is important. Let us look at some examples by way of illustration.

Women of Anatolia and the Golden Horde

As noted earlier, the account of the country of the Turks, *Bilad al-Rum*, or Anatolia as we have preferred to call it, opened with a brief but passionate praise of the country where '*God had brought together the good things dispersed through other lands*' and of its inhabitants as '*the kindliest of God's creatures*'. His very first impression of women was their appearance in public *unveiled*. Clearly he found that worthy of note. Later, during his stay in the camp of the Sultan of the Golden Horde, he recalled some of the Turk's customs, noting at the end his impression of their women. He said, '*I witnessed in this country a remarkable thing, namely the respect in which women are held by them, indeed they are higher in dignity than the men.*' An example was the wife (*khatun*) of a commander travelling in her richly caparisoned covered wagon with its windows and entrance open. The wives of traders and even the common people, he suggested, also travelled by horse-drawn covered wagon, less elegantly decorated, but also with open windows so that the occupant's face was visible, '*for the women of the Turks do not veil themselves*'. Some women would enter the market in this manner with goods to exchange for others. Sometimes a woman would be accompanied by her husband, '*and anyone seeing him would assume him to be one of her servants; he wears no garments other than a sheep-skin cloak with a cap to match*'. The nub of the matter was that men who appeared in public in this way demeaned themselves in the eyes of the traveller from Tangier because it made their wives' dignity seem greater than their own.

During his stay at the enormous mobile court of Muhammad Uzbek, Ibn Battuta met each of his four wives. The principle *khatun*, named Taitughli, was the sultan's favourite and although she was honoured for this fact she was said to be devoid of generosity. The most intriguing detail about her had been entrusted to him in confidence:

> *The sultan is enamoured of her because of a peculiar property in her, namely that he finds her every night just like a virgin … since the vagina of this* khatun *has a conformation like a ring. I never met anywhere anyone who said that he had seen a woman formed in this way, or heard tell of one other than this*

khatun, *except that I was told in China there is a class of women with this conformation. But nothing like that ever occurred to my experience nor have I discovered the truth of it.*

The remaining three wives of the sultan were much more agreeable. Number two was called Kabak and at the time of their visit Ibn Battuta found her reading the Quran. Number three was Bayalun who was Greek and the daughter of the Emperor of Constantinople. Conversation focused upon her guests' travels, and she wept with compassion for their similar fates, both being far from their native lands. She had a generous nature that was revealed later when Ibn Battuta travelled with her to Constantinople where she wished to visit her family and give birth to her child. The last wife Urduja most impressed the traveller. He described her as virtuous, amiable and one who '*showed us a beauty of character and generosity of spirit that cannot be surpassed*'. The sultan's daughter also showed the company great generosity and heaped favours upon them. Ibn Battuta proudly noted that the first two sultan's wives had accorded him the highest honour by personally offering him a bowl of *qumiss* to drink.

Sultanate of Delhi

By now he was accustomed to women of all classes who did not cover their heads or faces. Meeting the wives of a powerful ruler, however, was not an honour accorded him by the Sultan of Delhi. The only females Ibn Battuta saw in the great audience hall at the Delhi court were on the occasions of the two major Muslim religious festivals when musicians and dancers were presented:

> *first of all the daughters of the infidel Indian kings who have been taken as captives of war during that year and whom, after they have sung and danced, the Sultan presents to the amirs and distinguished foreigners, then after them the rest of the daughters of the infidels and these, after they have sung and danced, he gives to his brothers and kinsmen and relatives by marriage.*

Ibn Battuta offered no comment on this practice. He probably did not equate it with the practice of using slaves as prostitutes that he had condemned in Anatolia. Any twinge of conscience he may have felt was eased on subsequent days of the feast ceremonies when the sultan emancipated male slaves, then female slaves and then oversaw marriages between male and female slaves, and, finally, in a lavish flourish, distributed alms.

The Maldive Islands – again

As for the matter of dress code, it turned out that the women of the Maldives tested Ibn Battuta's patience most sorely. From another part of his account of Maldivian womenfolk cited above, he continued in a plaintive tone:

> they do not cover their heads, not even their ruler the Sultana, and they comb their hair and gather it to one side. Most of them wear only an apron from the navel to the ground, the rest of their bodies being uncovered. It is thus they walk abroad in the bazaars and elsewhere. When I was a religious judge there, I tried to put an end to this practice and ordered them to wear clothes, but I met with no success. No woman was admitted to my presence in a lawsuit unless her body was covered, but apart from that, I was unable to effect anything. Some of them wear shirts in addition to the waistcloth, their shirts having short and wide sleeves. I had some slave girls who wore garments like those worn in Delhi and who covered their heads, but it was more of a disfigurement than an ornament in their case, since they were not accustomed to it.

Ibn Battuta wrote more in sorrow than anger. He happily admitted the carnal pleasures he enjoyed during his stay on the islands. He compared the Maldivian women with those belonging to a Hindu tribe he had heard about in India, whose 'women especially are exceedingly beautiful and famous for their charms in intercourse and the amount of pleasure they give'. What distressed him was simply the immodest manner in which Maldive women dressed in public, an attitude conditioned by his religious scruples.

Otherwise, his view of Maldivians was positive on matters he also judged important, that 'The people of these islands are pious and devout, sound in belief, and sincere of intent; they keep to lawful foods, and their prayers are answered. When one of them sees another he says: "God is my Lord, Muhammad my Prophet, and I am an uneducated and miserable creature."' The phrase echoed common Muslim belief about the Prophet that the Quran must have been God-given since he was a poor and uneducated or illiterate (*ummi*) man and could not have invented the revelations as he had been accused of doing. Ibn Battuta accepted their rather limited adherence to *sharia* in following the dietary prescriptions and prayer, but stressed the important function of intention in their beliefs and practices. On the other hand, as we saw in his failed efforts to change women's dress habits, he strove to change other practices that concerned women after his appointment as religious judge to replace the incumbent whom he thought was useless. *'Lawsuits there are not like those in our land. The first bad custom I changed was the practice of divorced wives staying in the houses of their former husbands, for they all do so until they marry another husband.'* He also attempted to enforce stricter observance of prayers with punishments for slackers, apparently with some success.

Land of the Blacks (Sudan)

The final journey Ibn Battuta undertook was from Morocco southwards into the *Bilad al-Sudan*, literally, the Land of the Blacks according to the medieval Muslim geographers, or the Western Sudan. It covered the area adjoining the Sahara desert, stretching from the Atlantic Ocean to the gigantic loop of the River Niger, and today would roughly embrace the countries of Mauritania, Mali and Niger. These societies had acquired an Islamic identity through trade with Muslim North Africa, including Morocco, and by the eleventh century most Sudanese trading towns had a Muslim quarter while Muslims became important as advisors to local rulers. In Ibn Battuta's day, the kingdom of Mali was the dominant regime and Islam the cult of the ruler and court elite. Its current ruler was Sultan (or Mansa) Sulayman, brother of his illustrious predecessor Mansa Musa (1307–31) who had travelled to Cairo in 1324 and made his kingdom renowned for its fabulous wealth in gold. By the end of his estimated two-year visit (1352–54) Ibn Battuta would have just turned 50 years of age.

He had set out from Sijilmasa in the Maghrib (Morocco) and travelled by caravan for two months south to the city of Iwalatan, which he described as on the very edge of the Land of the Blacks. The caravan leader was from the Massufa, a Berber tribe akin to the Tuareg, whose men, like them, wore a veil that covered the face except for the eyes. This garment may have been intended as protection from the sand and dust of the desert, evil spirits or both. Most of the inhabitants of Iwalatan were from the Massufa and Ibn Battuta immediately took note of their women who were *'of outstanding beauty and are more highly regarded than the men'*.

Yet he found their lifestyle strange. It was, he said, a matrilineal society, the like of which he had seen only once before, among Hindus of Malabar in India. Nevertheless, the Massufa were Muslims, strict in prayer observance, studying the *sharia* and committing the Quran to memory. The women, too, were observant but, Ibn Battuta quickly added,

> *they have no shame in front of men and do not veil themselves. … Anyone who wants to take a wife among them does so, but they do not travel with their husbands, and even if one of them wished to, her family would prevent her. Women there have friends and companions among men outside the prohibited degrees of marriage, and in the same way men have women friends in the same category. A man goes into his house, finds his wife with her man friend, and does not disapprove.*

In short, he concluded in exasperation, *'the men have no jealousy'*.

This shocking state of affairs is recounted in two anecdotes. One involved the city's religious judge, who had performed the pilgrimage and was therefore entitled to be called a Hajji. The other tale was about a man who had lived in the Maghrib and therefore was assumed to understand at least the *sharia* basics. When Ibn Battuta entered the *qadi*'s home he found him with a very beautiful woman; embarrassed, he quickly made a move to withdraw. The woman laughed and the *qadi* insisted the lady was his friend. Later he learned that the *qadi* had even sought permission for the lady to accompany him on the pilgrimage. In the second episode, Ibn Battuta visited the home of an acquaintance from the caravan journey. There he found to his surprise, besides his host, a man and a woman seated together conversing on a canopied couch. The horror was that the woman was his host's wife! When asked how he could stand the situation, his host replied, 'The companionship of women and men among us is a good thing and an agreeable practice, which causes no suspicion; they are not like the women in your country.' Ibn Battuta found the response so flippant and unbearable that he left the house, never to return. He rejected all subsequent invitations.

Ibn Battuta's next stay was in Mali, capital of the Sultan of the Blacks where he rented a house. As he had done in his account of the Sultan of Delhi, he drew up a ledger of the good and bad points of the Blacks. The bad practices virtually all centred upon those females, the servants, slave girls and young girls who

appear naked before people, exposing their genitals. I used to see many like this
in Ramadan for it is customary for the military commanders to break the fast
in the Sultan's palace, where their food is brought to them by twenty or more
slave-girls, who are naked. Women who come before the Sultan are naked and
unveiled, and so are his daughters. … I have seen about a hundred naked slave-
girls come out of his palace with food; with them were two daughters of the
Sultan with full breasts and they too had no veil.

Their degree of nakedness exceeded even that of Maldivian women but, on this occasion, he apparently made no move to protest against it.

A last encounter with a nomadic Berber tribe, the Bardama, casts a ray of light, albeit faint, upon Ibn Battuta's conception of feminine beauty. Like the Massufa, the Bardama were in the business of caravan protection and Ibn Battuta noted their women were regarded in the same way, as more important than the men. They were also beautiful, and more: *'They are the most perfectly beautiful of women and have the most elegant figures; they are pure white and very fat. I have not seen in the country any who are as fat. They feed on cow's milk and pounded millet, which they drink, mixed with water, uncooked, night and morning.'* Ibn Battuta added that anyone who wished to marry among them would have to settle within the area of their migratory routes. On his way back to Morocco, he passed through cities where merchants did a brisk trade in domestic slaves; the caravan in which he travelled carried 600 female slaves. He wanted an educated female servant (*khadim*) but these were rare and expensive. In Azelik, the local *qadi* sent him one belonging to a friend of his and he purchased her for 25 *mithqals*. The original owner then wished to revoke the deal but provided Ibn Battuta with another, apparently even better-educated woman. In the event, she did not return to Morocco with Ibn Battuta. Instead, he was given a slave boy as a gift who was still with him at the time he dictated *The Travels* to Ibn Juzayy in Fez.

Women in the political arena

Three female figures, all from beyond the Arab world, are described briefly in scattered sections of *The Travels*. What bound them together was their attainment of positions of apparent power in their respective societies. Two of them, both Muslim, were actual, the third fictional, whose tale will be reserved for later. Ibn Battuta introduced his short account of the Sultana of the Maldives saying, *'It is a strange thing about these islands that their ruler is a woman, Khadija.'* Strange indeed judged from an almost uniform perspective of political rule throughout the medieval world, not least within Muslim domains. The reality, as Ibn Battuta himself indirectly indicated, was that actual power in the Maldives was firmly in the hands of the male members of the queen's inner circle, first with her successive husbands and then her son.

A second example occurs in a very short note in Ibn Battuta's account of the history of the Delhi sultanate. This concerned the Sultana Radiya who ruled the Indian sultanate for four years from 1236 to 1240. When her brother was put to death, the army conferred sovereignty on her as queen. *'She used to ride abroad just like the men, carrying bow and quiver and without veiling her face. After that she was suspected of relations with a slave of hers so people agreed to depose her and marry her to a husband. In consequence she was married to a relative and another of her brothers became king.'* So, she acted like a man on horseback, and in her relation with a slave as men did with their female slaves. Except that men rejected a woman's acting like a man in that sense, which they deemed shameful; hence she was dethroned just as she had been enthroned by men, who then married her off and restored her proper place in society. And the world was set to rights. Queens Radiya and Khadija went against Muslim norms of political rule, but for all that they were safely within the embrace of their communities, properly supervised or controlled by their male minders.

Religious and racial 'others'

Ibn Battuta, as remarked in several places, adhered to Maliki juristic thought and practice within the broad reach that was the majority Sunni Muslim community. Three other 'schools' of legal practice were the Shafii, Hanbali and Hanafi. The founder of the Maliki tradition was Malik b. Anas (d. 795), whose tomb Ibn Battuta had visited in Medina. In their religious legal judgements, agreement among the schools was much greater than their differences. At a rough estimate, there was a 75 per cent accord among scholars, while the remaining quarter of variations in opinion were based upon differences of rules and procedures in understanding or authenticating the sacred primary sources of the Quran and the traditions of the Prophet. Differing viewpoints, too, could be found within the same school. It was also important that within the juristic culture of medieval Islam, Sunni scholars recognized that no legal judgement could be deemed absolutely certain but only probable, despite the skill and knowledge of the individual jurist. Since the *sharia* expressed the will of Allah, the challenge faced by all jurists was to strive to understand what constituted His will so that Muslims could adhere to it in their daily lives. The exercise of juristic effort (*ijtihad*) was supported by a tradition from the Prophet that said a jurist would receive two rewards in the afterlife if his judgement was correct and one reward if it was wrong; in other words, there was no sin attached to the effort, whatever the result. By means of a collective scholarly enterprise over many generations an *approximate* understanding of that will was gradually achieved.

Ibn Battuta's view of Muslims

The juristic schools tended to be geographically concentrated by reason of historical influences in their development. The Malikis, for example, were firmly established in Morocco and in al-Andalus, while in Anatolia and India the Hanafi school was predominant. In certain major centres of learning, like Cairo and Damascus, jurists belonging to each of the four legal schools were trained in the religious colleges (*madrasas*). Ibn Battuta mentioned the names of the grand *qadis* of the schools at the time of his visit to Cairo, the Shafii being the highest in rank with the authority to appoint and dismiss any *qadi*. The Hanafi grand *qadi* had a reputation for severity and the Mamluk Sultan of Egypt was said to be in awe of him. In the great mosque of Damascus *imams* of each school officiated as prayer leaders in separate parts of the mosque for their own followers.

As in Cairo, *qadis* of each school were represented in Damascus as well. Not surprisingly, as it mirrored his own interests, Ibn Battuta described the Maliki judge of Damascus as one of its principal religious leaders who was also the grand *shaykh* of the Sufis. Likewise the Hanafi *imam* was also a leading Sufi and head of two monasteries (*khanqah*) in the city. Once again the Hanafi judge was deemed the most severe in court. He was one to whom '*wives and their husbands took their cases, and a man had only to hear his name and he would act justly by his wife of his own accord before coming before him*'. Ibn Battuta was not assessing strictness negatively but rather as an efficient means of protecting believers' interests while defending God's law. For example, in Herat (modern Afghanistan) the large population all followed the Hanafi rite and, although strict application of the law is not mentioned, the Maliki traveller's opinion was that '*its inhabitants were people of rectitude, abstention from unlawful pleasures, sincerity of religion and their city is kept pure of all vice*'. On the other hand, Turkish Muslims of Anatolia who were also Hanafi and firmly attached to the Prophet's Sunna possessed '*a virtue by which God Most High has distinguished them*', while at the same time, '*they consume* hashish *and think nothing wrong in that*'. He observed that in the city of Sanub some senior army officers seated on a bench outside the mosque were eating *hashish*, yet nowhere in Anatolia was disapproval of the practice heard. We have already seen how Ibn Battuta dealt with the Hanafi attitude towards alcohol among the Turks of the Golden Horde, explaining to his readers that it was acceptable according to their legal practice. From a practical viewpoint, Turkish Hanafi domination of Anatolia had the inestimable value of ensuring the region remained free from all heretical influence of religious innovators (sing. *mubtadai*). One of the pillars of the Meccan community was the virtuous and generous Hanafi *imam* and jurist who supplied food to sojourners and needy travellers. He ran up huge deficits every year '*to the amount of forty or fifty thousand dirhams, but God discharges them for him*'. From these few examples of Ibn Battuta's depiction of Hanafis, it can be inferred that his ability to appraise individuals in their specific contexts allowed him to reach a nuanced judgement of the whole school.

As for Malikis, his interest was certainly to inform his audience of the jurists' graves he had visited and those Malikis he had met, stayed with or heard about on his journeys. Yet this did not prevent him reporting from Aleppo that the chief *qadi* of the Hanafis, Nasr al-Din Ibn al-Adim, was '*a man of fine figure and character*', while the chief Maliki *qadi* he refused even to name because he had once obtained a post as notary in Cairo he did not deserve for want of qualifications. He criticized another Maliki scholar, a native of Fez then living in Mecca, who by virtue of his ignorance of the annals of early Islam unwittingly uttered an offensive remark in public concerning the ancestry of the current Meccan ruler. Ibn Battuta labelled the blunder '*a grievous sin*' in the circumstances. The Meccan ruler banished him from the city and he was never seen again. '*God preserve us from stumbling and slipping of the tongue*,' he shuddered, recalling the event.

When Ibn Battuta was appointed *qadi* in Delhi, he exclaimed to Muhammad b. Tughluq, '*O Master, I belong to the school of Malik and these people are Hanafis and I do not speak the language.*' He later learned to speak Persian but meanwhile the sultan assigned to him two assistants who would be guided by his advice, although Ibn Battuta was responsible for signing the relevant legal documents. He tells us virtually nothing of his activities as a jurist during his sojourn in Delhi, in contrast to measures he took related to women when he was *qadi* in the Maldive Islands.

Elsewhere we see him acting independently as a critic of a person's behaviour in the spirit of the Quran's injunction of, 'enjoining what is reputable and forbidding what is disreputable' (Q 3:104). This meant that when one witnessed a wrong, there was an obligation to see it rectified. The Quran was supported by the Prophet's tradition that said that whoever saw a wrong and could correct it with the hand should do so, otherwise with the tongue or, failing that, minimally, with the heart. The legal understandings drawn from these prescriptions were complicated but could be illustrated by an incident that Ibn Battuta witnessed in Egypt during his first journey up the Nile. He was staying in the large town of Munyat al-Khasib when, one day, he entered the public bath house and found the male clients inside to be totally naked. His reaction was that '*This appeared a shocking thing to me, and I went to the governor and informed him of it. He ordered the lessees of all the bathhouses brought before him and agreements were drawn up on the spot making them subject to penalties if any person should enter a bath without a waist-wrapper.*' The wrong in this case was the men's immodesty in exposing themselves to each other in the bath house. Since the town *qadi* was a Maliki, as possibly the governor was as well, the authorities' swift reaction to Ibn Battuta's complaint may have been facilitated. This was acting with 'the hand'. Yet, as we have seen, Ibn Battuta was helpless to correct Maldivian women's custom of dressing semi-naked, even while he was *qadi*, except in the limited cases of their appearance before him in court. In the Sudan, he could make his indignation known only by 'the tongue' when he saw men and women mixing socially in a person's house; and, least vigorous of all, he seems to have kept protest confined to his heart when he saw slave girls and the sultan's daughters going about completely naked. On the other hand, one recalls that Ibn Battuta described the Muslims of the Maldives and the Sudan as people sincere in pursuit of their faith, however limited their attainments.

The Rafidis

On other occasions, he criticized individuals in the same spirit of righting a perceived wrong. In one instance his reaction may have been more complex. He was visiting the coastal town of Tyre in Syria, which he found in ruins at the time. Outside Tyre was a village which, he noted, was inhabited mainly by Rafidis. He picks up the story:

> *I stopped there at a place with some water to make the ritual ablutions before prayer, and one of the men of this village also came to make his ablutions. He began by washing his feet, then he washed his face, without rinsing out his mouth or snuffing water up his nostrils and ended by wiping his hand over a part of his head. I reproved him for doing this, but he said to me, 'In building, the place to begin is at the foundation.'*

His Sunni audience would have reacted in the same scandalized manner. The Shia Muslim preparation for prayer was to perform the ritual ablution beginning with the feet, that is, the 'foundation' of the body. Sunni Muslims commenced the ablution in what they held to be the ritually correct sequence of face, hands and then the feet. Ritual differences as seemingly simple as these were never innocent from an opponent's viewpoint, whichever side he was on. Correct ritual was emblematic of belonging to a community with a warrant of divine approval; get it wrong and approval was believed removed. Once, the tables were turned and Ibn Battuta found himself suspected of being a Rafidi by a group of Hanafis in Anatolia. A perceptible ritual difference was again the cause. The Hanafis prayed in the standing position with their arms bent upward from the elbow but were ignorant of the fact that Maliki practice was to let the arms hang down. When the Hanafis had spotted Ibn Battuta perform his prayers incorrectly (or differently) in the mosque they concluded he could be a heretic, or Rafidi. So, who were the Rafidis?

Sunni Muslim scholars did not use the term with any great precision. The famous Sunni theologian al-Ashari (d. 935), in a work on Muslim sects and the 'orthodox' Sunni community, explained the Rafidi as one of three main groups of the Shia or as yet another Shia group called the Imamiya. The term may best be described as a general label of abuse that Sunnis used for people they considered to be Shia, without applying it exclusively to any particular subdivision. In straightforward terms, Shia

stood for Shiat Ali or 'party of Ali'. They were Muslims who accepted
Muhammad as the Prophet of Allah and who believed his immediate
legitimate successor should have been his cousin and son-in-law Ali b.
Abi Talib, regarded as the first Shia Imam, who had married the Prophet's daughter Fatima, from whose issue the subsequent line of male Imams
were descended. The Shia therefore declared as illegitimate usurpers the
first three actual successors to Muhammad as leaders of the Muslim
community. These had been the Prophet's Companions and later the first
three caliphs, Abu Bakr, Umar and Uthman. It was all a matter of with
whom, and by what means, the post-Prophetic leadership of Muslims had
become vested.

From a collection of Ibn Battuta's references to non-Sunni Muslims,
it is obvious he had only the vaguest understanding of how the later sub-
groups of Shia emerged or why and what distinguished one group from
another. André Miquel correctly considered that Ibn Battuta's perception of the Shia was based upon his deep dislike of what he regarded as
their extreme behaviour and beliefs, stemming from a grossly exaggerated adoration of the Prophet's family that centred upon Ali, his wife
Fatima and their children.[8] One Sunni–Shia difference in ritual prayer
has already been mentioned. Another was noted when Ibn Battuta travelled to the beautiful city of date palms, al-Qutayf, on the Arabian mainland near the island of Bahrain. The inhabitants comprised different
Arab clans who were '*extremist Rafidis* (rafidiyya ghulat) *who display their
heresy openly without fear of anyone*'. The heresy related to the call to prayer
made publicly by the *muadhdhin* five times a day. The Sunni prayer call
consisted of seven short phrases. Ibn Battuta explained that the Rafidis
inserted an extra formula after the universal words of 'testifying', which
were 'I testify that there is no god but Allah' and 'I testify that Muhammad is the Messenger of Allah'. The Rafidi addition was 'I testify that
Ali is the Friend of Allah'. Two other phrases were added, the last placed
after the universal exclamation of 'God is Great' (*Allahu akbar*) which
was the most openly challenging: 'Muhammad and Ali are the best of
mankind; whoever opposes them becomes an infidel.' Sunnis held Ali in
deep reverence as the greatest of the Prophet's Companions, but he was
not Muhammad's equal as a prophet. The Shia regarded Ali as possessing
the same divine spark with which God had graced Muhammad.

References to other dissident Shia groups are made by Ibn Battuta.

In northern Syria he visited some of the strongly fortified castles that dotted the region. Other castles he could not visit because they belonged to the dangerous sect of Ismailis also known as the *fidawiyya*. Their contemporary role was, literally, 'intriguing', since they were employed by none other than the Sunni Mamluk Sultan of Egypt and Syria, al-Malik al-Nasir, one of Ibn Battuta's seven great world leaders. Figuratively he called them the 'Sultan's Arrows', for *'when he desires to send one of them to assassinate some foe of his, he pays him his blood money. If he escapes after carrying out the deed, the money is his, but if he is caught it goes to his children. They have poisoned knives with which they strike their victims but sometimes they fail and are themselves killed.'* The infamous reputation of these assassins spread to medieval Europe where people believed the killers were sent on their deadly missions under the euphoric spell of hashish, the Arabic word from which the English term 'assassin' is derived. Ibn Battuta may have privately condemned the activities of these heretics but did not say so. Rather he entertained his readers with a tale of al-Malik al-Nasir's long-standing pursuit, employing assassins, of the man known to have been implicated in the murder of his brother.

Another dissident sect of the Shia were called Nusayris, whom he encountered in the area along the coastal area of northern Syria. Ibn Battuta detailed their heretical views and practice:

> *they hold the belief that Ali b. Abi Talib is a god. They do not perform the ritual prayers, nor are they circumcised, nor do they fast. When they were commanded to build a mosque in each village, they placed it far from their houses without using it or maintaining its condition. It often serves as a refuge for their cattle and asses. Frequently, too, a stranger comes to a village of theirs, stops at the mosque and recites the call to prayer out loud. They yell at him, 'Stop braying, your fodder is coming to you!'*

They clearly had no redeeming features whatsoever.

The Carmathians (*Qaramita*) were another group with a political agenda. They originated as a rebel federation of Arabs organized in lower Iraq after the revolt of East African Zanj slaves in 877. The Carmathian movement began to lay waste southern Iraq, they severed the pilgrim routes to Mecca and in 930 they seized the Holy City and made off with the Black Stone from the Kaaba within the sacred sanctuary, only restoring it some 20 years later. Ibn Battuta made passing reference to the episode, noting that the stone had been repaired, for when he saw it, four pieces had been stuck together, the usual story being that *'the Qarmati – God curse them – broke it, but it has also been said that someone else smashed it'*. He rightly cursed them for the theft, but in a spirit of fairness suggested they may not have been responsible for its damage.

Another Rafidi group, so-called by Ibn Battuta, may actually have more precisely been a splinter faction of Nusayris who publicly insulted the memory of the Prophet's Companions, especially the Ten Companions among whom were the first four caliphs, including Ali, who, of course, was exempted from Rafidi insult. Among a similar group, members who sold their goods by auction in the market refused to cry out the number 'ten', but only 'nine and one'. To Ibn Battuta, this was indeed an extraordinary thing! He identified as Rafidis, too, those who attacked caravans, those active in Khurasan who captured some of its major cities, and those who created civil discord in the Iraqi city of al-Hilla by constant feuding amongst themselves. The city of Mashad Rida in Khurasan was named after a descendant of Ali, the eighth Shia Imam, Ali al-Rida, and was where his tomb was also located. The sanctuary was surmounted by a great dome inside a hospice with an adjoining mosque and *madrasa*. The chamber was heavily carpeted, and facing al-Rida's tomb was the tomb of the famous Abbasid caliph and Commander of the Faithful (*'God be pleased with him'*, says Ibn Battuta), Harun al-Rashid (d. 809). The point of this anecdote is that *'When a Rafidi enters to visit the tomb of al-Rida, he kicks the tomb of al-Rashid with his foot and pronounces a blessing on al-Rida.'* In whatever way he understood the Rafidis, it is worth noting that he never labelled them as 'infidels' (*kuffar*, sing. *kafir*) and equated them with Hindus and the pagans of Africa.

Ibn Battuta's 'profound distaste' for the 'loathsome practices' of the Shia has sometimes been exemplified (here, in the words of Roxanne Euben) by his refusal to enter the pretty town of palm-groves in southern Iraq called Bir Mallaha because its inhabitants were Rafidis.[9] Instead, he and his party camped outside the town. Yet, the very next city on his itinerary was al-Hilla, whose inhabitants he described as Imamis of the Twelver sect, that is, a Shia group who believed in a line of 12 Imams or religious leaders descended from Ali. Ibn Battuta described the Imamis of al-Hilla as divided into two factions in constant conflict with one another. From al-Hilla he proceeded to the town of Karbala, the site of a battle in 680 in which al-Husayn, son of the Imam Ali, was murdered (or martyred, depending on your viewpoint) and then beheaded by the dissolute caliph al-Yazid. Ibn Battuta described his sanctuary and gave his blessing of peace (*al-salam alayhumma*) upon *both* son and father. As for the inhabitants of Karbala, they were also Imamis engaged in factional strife that had brought the town to ruin.

Evidently distressed by extreme Rafdi/Imami behaviour, and their ritual errors, Ibn Battuta nonetheless recognized that behind these excesses there were qualities of piety and hospitality he admired, as he discovered when visiting the domed shrine and tomb of Ali in Najaf, discussed in the previous chapter. In Palestine, near Hebron, he had ventured into the cave where he saw the tomb of al-Husayn's daughter, named Fatima after her grandmother, and upon them both he conferred his blessing of peace. In Ascalon on the Palestinian coast he visited the sanctuary where the relic of al-Husayn's head had been kept before being moved to a shrine in Cairo that he had also visited. While in Medina, he had noted among the city's sanctuaries those of Ali's brother and nephew and that of al-Hasan, the elder brother of al-Husayn. In the great mosque of Damascus, prayers were said in a sequence beginning with the senior prayer leader of the Shafii, followed by the prayer leaders of the sanctuaries of Ali and then of al-Husayn, completed by the remaining Sunni prayer leaders. These examples illustrate how Ibn Battuta felt able, on occasion, to enter common territory with the Shia.

A final Shia sub-sect to consider were the Zaydis, named after the grandson of al-Husayn and established early in the ninth century throughout the highlands of the Yemen, who had strong relations with the religious leadership in Mecca and Medina. During his first pilgrimage, Ibn Battuta was accompanied from Damascus by, among others, the *qadi* of the Zaydis, Sharaf al-Din Qasim b. Sinan. No more is said of him than this, but there is no hint of animosity towards his travel companion. His description of Ramadan in Mecca involved great preparations in the sacred mosque, renewing the floor mats and increasing the candles and torches until *'the Sanctuary gleams with light and glows, radiant and resplendent'*. Each night, the prayer leaders of the different rites gathered together their own followers to recite the Quran. Apart from representation of the four Sunni rites, he mentioned the Zaydis as well, although he noted, the Shafii *imams* were the most zealous in their devotional exercises. *'There is not a corner or spot left in the sanctuary but it is occupied by a Quran reciter leading a group in prayer, so that the mosque is filled with a babble of reader's voices, and all spirits are softened, all hearts wrung, and all eyes bathed in tears.'* There was, at least, one Shia sect that Ibn Battuta regarded, in this sacred place and occasion, fully a part of the Muslim *umma*.

Of equal or perhaps greater interest is the tale of a miraculous grace performed by the Yemeni Ahmad b. al-Ujayl, an *'ascetic and humble devotee ... who was one of the greatest men of those favoured with miraculous powers'*. This story involved the great theological debate that had raged in the early days of Islam over whether man possessed free will to do what he wished or was predetermined in all his actions by God. Ahmad b. al-Ujayl, evidently of Sunni orientation, awaited the visit of a group of Zaydis outside his hospice in the Yemeni city of Zabid where Ibn Battuta had noted the great beauty of its women. Greetings were exchanged, discussion arose and with it the question of predestination which the Zaydi visitors did not believe in; they supported human free will because, they argued, *'everyone was responsible for carrying out the ordinances of God and therefore creates his own actions'*. Human responsibility for one's actions was the key to their theological position. Ahmad b. al-Ujayl replied:

> *Well, if the matter is as you say, rise up from this place where you are. They tried to rise up and could not, and the* shaykh *left them as they were and went into the hospice. They remained thus until, when the heat afflicted them sorely and the blaze of the sun smote them, then they complained loudly of what had befallen them. The* shaykh's *associates went to him and said, 'These men have repented to God and recanted their false doctrine.'*

Ahmad went to them and took their pledge to return to and maintain the truth. They remained his guest for three days and returned to their respective homes. Ibn Battuta does not enter into the details of this thorny theological question. His views were probably not passively fatalistic but more in line with the notion that the individual acquired responsibility for actions that God created for him. Such a position would account for actions where conflicting desires had afflicted him during his travels.

Return to the Land of the Blacks (Sudan)

Ibn Battuta's first impression of Iwalatan was not a happy one. It was, he said, the first place in the Land of the Blacks and, according to him, was a mixed city of Muslim Massufa Berber merchants and Africans. The Sultan of Mali had sent as his deputy a slave called Husayn to supervise the merchandise brought to Iwalatan by the recent caravan. As Ibn Battuta understood the situation, Husayn spoke to the Massufa merchants through an interpreter, *'as a sign of his contempt for them. ... At this I was sorry I had come to their country, because of their bad manners and contempt for white people.'* Although unaware of it, what he had observed was the local practice of using an interlocutor between two parties at court or in business arrangements like these, and no contempt was implied. The Sultan of Mali, Mansa Sulayman, used the *qadi* and preacher as interlocutors when he later met the traveller for the first time. A second incident occurred shortly thereafter. Ibn Battuta had ventured near a riverbank to relieve himself when *'one of the Blacks came and stood in the space between me and the river; I was amazed at his appalling manners and lack of decency. I mentioned it to someone who said: "He did that only to protect you from a crocodile nearby by putting himself between you and it."'* After a lifetime of wandering through different countries among different peoples, Muslim and otherwise, Ibn Battuta found himself still on a cultural learning curve; and, experienced as he was, he learned quickly.

When Ibn Battuta arrived at the Sultan of Mali's capital, he proceeded straight to the 'quarter of the white people (*al-bidan*)' inhabited by North African merchants and religious personnel. Several people came to welcome him, first the *qadi*, Abd al-Rahman: *'He is Black, a pilgrim* (hajj), *an excellent man with noble qualities; he sent me a cow as a welcoming gift. I met the interpreter, Dugha, one of the most distinguished and important of the Blacks; he sent me a bull.'* And a friend, Ibn al-Faqih, who had rented a house for him opposite his own in the white quarter, was married to the daughter of the sultan's paternal uncle, producing a family of mixed race. Ibn Battuta's language of colour was being transformed; 'black' becomes a term for 'native', one who naturally belonged to the Land of the Blacks. It had an extended positive sense to mean a 'black' Muslim, and a negative sense when 'black' referred to a pagan African. 'White' seemed to refer to North African Muslims in general and to a Moroccan Muslim in particular. One of the positive qualities of Blacks Ibn Battuta listed was that *'they do not interfere with the property of white men who die in their country, even if it amounts to vast sums; they just leave it in the hands of a trustworthy white man until whoever is entitled to it takes possession of it'*. In similar language for precisely the same circumstances, he had described the attitude of 'the people of India', a term that implied 'infidel', but used also in a positive sense. Ibn Battuta's reactions are certainly not those informed by our modern sensitivities to race relations, but neither do they reflect the crudities of race hatred expressed in our own modern Western societies. As ever perceptive, Roxanne Euben has described Ibn Battuta's reactions to the Land of the Blacks as two-sided, 'reflecting a complex dialectic of racial, ethnic, and linguistic difference and religious and moral commonality ... [and] rather than serving as a consistent marker of political and cultural borders, race recedes in the *Rihla* [*The Travels*] amidst the commonality of religious practice'.[10]

Moreover, skin colour became a 'difference without distinction', as Euben further remarked. The most famous of Mali rulers, Mansa Musa, was *'generous and virtuous. He loved the white people and did favours for them ... but the Blacks disliked Mansa Sulayman because of his avarice'*, a view Ibn Battuta at first heartily concurred with. He recounted an anecdote of Mansa Musa's generosity in order to compare it with Mansa Sulayman's stinginess. He was *'a miserly king and a large welcome gift is not to be expected from him'*, said Ibn Battuta, imagining that, at best, the gift might only be robes of honour and some money. The gift belatedly was delivered to him and consisted of *'three rounds of bread, a piece of fried beef, and a container of curdled milk. When I saw it I laughed and was greatly surprised at their exaggerated opinion of something contemptible.'* It transpired that the nature of the gift had stemmed from another misunderstanding, this time on the sultan's part. The matter was smoothed over during Ramadan, as the sultan customarily distributed money to his courtiers and Ibn Battuta received a share. When he finally departed to return to Morocco, the sultan gave him a gift of 100 *mithqals* of gold.

Ibn Battuta met many individual black Muslims who drew his praise. In his catalogue of their good qualities as a people (to balance the women's characteristics he disapproved of) many focused upon the earnestness of their religious faith and practice. *'If a man does not come early to the mosque he will not find a place to pray because of the dense crowd.'* Thus men would send their servants beforehand to spread the prayer mat out to reserve a place. '*They dress in clean white clothes on Fridays; if one of them has only a threadbare shirt he washes it and cleans it and wears it for prayers on Friday. They pay great attention to memorizing the Quran.*' Ibn Battuta was struck with amazement to see children who were backward in learning the Quran placed in shackles until they learned it. Other qualities touched upon society as a whole: the sultan's policy of avoiding injustice and '*the universal security in their country, for neither the traveller nor the resident there has to fear thieves or bandits*'. The sultan's domains in this respect merited plaudits just as the Rafidis and Imamis were denounced for causing civil disorder in the cities and areas where Ibn Battuta had witnessed conflict or experienced the threat of plunder.

Race, or better, 'colour', and religion finally became hopelessly intermeshed in an anecdote Ibn Battuta related about the great Sultan Mansa Musa and his white religious judge. The *qadi*, probably a Moroccan and a Maliki, claimed he had been robbed of 4,000 *mithqals* the sultan gave him for expenses. Intensive investigations were ordered and the money at last was recovered when it was learned that the *qadi* himself had buried it in his garden. The sultan banished the culprit '*to the land of the infidels who eat the sons of Adam*', cannibals, that is, in modern parlance. After several years in exile the sultan allowed him to return to Morocco. Ibn Battuta explained the *qadi*'s remarkable survival, doubtless drawing upon his knowledge of folk gastronomy: '*The infidels had not eaten him because he was white, for they say that eating a white man is harmful because he is unripe. They claim that a Black is ripe.*' No further comment was added; the stolen goods were recovered, punishment was meted out and the culprit spared a fate that Ibn Battuta would not have wished upon anyone.

'People of the Book'

The expression 'People of the Book' is Quranic (Q 5:68) and designates both Jews and Christians, collectively or separately, as believers in a revealed book sent down by God to His chosen Prophet. The books and their recipients mentioned in the Quran are the Torah revealed to Moses, the Gospels to Jesus and the Psalms to David. From the Muslim perspective, the People of the Book later betrayed the favour God had shown them by concealing, changing or substituting words or passages of their original revelation. Were they to refer to scripture in its original form they would find each confirmed the message of the Prophet Muhammad. The Quran states this notion clearly: 'He has sent down to you the Scripture [Quran] in truth, confirming what came before it. And He sent down the Torah and the Gospel, previously, as guidance for the people' (Q 3:3–4). Christians and Jews, from their separate viewpoints, each totally rejected the notion that their own sacred books were anything less than repositories of the final divine truth; therefore it followed that Muhammad was dismissed by them as a false prophet and the Quran as his own composition. Significant communities of Jews and Christians continued to live under Muslim rule from the eighth-century conquests onwards. They were known in Islamic law as 'people of the covenant' (*ahl al-dhimma*), which ensured protection of their particular communal institutions through the control of their own religious leaders in return for a poll tax called *jizya* levied on the heads of Jewish and Christian households and paid to Muslim authorities. It was not a perfect system but it survived for centuries as an early, albeit crude, experiment in the history of inter-faith community relations; it did prove superior to European Christian relations with their Jewish populations throughout the pre-modern period.

The subsequent history of Muslim relations with the People of the Book cannot concern us here. A few references by Ibn Battuta suggest that he was aware of contemporary confrontation along mutually contested frontiers between Muslims and Christians of Western Europe and of Byzantium in the Eastern Mediterranean. First, on the eastern boundary of Byzantium, his introduction to the Sultan of the Golden Horde, Muhammad Uzbek, described him as '*mighty in sovereignty, exceedingly powerful ... victor over the enemies of God, the people of Constantinople the Great, and diligent in Holy War* (jihad) *against them*'. More immediately active was the prince and commander of Yazmir (Smyrna, modern Izmir) on the western Anatolian coast who '*was continually engaged in* jihad *against the Christians. He had war-galleys with which he used to make raids on the environs of Constantinople the Great and to seize prisoners and booty*'. Eventually the pope had to appeal to the Christians of Genoa and France to attack the prince. Ibn Battuta was probably not aware of a conflict situation before his arrival in the region. More than a century would pass before the Byzantine capital was successfully conquered (1453) by Muslim Ottoman forces. He had fortuitously met the son of the eponymous founder of the

Ottoman dynasty who had captured the city of Bursa from the Greeks. The son, Urkhan Bak, '*also fights the infidels continually and keeps them under siege*'. Constantinople was not on Ibn Battuta's doorstep as was the kingdom of Granada across the strait of Gibraltar in al-Andalus where Muslims were conducting a long and eventually losing struggle against the Christian re-conquest of the entire Iberian peninsula. On his return to Morocco from the east, Ibn Battuta stayed a while in his native Tangier before moving to nearby Ceuta where he was obliged to recuperate from a lengthy illness. '*Then,*' he said, '*God cured me and I wanted to take part in the Holy War and the frontier fighting.*' The wish was unfulfilled. Instead he took comfort in the knowledge that the Marinid sultans of Morocco had long been engaged against the Christian forces, a point underscored in the opening passage of *The Travels*.

Muslims and Christians were divided on more than differences over the nature of their respective scriptures; theology, religious law and rituals were other areas that separated the two traditions. On an individual level, however, attitudes between members of either faith were more complex and seldom irredeemably hostile. Ibn Battuta noted that Anatolia had been conquered from the Christian Greeks who were now '*under the protection of Muslims*', which involved the payment of special *jizya* tax. He regarded that as the proper function of the new order. Taxpaying Christians in places also suffered various humiliations, at, for example, the Church of the Holy Sepulchre in Jerusalem. Ibn Battuta also expressed his irritation at hearing the noise of church clappers in al-Kafa, the Christian city of Genoese merchants on the northern Black Sea coast. On the other hand he recorded a number of places in Syria and Palestine where Christian churches or monasteries provided hospitality to all comers, conduct that touched his particular interests and religious values. He noted with pleasure occasions of meeting a convert from Christianity who had become a pious and sincere Muslim. At the same time when a Muslim devotee offered to take him to visit a local Christian monk known for his arduous ascetic exercises, he refused, '*although afterward I regretted not having met him when I found out the truth of what people said about him*'.

Ibn Battuta's journey to Constantinople in the company of Sultan Uzbek's Greek wife, Bayalun, was also a bitter-sweet experience. As the party crossed over from the territories of her Turkish husband into those of her Byzantine father, Ibn Battuta expressed sorrow at the pronounced transformation he observed. Bayalun proceeded to Constantinople with her own people and '*left her mosque behind so that the call to prayer was discontinued. Wines were brought to her and she would drink them and one of her personal attendants told me that she also ate pork.*' Despite the change, he remarked on her unwavering generosity and kindness towards him. The account of his days in Constantinople was positive, although he recalled he could only describe the exterior of the great church, Aya Sophia, as he had never seen its interior. The reason was that upon entering he would have been obliged to prostrate himself before the Cross, an act he refused to perform. A monk he met who discovered he had visited the sacred sites in the Holy Land, touched Ibn Battuta's foot with his hand and passed it over his face. Ibn Battuta said, '*I was amazed at their belief in the merits of one who, though not of their religion, had entered these places.*'

Understandably Ibn Battuta's encounters with Christians were relatively few, and with Jews fewer still. Most notable was his outspoken anger against an elderly Jew who had entered the presence of the Sultan of Birgi in Anatolia. He seated himself before the sultan but on a level above the Quran readers. Ibn Battuta berated the man for this insulting behaviour that caused him to withdraw in distress. His anger, he conceded, may have been stirred by a deeper animosity which he left unexplained. On other occasions Ibn Battuta's meetings with Jews were casual yet cordial. A Syrian Jew who spoke Arabic assisted him in Constantinople as an interpreter and advisor. He met another Jew from al-Andalus in the market place of al-Machar in the Crimea. He told Ibn Battuta that he had journeyed four months overland across southern Europe from the Iberian peninsula to Constantinople, and then crossed Anatolia to al-Machar. Ibn Battuta was amazed at this feat but was assured by experienced merchants that the journey time was quite feasible.

All of these tales are of 'others', mainly Muslim but some not, who lived within the domain of Islam, that intricate Arabesque that symbolized the eternal watchful relationship between God and the *umma*. From Ibn Battuta's perspective, these were 'others' in a relative sense because they all belonged within by virtue of their faith as Muslims or as People of the Book living under Muslim protection (*dhimma*). The situation in India was indeterminate and fluid, as some if by no means all Hindus were under Muslim political rule. The Western fringe of the *umma* was his own native turf of Morocco, and if there was an Eastern edge it would be

Sumatra in South East Asia. This territory was ruled by Sultan al-Malik al-Zahir, who Ibn Battuta could say was *'one of the noblest and most generous of kings … a lover of jurists … who often fights against the infidels. He is unassuming and walks to the Friday prayer on foot. The people of his country are Shafiis, eager to fight infidels and readily go on campaign with him. They dominate the neighbouring infidels who pay* jizya *to have peace.'*

Beyond the *umma*'s Eastern perimeter, there were 'others' in an absolute sense. The very next sultan Ibn Battuta visited was the Sultan of Java, an infidel who summoned him when he heard his ship had landed. Ibn Battuta saluted the ruler boldly, perhaps with a tinge of impudence: *'Greetings* (salam) *to whoever follows the true guidance!'*, and noted, possibly with relief, that only the word *salam* had been understood. Nevertheless he was given hospitality for three days and then instructed to leave. His next voyage was to the China coast.

Epilogue

The China narrative occupies a mere 22 pages out of close to 1,000 pages of the entire four-volume *Travels* in the Gibb-Beckingham translation. It takes up as much space as Ibn Battuta's account of his entire return journey from China to Morocco. The authenticity of his China adventures has been questioned, although a final scholarly consensus has yet to be reached. Nonetheless Ibn Battuta seems to have wanted to set the short China narrative symbolically apart from the rest of his travels. He sought to flag it up as a region beyond and apart from the *umma* and yet its sultan, an infidel, still found a place on the Tangerine's list of the world's seven great sovereigns. The symbolic separation of the China story is marked by being framed by two tales of the exotic and the monstrous, each related immediately before and after his China visit which involved navigating a mysterious sea leading to and from the China coast.

The first tale concerns Urduja, princess of Tawalisi. Ibn Battuta claimed to have picked up the story during his voyage on the eastern seas aboard a Chinese junk. They had to overcome the dangerous crossing of the so-called Tranquil Sea before arriving at a port called Kailukari in the country of Tawalisi, whose king bore the same name. As noted in Chapter I, the country has never been satisfactorily identified, albeit not for want of scholarly effort. In fact, the matter of its existence was irrelevant to Ibn

Battuta's purpose. The tale is a concoction of motifs drawn from tales of 'warrior women' that belonged to a vast corpus of folktales and popular epics that circulated throughout the Muslim world in Arabic, Persian and Turkish, incorporating scores of stories not only similar to those in *The Thousand and One Nights* but often overlapping with them in content.

This episode in brief depicts the inhabitants of Tawalisi as idol worshippers, although brave and intrepid, whose women rode horses and understood archery and fought like men. The port city, where the junk had anchored, was governed by Princess Urduja, the ruler's daughter. Conforming to custom, she invited captain, crew and passengers to a banquet. Ibn Battuta initially refused as a matter of conscience because, he said, *'they are infidels and it is not lawful to eat their food'*. He subsequently relented and entered his hostess's presence. Female employees were in attendance and her ministers were also women, whom, he judged, were well past child-bearing age. Urduja's army contained serving women and slaves who fought like men, and her own military prowess had resulted in a single-handed victory against a rival king whose head she brought home on a spear. Many were said to have sought her hand in marriage, only to back away when she responded, 'I shall marry only a man who fights against me and defeats me.' All of these details relating to Urduja were customized by Ibn Battuta to create his status as participant observer and lend the story an aura of verisimilitude. When, during conversation, Urduja learned he had been in India she is made to remark, 'I must invade India and take possession of it. Its wealth and its soldiers please me' and Ibn Battuta cordially agreed she should do so. Urduja's characteristics conformed to the picture of the 'warrior woman' of popular folklore who not only bore arms but also wielded authority and who refused to marry any man who could not vanquish her in battle.[11] With the exception of her royal father, the country appeared to be the complete inversion of or represent a challenge to traditional patriarchal social order. The point of the tale was as a warning of the equally unnatural state of affairs that lay beyond in China and the dangers that it posed for the unwary Muslim traveller.

The second brief tale occurred during the return from China when their junk became lost in an 'unknown sea' when they again had expected to be approaching Tawalisi. Suddenly a strange mountain was seen to rise out of the sea in the distance. *'If the wind drives us on to it, we shall perish'*, everyone feared as they prepared to meet their end in prayers of repentance and supplication. They then observed in terror as the mountain rose out of the sea and into the air! Ibn Battuta asked what it was and they said, 'What we took for a mountain is the rukh and if it sees us we shall surely die.' Mercifully, Ibn Battuta says, God sent them His blessing in the form of a favourable wind that steered them away from danger and, by now somewhat bemused, he concluded, *'We did not see it or know its true shape.'* As with the 'warrior woman' tale he did not have to explain to his audience what a Rukh was, as it formed part of popular Arab lore of the weirdly unnatural and dangerous.

Sindbad the Sailor had seen a Rukh at close hand on the second of his famous voyages told in *The Thousand and One Nights.* His ship had left him behind on a strange island and after wandering about it aimlessly he came across a huge, white, shiny dome. He found no entrance to it, nor was he able to scale its slippery sides, so he walked around it and measured its circumference at 50 good paces. Then suddenly darkness fell and, looking upwards, he discovered the cause was none other than 'an enormous bird, of gigantic girth and inordinately wide of wing which, as it flew though the air, veiled the sun and hid it from the island'. Sindbad then remembered tales told by travellers and pilgrims of an island where there dwelled a huge bird called the Rukh which fed its young on elephants. He then realized the large, white, shiny dome was none other than the Rukh's egg![12] Marco Polo knew the Rukh inhabited the islands south of Madagascar. He said it was the same creature that Europeans in error called a gryphon, half-bird, half-lion, except, he assured his readers, that it was actually a colossal eagle as Muslim witnesses had informed him.[13] This second tale of a monster of nature paralleled that of the unnatural social order of the 'warrior woman', both as warning beacons to any who dared venture beyond their reach.

To return to the China narrative, Ibn Battuta depicted it as a land inhabited by infidels under infidel rule. Yet for all that, China was far from uncivilized. Small Muslim merchant communities occupied special quarters of some Chinese cities and warmly welcomed brethren *'from the land of Islam'.* He witnessed positive aspects of China that he commended. One lasting impression of his stay was the high quality of many food products, although he mentioned no meal in which he partook. *'All the fruits we have in our country are there as good or better. Corn is very plentiful*

and I have seen none better. It is the same with lentils and chickpeas.' Perhaps
the specific attraction that China held for him was that the last predicted
act of grace involving him would be fulfilled there, as indeed it was as
we saw in the previous chapter. On the other hand, if ambivalence was
felt towards any region of his travels it was towards China. Not only did
an infidel sultan rule, but Ibn Battuta feared that Muslims would not
always be free to conduct their lives with the proper devotion. Better the
porous boundaries between Muslim and Hindu in India so long as the
state was governed by a Muslim. His ambivalence is best expressed in his
own words:

> *for all its magnificence, it did not please me. I was deeply depressed by the
> prevalence of infidelity and when I left my lodging I saw many offensive things
> which distressed me so much that I stayed at home and went out only when it
> was necessary. When I saw Muslims it was as though I had met my family and
> relatives.*

In this context Ibn Battuta described a chance meeting with a Muslim
jurist, when both men embraced and wept upon discovering they were
from neighbouring towns in Morocco. He had not expressed such
emotion before with any fellow countryman he met within the *umma* as
he understood it. He had journeyed to many of its edges if not along its
entire perimeter, experienced its rich cultural complexities and, with the
exception of the lands beyond the Tranquil Sea, felt at home wherever
he could rest his head at night. In China he acknowledged it was time to
return, at least to the spiritual safety within the *umma*.

A few pages later as his narrative was drawing to a close, Ibn Battuta
was back in Morocco and there declared that *'I had laid down my travelling staff in this noble country after confirming with superabundant impar-
tiality that it is the best of countries.'* The passage then shifts abruptly to
a truly 'superabundant' glorification of the Commander of the Faithful,
Abu Inan, his patron. Yet this lengthy, unctuous passage fails to deflect
attention away from truer, heartfelt sentiments: that on his return voyage
home from Alexandria, the affection and love expressed for his family,
friends and country were fused upon arrival with the deeply painful news
of his mother's recent death from the plague. He visited her grave but did
not remain long in Morocco and was soon off again, first to al-Andalus
and then to the kingdom of Mali. Upon his return from this very last

journey and during a trek through the Atlas mountains towards Fez, he was met by the bleakest and harshest of wintry conditions he said he had ever experienced. Two homecomings: one marked by personal loss and the other by extreme discomfort.

Ibn Battuta's real 'coming home' was through reliving the travels, recounting them to Ibn Juzayy so that others might vicariously share in his own physical and spiritual experiences. In the years left to him, a decade or so at least, there is no certain evidence as to his whereabouts or activities. Did he expect to enjoy fame and fortune or was he disappointed and bitter at his failure to achieve either? Did he withdraw into relative obscurity, perhaps serving his community again as a religious judge? Or did he retreat more completely, to be left alone with only his memories? This last possibility is unlikely given the traveller's gregarious nature. He was also conscious, as he reminded his readers at one point, that he was one of the greatest travellers of his age. However, he could not have imagined for a moment that by the fortunate alliance of indomitable traveller, enthusiastic patron and dedicated editor his *Travels* would one day be appreciated as the most original narrative of its kind to emerge from the medieval Muslim or Christian world.

＊⤳ ⤶＊

Notes

Chapter 1. Travel Tales, Their Creators and Critics

1. On al-Masudi's historical method, see Tarif Khalidi, *Islamic Historiography: The Histories of Masudi* (Albany, NY: State University of New York Press, 1975), chapter 2.

2. Al-Muqaddasi, *The Best Divisions for Knowledge of the Regions*, trans Basil Collins (Reading: Garnet Publishing, 2001), p 41.

3. Adomnan on Arculf, 'The Holy Places', in John Wilkinson, *Jerusalem Pilgrims: Before the Crusades* (Warminster: Aris & Phillips, 1977), p 93.

4. Hugeburc on the 'Life of St Willibald' (excerpts), in *ibid.*, p 135.

5. Marco Polo, *The Travels*, trans Ronald Latham (Harmondsworth: Penguin Books, (1958) 1979); Rustichello's comments are in the Prologue, pp 33–4.

6. *The Travels of Ibn Battuta AD 1324–1354*, trans H.A.R. Gibb (New Delhi: Munshiram Mooharlal Publishers, 2004); Ibn Juzayy's comments are in vol. 1, p 6.

7. John Larner, *Marco Polo and the Discovery of the World* (New Haven: Yale University Press, 1999), p 97.

8. For this account from Ibn Khaldun's *Prolegomena*, see Ibn Battuta, *Voyages d'Ibn Batoutah*, Arabic text and French translation by C. Defremery and B.R. Sanguinetti (Paris, (1852–58) 1874–79), vol. 1, pp 464–7.

9. Ibn Battuta, *Travels in Asia and Africa*, selections translated by H.A.R. Gibb (Delhi: Pilgrims Book, (1929) 1998), pp 12–13; see also his discussion on chronology in Ibn Battuta, *The Travels*, Appendix, vol. 2, pp 528–37.

10. Ivan Hrbek, 'The chronology of Ibn Battuta's Travels', *Archiv Orientalni* 30 (1962), pp 473–83, at p 481.

11. Harry Norris, 'Ibn Battuta's journey in the North-Eastern Balkans', *Journal of Islamic Studies* 5/2 (1994), pp 209–20, at p 219.

12. Ross Dunn, *The Adventures of Ibn Battuta: A Muslim Traveller of the Fourteenth Century* (London: Croom Helm, 1986), p 253.

13. Marco Polo, *The Travels*, p 14.
14. Ibn Jubayr, *The Travels of Ibn Jubayr*, Arabic edition by William Wright (London: Luzac, 1907), p 17.
15. Charles Pellat, *Encyclopaedia of Islam*, new edition (Leiden: Brill, 1960–2002), article on 'Ibn Djubayr'.
16. J.N. Mattock, 'Ibn Battuta's use of Ibn Jubayr's Rihla', *Proceedings of the Ninth Congress of the Union Européene des Arabisants et Islamisants*, ed Rudolph Peters (1981), pp 208–18, at p 218 (emphasis added).
17. Ibn Jubayr, *Ibn Yubayr: A traves del Oriente (Rihla)*, trans Felipe Maillo Salgado (Madrid: Alianza Editorial, 2007), p 49.
18. Ibn Jubayr, *The Travels*, Arabic edition by William W. Wright, p 218; Broadhurst translation, p 226.
19. Ibn Battuta, *The Travels*, trans Gibb; on Medina see vol. 1, p 164, fn. 42; p 178, fn. 84.
20. *Ibid.*, on Mecca, vol. 1, p 190, fn. 9.
21. Mattock, 'Ibn Battuta's use of Ibn Jubayr's Rihla', pp 210–11.
22. Ibn Jubayr, *The Travels of Ibn Jubayr*, trans R.J.C. Broadhurst (London: Jonathan Cape, 1952), p 185.
23. Amikam Elad, 'The description of the travels of Ibn Battuta in Palestine: Is it original?', *Journal of the Royal Asiatic Society* (1987), pp 256–72, at p 266.
24. On Mandeville's *persona*, see *The Travels of John Mandeville*, trans C.W.R.D. Moseley (Harmondsworth: Penguin Books, 1983), p 18.
25. Roxanne Euben, *Journeys to the Other Shore: Muslim and Western Travelers in Search of Knowledge* (Princeton: Princeton University Press, 2006), pp 63–89 for a discussion of Ibn Battuta.
26. Abderrahmane El Moudden, 'The ambivalence of *rihla*: community, integration and self-definition in Moroccan travel accounts, 1300–1800', in Dale Eickelman and James Piscatori (eds), *Muslim Travellers: Pilgrimage, Migration and the Religious Imagination* (London: Routledge, 1990), pp 69–84, at pp 69, 79, 82.

Chapter 2. The Travels

1. Larner, *Marco Polo*, p 64.
2. Marco Polo, *The Travels*, p 290.
3. William of Rubruck, *The Mission of Friar William of Rubruck: His Journey to the Court of the Great Khan Mongke, 1253–1255*, trans Peter Jackson with introduction, notes and appendices by P. Jackson with David Morgan (London: Hakluyt Society, 1990), pp 140–1.

4. John of Plano Carpini, 'History of the Mongols', in Christopher Dawson (ed), *The Mongol Mission: Narratives and Letters of the Franciscan Missionaries in Mongolia and China in the 13th and 14th Centuries* (London: Sheed & Ward, 1955), quoted pp xv–xvi.

5. Ibn Jubayr, *The Travels*, Broadhurst translation, pp 27, 29–30.

Chapter 3. Tales of Food and Hospitality

1. Al-Tabrizi, *Mishkat al-Masabih*, trans James Robson (Lahore: Muhammad Ashraf, 1990), vol. 2, p 877 (lawful and unlawful food).

2. Al-Muqaddasi, *The Best Divisions*, p 167.

3. Joseph Chelhod, 'Ibn Battuta, Ethnologue', *Revue de l'Occident Musulman et de la Méditerranée* 25 (1978), pp 5–24, at p 10.

4. On *buri*, see Anonymous, *Kanz al-Fawaid fi tanwi al-mawaid*, ed Manuela Marin and David Waines (Beirut/Stuttgart: Franz Steiner Verlag, 1993), recipe 254, p 99.

5. On *buri*, see Ibn Razin al-Tujibi, *Kitab Fadalat al-Khiwan fi Tayyibat al-Taam wal-Alwan*, ed Muhammad bin Shaqrun (Rabat, 1984), p 198.

6. On *naida*, see al-Muqaddasi, *The Best Divisions*, p 172, where he calls it a sweet pastry.

7. On uses of *dibs*, see Anonymous, *Kanz al-Fawaid*, index; a recipe for *sabuniyya* is on p 115, number 302.

8. On moral peril, see al-Ghazali, *Breaking the Two Desires*, trans T.J. Winter (Cambridge: Islamic Texts Society, 1995), p 106; on table etiquette, see al-Ghazali, *On the Manners Relating to Eating*, trans D. Johnson-Davies (Cambridge: Islamic Texts Society, 2000), pp 29–45.

9. On the Prophet on spiritual hunger, see al-Ghazali, *Breaking the Two Desires*, p 108.

10. On rice and rice bread, see Marius Canard, 'Le riz dans le Proche Orient aux premiers siècles de l'islam', *Arabica* (1999), pp 120–5; Ibn Qayyim al-Jawziyya, *Medicine of the Prophet*, trans Penelope Johnstone (Cambridge: Islamic Texts Society, 1998), pp 206–7; Ibn Sayyar al-Warraq, *Kitab al-Tabikh*, ed Kay Ohrnberg and Sahban Mroueh (Helsinki: Finnish Oriental Society, 1987), p 12; Anonymous, *Kanz al-fawaid*, rice recipes numbers 64, A33.

11. For a poem on *sawiq*, see Ibn Sayyar al-Warraq, *Annals of the Caliphs' Kitchens*, English translation, introduction and glossary by Nawal Nasrallah, (Leiden: Brill, 2007), p 127.

12. Ibn Mujawir, *A Traveller in Thirteenth-Century Arabia: Ibn Mujawir's Tarikh al-Mustabsir*, trans and ed G. Rex Smith (London: Hakluyt Society, 2000),

pp 34, 36.

13. On dates, see Ibn Qayyim al-Jawziyya, *Medicine of the Prophet*, p 211.

14. On dreams and visions, see al-Tabrizi, *Mishkat al-Masabih*, vol. 2, p 962; Annemarie Schimmel, *And Muhammad is His Messenger: The Veneration of the Prophet in Islamic Piety* (Chapel Hill: University of North Carolina Press, 1985), pp 67–80.

15. For *jammun*, see *Hobson-Jobson: The Anglo-Indian Dictionary*, ed Henry Yule and A.C. Burnell (Ware: Wordsworth Editions, (1886) 1996), p 449.

16. On the betel, see Alan Davidson, *The Penguin Companion to Food* (London: Penguin Books, 2002); see also *Hobson-Jobson* on *areca* and *betel*.

17. *Atraf al-tib*, defined in Anonymous, *Kanz al-fawaid*, recipe 434.

18. For *fufal* in medicinal preparations, see Ibn al-Tilmidh, *The Dispensatory of Ibn at-Tilmid*, Arabic text, English translation, study and glossaries by Oliver Kahl (Leiden: Brill, 2007), recipes 133, 323.

19. On the properties of the coconut, see Efraim Lev and Zohar Amar, *Practical Materia Medica of the Medieval Eastern Mediterranean According to the Cairo Geniza* (Leiden: Brill, 2008), pp 383–4.

20. On the *rubb*, see Ibn al-Tilmidh, *The Dispensatory*, chapter 6, receipts 161–9; Ibn Sayyar al-Warraq, *Annals of the Caliphs' Kitchens*, pp 488–90.

21. On *tharid* in a Prophetic tradition, see Ibn Qayyim al-Jawziyya, *Medicine of the Prophet*, p 213; for *tharid* recipes, see Ibn Sayyar al-Warraq, *Kitab al-tabikh*, p 162.

22. John of Plano Carpini, in Dawson (ed), *The Mongol Mission*, p 16.

23. On the Turks' use of bread and sweetmeats, see Paul D. Buell, 'Mongol Empire and Turkicization: The evidence of food and foodways', in R. Amita-Preiss and D.O. Morgan (eds), *The Mongol Empire and its Legacy* (Leiden: Brill, 2000), pp 200–3.

24. On *qumiss*, see 'The journey of William of Rubruck', in Dawson (ed), *The Mongol Mission*, pp 98–9.

25. On figs as a cure for gout, see the caution expressed by Ibn Qayyim al-Jawziyya, *Medicine of the Prophet*, p 212.

26. Jackson, *The Sultanate of Delhi*, pp 126, 155.

27. Davidson, *The Penguin Companion to Food*, 'jackfruit'; see also *Hobson-Jobson*, 'jack'.

28. For *luqaymat al-qadi, qahiriyya, samusak*, see the anonymous cookbook *Kanz al-fawaid* for recipes of each preparation. *Luqaymat al-qadi*, or 'judge's little mouthfuls', recipe 286, where they are described as having the shape and size of dinar coins; for the sweet dish, *qahiriyya*, or 'vanquisher', see recipe 322;

samusak, called *sanbusak* in the cookbook, comes in both sweet and savoury preparations, recipes 115 and 116.

Chapter 4. Tales of Sacred Places, Saints, Miracles and Marvels

1. The expression 'juridical Sufism' is Vincent J. Cornell's, from his excellent study of Moroccan Sufism, *Realm of the Saint: Power and Authority in Moroccan Sufism* (Austin: University of Texas Press, 1998), pp 67, 109–11.

2. Marshall Hodgson, *The Venture of Islam* (Chicago: University of Chicago Press, (1958) 1974), vol. 2, p 203.

3. See William Chittick, *Sufism: A Beginner's Guide* (Oxford: Oneworld, 2008), quoted p 21.

4. Cornell, *Realm of the Saint*, p 94.

5. Sufi sayings on travel are from Abul-Qasim Al-Qushayri, *Al-Qushayri's Epistle on Sufism*, trans Alexander Knysh (Reading: Garnet Publishing, 2007), pp 297–302; on Sufism in general see pp 288–92.

6. Epitaphs on graves are cited in Christopher Taylor, *The Cult of Saints in Late Medieval Egypt* (Ann Arbor: University Microfilms International, 1989), p 85.

7. For *hadiths* on grave visitation, see al-Tabrizi, *Mishkat al-Masabih*, vol. 1, pp 369–70.

8. Ibn al-Hajj cited in Taylor, *The Cult of Saints*, p 97; for the Arabic text, see Ibn al-Hajj, *Kitab al-Madkhal* (Cairo: Dar al-Fikr, 1982), pp 267–8.

9. On graveyard guides and guidebooks, see Taylor, *The Cult of Saints*, pp 100–20.

10. On al-Khidr and Ilyas, see Al-Kisai, *The Tales of the Prophets of al-Kisai*, trans W.M. Thackston (Boston: Twayne Publishers, 1978), pp 247–51, 262–70.

11. Ibn Ishaq's story of the night journey is told in Ibn Ishaq, *The Life of Muhammad: A Translation of Ibn Ishaq's Sirat Rasul Allah*, trans Alfred Guillaume (Karachi: Oxford University Press, (1955) 1980), p 182.

12. On Jesus as a Muslim prophet, see Al-Kisai, *Tales of the Prophets*, pp 326–36.

13. The poet al-Saadi is discussed by Katouzian, 'Sufism in Sa'di', in Lewis Lewisohn, *The Heritage of Sufism* (Oxford: Oneworld, 1999), vol. 2, p 201.

14. On the institution *salih*, see Cornell's fundamental discussion in *Realm of the Saints*, pp 3–31.

15. Michael Gilsenan's discussion of miracles as 'indications of divine power' is in his *Recognising Islam* (London: Croom Helm, 1982), pp 79–80.

16. On Barani's views, see David Waines, 'Ibn Battuta on public violence', in A. Vrolijk and J.P. Hogendijk (eds), *O Ye Gentlemen: Arabic Studies on Science and*

Literary Culture (Leiden: Brill, 2007), pp 242–3.

Chapter 5. Tales of the 'Other'

1. Ibn Battuta, *Travels in Asia and Africa*, selections translated by Gibb, p 12.
2. On Hindus and the poor, see Euben, *Journeys to the Other Shore*, p 83.
3. Remke Kruk, 'Ibn Battuta: Travel, family life and chronology', *al-Qantara* 16/2 (1995), pp 369–84, at p 370.
4. *Ibid.*, p 376.
5. Al-Ghazali, cited in Ahmad ibn Naquib Al-Misri, *Reliance of the Traveller*, Arabic text and translation by Nuh Ha Mim Keller (Maryland: Amana Publications, 1991), p 525.
6. Marina A. Tolmacheva, 'Ibn Battuta on women's travel in the Dar al-Islam', in B. Frederick and S.H. McLeod (eds), *Women and the Journey* (Washington: Washington State University Press 1995), p 126.
7. Kruk, 'Ibn Battuta', p 375.
8. André Miquel, 'L'Islam d'Ibn Battuta', *Bulletin d'Etudes Orientales* 30 (1978), pp 75–83, at p 78.
9. Euben, *Journeys to the Other Shore*, p 69.
10. *Ibid.*, pp 79–80.
11. Remke Kruk, 'Warrior women in Arabic Popular Romance: Qannasa bint Muzahim and other valiant ladies', *Journal of Arabic Literature* 24 (1993), pp 213–30.
12. On Sindbad and the Rukh, see *The Arabian Nights*, abridged translation by Richard Burton (New York: The Modern Library, 2001), p 342.
13. For the Rukh in Marco Polo, see *The Travels*, trans Latham, pp 300–1.

Glossary

abid	pious.
akhi	leader of a communal group of young men (*fityan*) noted for their hospitality to travellers in Anatolia.
alim (pl. *ulama*)	'person of knowledge', 'learned', 'scholar'; generally applied to an expert in the field of *hadith*, *fiqh* or *sharia*.
anbah	mango.
arruz	rice.
atraf al-tib	aromatic spice mixture.
aya (pl. *ayat*)	literally 'sign', referring to a verse from the Quran, and the 'signs' of God's creation in nature and the cosmos.
baraka (pl. *barakat*)	blessing(s). A spiritual power associated with holy persons, sacred places and objects such as relics. Believed to have a real existence that could be transmitted to persons who come into contact with individuals or things thought to possess that power.
barki	together with *shaki*, the 'jack fruit' found in India.
bawariji	carver of meat.
dayr	Christian monastery.
dhikr	remembrance, recollection (of God). A ritual among Sufis, during which divine names or holy phrases are chanted in rhythmic fashion resulting in a state of meditation or ecstasy.
dhimmi	protected person or community, first of the Jewish or Christian faith then, by extension, Zoroastrians, all of whom possessed sacred scriptures; those who lived in a relationship of protection (*dhimma*) under a Muslim ruler against payment of a poll tax.
dibs	sweet paste made from grapes or dates.

diyafa   hospitality gift, given to a traveller by his host.

dua   supplication to God.

faqih   jurist of Islamic religious law.

faqir (pl.   poor brother or brethren, a term used of Sufis who practised
fuqara)   spiritual poverty (*faqr*) and were said to have transcended the
                  world regardless of economic status.

fityan   young men, members of an *akhi* organization in Anatolia.

funduq   inn, hostelry, akin to a larger institution for commercial travel-
                  lers, the *khan* or caravanserai, found in both rural and urban
                  locations.

fuqqaa   barley water, or barley beer.

hadith   'Prophetic tradition', an anecdote attributed to the Prophet
                  Muhammad or a story of his deeds and words related by his
                  Companions; the vast tradition literature, collectively also
                  called *hadith*, constituted one of the authoritative bases of
                  Islamic law (*sharia*).

hajj   pilgrimage to Mecca which every adult Muslim of sound mind,
                  body and the necessary means must perform once during their
                  lifetime in the last month of the Muslim year, Dhu-l Hijja.

hal (pl.   literally, 'state' or 'states', to be distinguished from 'stages' (sing.
ahwal)   *maqam*) along the Sufi path of spiritual absorption into the
                  Real (God); 'states' are beyond the individual Sufi's control but
                  rather descend from God into the heart. The 'stages' constitute
                  the ascetic and ethical discipline of the Sufi, while the 'states'
                  form a parallel psychological progress.

ibada (pl.   obligatory form of Muslim worship such as prayer, fasting,
ibadat)   pilgrimage and the giving of alms.

idam   'savory condiment', 'seasoning'.

jizya   tax paid by the head of Jewish or Christian families living
                  under the protection (*dhimma*) of a Muslim ruler.

Kaaba   cube-like construction covered with a black brocaded cloth (the
                  kiswa) housing the Black Stone; according to tradition it was
                  built by the prophet Abraham at Mecca and became the focal
                  point of prayer by all Muslims.

kafir (pl. *kuffar*)	term used for 'unbeliever', that is a non-Muslim, who is deemed unworthy of God's compassion and mercy owing to an attitude of ingratitude towards God's works.
kaak (sing. diminutive plural, *kuaykat*)	small cakes made from barley.
karama (pl. *karamat*)	miracle, granted by God and performed by a saint that was often seen as evidence of his close relationship to God; to be distinguished from a prophet's miracle, also granted by God and called *mujiza*.
khanqa	'monastery'; an endowed foundation supervised by a *shaykh* with provision for the maintenance of Sufis.
khatib	Muslim preacher with special duty to deliver the sermon at the Friday congregational prayer.
khatun	socially prominent lady, wife.
khirqa	robe of initiation, given by a Sufi *shaykh* to a disciple.
kiswa	coloured, brocaded covering of the Kaaba walls in Mecca.
kurkum	turmeric (called *zard shubah* in India).
madrasa	college for the higher study of Islamic orthodox doctrine and religious law.
Mamluk	literally 'owned', 'belonging to', referring to a slave or Mameluke, member of a military caste and the name of the dynasty that ruled Egypt and Syria from the mid-thirteenth to the early sixteenth century.
maqam (pl. *maqamat*)	'stage(s)' on the Sufi spiritual path that can be mastered by one's own effort (see also *hal*).
mashhad (pl. *mashahid*)	sanctuary of holy person.
al-mishmish al-lawzi	almond apricot, also called white apricot, whose kernel was like a sweet almond.
muamalat (pl.)	the part of Islamic religious law that pertains to social relations such as commercial, criminal or family affairs.
mujawir	'sojourner', one who remains in the Holy Cities of Mecca or Medina beyond the pilgrimage season for several years.

mujiza	prophet's probative miracle as distinct from an act of grace of a saint (*karama*).
murid	novice in a Sufi order under the supervision of a *shaykh* or spiritual guide.
mushunk	type of pea.
naida	sweet, honey-like, made from soaked, dried, crushed wheat.
narjil	coconut.
niqris	gout.
qadi	Muslim religious judge.
qamar al-din	dried apricot.
qumiss	staple beverage among Turkish nomads made from mare's milk.
qurs	round flat loaf of bread, usually made of barley.
qutb	literally 'tent pole' or 'axis'; a term used to designate a Sufi saint regarded as the greatest of his day and therefore the supreme 'Saint of the Age'.
Rafidi	Rafidite was a pejorative name employed by Sunni Muslims against the Shia in general or to a particular group of them.
ribat, rabita	literally, a place where horses are tethered; could apply to an institution such as a caravanserai, but commonly a hospice used by Sufis.
rihla	'travel', a term given to accounts of travels undertaken for the sake of making the pilgrimage to Mecca, or for the broader purpose of gathering religious knowledge.
rubb	thick, concentrated juice (of fruit).
salih	virtuous person, morally upstanding and socially constructive; a term that sums up the basic qualities of sainthood in Morocco, hence 'saint'.
sama	literally 'hearing', a Sufi ritual involving group listening to the recitation of Quranic verses, religious poetry, or music, leading to a state of ecstasy.
sayalan	date honey.
shahid (pl. *shuhada*)	martyr.
sharia	Islamic law, the material bases of which are the Quran and Prophetic traditions (*hadith*) that are interpreted through the efforts of legal scholars or jurists (*faqih*).

shaykh	literally, 'elder' or 'chief', and could apply to a scholar, political leader or, as in Sufism, spiritual leader or guide.
Shia	minority community within the Muslim world-wide *umma* which holds that legitimate leadership of the community after the Prophet's death had been designated to Muhammad's cousin Ali, married to his daughter Fatima. A line of male descendants were known as the Imams, their spiritual leaders.
Sufi	from the Arabic *suf*, 'wool', as the woollen robe symbolized the ascetic life; a Muslim 'mystic'. Although not every saint (*wali allah*) may have been a Sufi, many scholars (*alim*) or legal experts (*faqih*) were Sufis; there was no rigid distinction between a Sufi and any other Muslim intellectual.
sunna	the customary and exemplary practice of the Prophet Muhammad.
Sunni	name given to the majority of Muslims who hold that legitimate succession of the community after the Prophet Muhammad fell to those of his Companions elected to the leadership. Sunnis are also committed to following the example (*sunna*) set by the Prophet Muhammad as preserved and transmitted by his Companions; followers of the four 'orthodox' schools of law.
taifa	medieval Moroccan term for a Sufi order.
tawba	'repentance', or a turning away from sin towards actions approved or commanded by God.
tunbul	betel leaves, used with *fulfal*, areca nuts to honour guests.
umma	universal Muslim community as a whole, formed from the nucleus established by the Prophet Muhammad in Medina.
wali allah	literally, 'Friend of God', a renowned saint.
zahid	ascetic, one who practises *zuhd*, self-denial.
zawiya	hospice, generally applied to a Sufi institution.

Select Bibliography

Reference works

Encyclopaedia of Islam, new edition (Leiden: Brill, 1960–2002)
Encyclopaedia of the Quran (Leiden: Brill, 2001–2006)

Primary sources and translations

Al-Abdari, Abu Abdallah Muhammad, *Rihla al-Abdari (al-Rihlat al-Maghrabiyy),* ed Muhammad al-Fasi (Rabbat, 1968)

Anonymous, *Kanz al-Fawaid fi tanwi al-mawaid,* ed Manuela Marin and David Waines (Beirut/Stuttgart: Franz Steiner Verlag, 1993)

The Arabian Nights, abridged translation by Richard Burton (New York: The Modern Library, 2001)

Benjamin of Tudela, *The Itinerary of Benjamin of Tudela* (New York: Joseph Simon, 1983)

Dawson, Christopher (ed), *The Mongol Mission: Narratives and Letters of the Franciscan Missionaries in Mongolia and China in the 13th and 14th Centuries* (London: Sheed & Ward, 1955)

Deluz, Christiane, *Jean de Mandeville: Le Livre des Merveilles du Monde,* édition critique (Paris: CNRS Editions, 2000)

Al-Ghazali, *Breaking the Two Desires,* trans T.J. Winter (Cambridge: Islamic Texts Society, 1995)

___, *On the Manners Relating to Eating,* trans D. Johnson-Davies (Cambridge: Islamic Texts Society, 2000)

Ibn Battuta, *Cathay and the Way Thither,* vol. 4, *Ibn Battuta,* trans and ed Henry Yule (new edition by Henri Cordier) (New Delhi, (1916) 1998)

___, *The Rehla of Ibn Battuta (India, Maldive Islands and Ceylon),* trans with commentary by Mahdi Husain (Baroda: Oriental Institute, 1953)

___, *Rihla Ibn Battuta,* ed Abd al-Hadi al-Tazi, 5 vols. (Rabat: Royal Maghrib Academy, 1997)

___, *Travels in Asia and Africa*, selections translated by H.A.R. Gibb (Delhi: Pilgrims Book (1929) 1998)

___, *The Travels of Ibn Battuta AD 1325–1354*, trans H.A.R. Gibb, 3 vols. (New Delhi: Munshiram Mooharlal Publishers, 2004)

___, *The Travels of Ibn Battuta AD 1325–1354*, vol. 4, trans with annotations by H.A.R. Gibb and C.F. Beckingham (London: Hakluyt Society, 1994)

___, *The Travels of Ibn Battutah*, abridged and annotated by Tim Mackintosh-Smith (Oxford: Picador, 2002)

___, *Voyages d'Ibn Batoutah*, Arabic text and French translation by C. Defremery and B.R. Sanguinetti, 4 vols. (Paris, (1852–58) 1874–79)

Ibn al-Hajj, *Kitab al-Madkhal*, 4 vols. (Cairo: Dar al-Fikr, 1982)

Ibn Ishaq, *The Life of Muhammad: A Translation of Ibn Ishaq's Sirat Rasul Allah*, trans Alfred Guillaume (Karachi: Oxford University Press, 1955 (1980))

Ibn Jubayr, *Ibn Yubayr: A Traves del Oriente (Rihla)*, trans Felipe Maillo Salgado (Madrid: Alianza Editorial, 2007)

___, *The Travels of Ibn Jubayr*, Arabic edition by William Wright (London: Luzac, 1907)

___, *The Travels of Ibn Jubayr*, trans R.J.C. Broadhurst (London: Jonathan Cape, 1952)

Ibn Mujawir, *A Traveller in Thirteenth-Century Arabia: Ibn Mujawir's Tarikh al-Mustabsir*, trans and ed G. Rex Smith (London: Hakluyt Society, 2000)

Ibn Qayyim al-Jawziyya, *Medicine of the Prophet*, trans Penelope Johnstone (Cambridge: Islamic Texts Society, 1998)

Ibn Razin al-Tujibi, *Kitab Fadalat al-Khiwan fi Tayyibat al-Taam wal-Alwan*, ed Muhammad bin Shaqrun (Rabat, 1984)

Ibn Sayyar al-Warraq, *Annals of the Caliphs' Kitchen*, English translation, introduction and glossary by Nawal Nasrallah (Leiden: Brill, 2007)

___, *Kitab al-Tabikh*, ed Kay Ohrnberg and Sahban Mroueh (Helsinki: Finnish Oriental Society, 1987)

Ibn al-Tilmidh, *The Dispensatory of Ibn at-Tilmid*, Arabic text, English translation, study and glossaries by Oliver Kahl (Leiden: Brill, 2007)

Al-Kisai, *The Tales of the Prophets of al-Kisai*, trans W.M. Thackston (Boston: Twayne Publishers, 1978)

Mandeville, John, *The Travels of John Mandeville*, trans C.W.R.D. Moseley (Harmondsworth: Penguin Books, 1983)

Al-Misri, Ahmad ibn Naquib, *Reliance of the Traveller*, Arabic text and translation by Nuh Ha Mim Keller (Maryland: Amana Publications, 1991)

Al-Muqaddasi, *The Best Divisions for Knowledge of the Regions*, trans Basil Collins

(Reading: Garnet Publishing, 2001)

Polo, Marco, *The Travels*, trans Ronald Latham (Harmondsworth: Penguin Books, (1958) 1979)

Al-Qushayri, Abul-Qasim, *Al-Qushayri's Epistle on Sufism*, trans Alexander Knysh (Reading: Garnet Publishing, 2007)

Al-Tabrizi, *Mishkat al-Masabih*, trans James Robson, 2 vols. (Lahore: Muhammad Ashraf, 1990)

Voyage du Marchand Arabe Sulayman en Inde et en Chine rédigé en 851 suivi de remarques par Abu Zayd Hasan (vers 916), trans Gabriel Ferrand (Paris: Editions Bossard, 1922)

Wilkinson, John, *Jerusalem Pilgrims: Before the Crusades* (Warminster: Aris & Phillips, 1977)

William of Rubruck, *The Mission of Friar William of Rubruck: His Journey to the Court of the Great Khan Mongke, 1253–1255*, trans Peter Jackson with introduction, notes and appendices by P. Jackson with David Morgan (London: Hakluyt Society, 1990)

Wright, Thomas, *Travels in Palestine* (New York: KTAV Publishing House, (1848) 1968)

Secondary sources

Agius, Dionisius A. and Ian R. Netton (eds), *Across the Mediterranean Frontiers: Trade, Politics, and Religion, 650–1450* (Selected proceedings of the International Medieval Congress, University of Leeds, 10–13 July 1995, 8–11 July 1996) (Turnhout: Brepols, 1997)

Aigle, Denise (ed), *Miracle et Karama: Hagiographies médiévales comparés* (Turnhout: Brepols (Bibliothèque de l'école des hautes études sciences religieux, vol. 109), 2000)

Allen, Roger and D.S. Richards, *Arabic Literature in the Post-Classical Period* (Cambridge: Cambridge University Press, 2006)

Amita-Preiss, R. and D.O. Morgan, *The Mongol Empire and its Legacy* (Leiden: Brill, 2000)

Berkey, Jonathan P., *Popular Preaching and Religious Authority in the Medieval Islamic Near East* (Seattle: University of Washington Press, 2001)

Blair, Sheila S., 'Sufi saints and shrine architecture in the early fourteenth century', *Muqarnas* 7 (1990), pp 35–49

Bousquet, G.-H., 'Ibn Battuta et les institutions musulmans', *Studia Islamica* 24 (1966), pp 81–106

Buell, Paul D., 'Mongol Empire and Turkicization: The evidence of food and foodways', in R. Amita-Preiss and D.O. Morgan (eds), *The Mongol Empire and its Legacy* (Leiden: Brill, 2000), pp 200–23

Campbell, Mary B., *The Witness and the Other World: Exotic European Travel Writing 400–1600* (Ithaca: Cornell University Press, 1988)

Canard, Marius, 'Le riz dans le Proche Orient aux premiers siècles de l'islam', *Arabica* (1959), pp 113–31

Chelhod, Joseph, 'Ibn Battuta, Ethnologue', *Revue de l'Occident Musulman et de la Méditerranée* 25 (1978), pp 5–24

Chittick, William, *Sufism: A Beginner's Guide* (Oxford: Oneworld, 2008)

Constable, Olivia Remie, *Housing the Stranger in the Mediterranean World: Lodging, Trade and Travel in Late Antiquity and the Middle Ages* (Cambridge: Cambridge University Press, 2003)

Cook, Michael, *Forbidding Wrong in Islam* (Cambridge: Cambridge University Press, 2003)

Cornell, Vincent J., 'Ibn Battuta's Opportunism: The networks and loyalties of a medieval Muslim scholar', in Miriam Cooke and Bruce Lawrence (eds), *Muslim Networks from Hajj to Hiphop* (Chapel Hill: University of North Carolina Press, 2005)

___, *Realm of the Saint: Power and Authority in Moroccan Sufism* (Austin: University of Texas Press, 1998)

Davidson, Alan, *The Penguin Companion to Food* (London: Penguin Books, 2002)

Dunn, Ross, *The Adventures of Ibn Battuta: A Muslim Traveller of the Fourteenth Century* (London: Croom Helm, 1986)

Eickelman, Dale E. and James Piscatori (eds), *Muslim Travellers: Pilgrimage, Migration and the Religious Imagination* (London: Routledge, 1990)

Elad, Amikam, 'The description of the travels of Ibn Battuta in Palestine: Is it Original?', *Journal of the Royal Asiatic Society* (1987), pp 256–72

Euben, Roxanne L., *Journeys to the Other Shore: Muslim and Western Travelers in Search of Knowledge* (Princeton: Princeton University Press, 2006)

Fanjul, Serafin, 'Elementos folkloricos en la Rihla de Ibn Battuta', *Revista del Instituto Egipcio de Estudios Islamicos en Madrid* 21 (1981–82), pp 153–79

Fauvelle-Aymar, Francois-Xavier and Bertrand Hirsch, 'Voyage aux frontières du monde: Topologie, narration et jeux de miroir dans la Rihla de Ibn Battuta', *Afrique et Histoire* 1 (2003), pp 75–122

Friedman, John Block and Kristen Mossler Figg (eds), *Trade, Travel and Exploration in the Middle Ages: An Encyclopedia* (London: Garland Publishing, 2000)

Gilsenan, Michael, *Recognizing Islam* (London: Croom Helm, 1982)

Goldziher, Ignaz, 'Veneration of saints in Islam', in his *Muslim Studies*, trans C.R. Barber and S.M. Stern (London: George Allen & Unwin, 1971), vol. 2, pp 255–341

Goody, Jack, *Cooking, Cuisine and Class* (Cambridge: Cambridge University Press, 1982)

von Grunebaum, G. and Roger Caillois (eds), *The Dream and Human Societies* (Berkeley: University of California Press, 1966)

Hambly, Gavin R.G. (ed), *Women in the Medieval Islamic World* (London: St Martin's Press, 1998)

Hobson-Jobson: The Anglo-Indian Dictionary, ed Henry Yule and A.C. Burnell (Ware: Wordsworth Editions, (1886) 1996)

Hodgson, Marshall, *The Venture of Islam*, 3 vols. (Chicago: University of Chicago Press, (1958) 1974)

Hrbek, Ivan, 'The chronology of Ibn Battuta's Travels', *Archiv Orientalni* 30 (1962), pp 409–86

Islam, Riazul, *Sufism in South Asia: Impact on Fourteenth Century Muslim Society* (Karachi: Oxford University Press, 2002)

Janicsek, Stephen, 'Ibn Battuta's journey to Bulghar: Is it a fabrication?', *Journal of the Royal Asiatic Society* (1929), pp 791–800

Janssens, Herman, *Ibn Batouta, 'Le voyaguer de l'Islam'* (Brussels, 1948)

Khalidi, Tarif, *Islamic Historiography: The Histories of Masudi* (Albany, NY: State University of New York Press, 1975)

King, Noel, 'Reading between the lines of Ibn Battuta', *Milla wa Milla* (Australian Bulletin of Comparative Religion) 19 (1979), pp 26–33

Kruk, Remke, 'The Arabian Nights and the popular epics', in Ulrich Marzolph and Richard van Leeuwen (eds), *The Arabian Nights Encyclopedia* (Oxford: ABC Clio, 2004), vol. 1, pp 30–4

___, 'Clipped wings: Medieval Arabic adaptations of the Amazon myth', *Harvard Middle Eastern and Islamic Review* 1/2 (1994), pp 132–51

___, 'Ibn Battuta: Travel, family life and chronology', *al-Qantara* 16/2 (1995), pp 369–84

___, 'The Princess Maymunah: Maiden, mother, monster', *Oriente Moderno* 22/2 (2003), pp 425–42

___, 'Warrior women in Arabic Popular Romance: Qannasa bint Muzahim and other valiant ladies', *Journal of Arabic Literature* 24 (1993), pp 213–30

___, and Claudia Ott, 'In the popular manner: Sira-recitation in Marrakesh anno 1997', *Edebiyat* (Journal of Middle Eastern Literatures) 10/2 (1999), pp 183–95

Larner, John, *Marco Polo and the Discovery of the World* (New Haven: Yale University Press, 1999)

Lev, Efraim and Zohar Amar, *Practical Materia Medica of the Medieval Eastern Mediterranean According to the Cairo Geniza* (Leiden: Brill, 2008)

Lewicki, Tadeusz, *West African Food in the Middle Ages* (Cambridge: Cambridge University Press, 1974)

Lewisohn, Lewis, *The Heritage of Sufism*, 3 vols. (Oxford: Oneworld, 1999)

Lutfi al-Sayyid-Marsot, Afaf (ed), *Society and the Sexes in Medieval Islam* (Malibu: Undena Publications, 1979)

Lyons, Malcolm, *The Arabian Epic: Heroic and Oral Storytelling*, 3 vols. (Cambridge: Cambridge University Press, 1995)

Mackintosh-Smith, Tim, *The Hall of a Thousand Columns: Hindustan to Malabar with Ibn Battutah* (London: John Murray, 2005)

___, *Travels with a Tangerine: A Journey in the Footnotes of Ibn Battutah* (Oxford: Picador, 2001)

von Martels, Zweder (ed), *Travel Fact and Travel Fiction: Studies on Fiction, Literary Tradition, Scholarly Discovery and Observation in Travel Writing* (Leiden: Brill, 1994)

Mattock, John, 'Ibn Battuta's use of Ibn Jubayr's Rihla', *Proceedings of the Ninth Congress of the Union Européene des Arabisants et Islamisants*, ed Rudolph Peters (1981), pp 208–18

McGregor, Richard and Adam Sabra, *Le développement du soufisme en Egypte à l'époque mamelouke* (Institut français d'archéologie orientale, Caire (Cahiers des Annales islamologiques 27, 2006))

Miquel, André, 'L'Islam d'Ibn Battuta', *Bulletin d'Etudes Orientales* 30 (1978), pp 75–83

Mollat, Michel, 'Ibn Battoutah et la mer', *Travaux et Jours* 18 (1966), pp 53–70

Montanari, Massimo, *The Culture of Food* (Oxford: Blackwell, 1996)

Morgan, David, 'Ibn Battuta and the Mongols', *Royal Asiatic Society of Great Britain and Ireland* 11/1 (2001), pp 1–11

El Moudden, Abderrahmane, 'The ambivalence of *rihla*: Community, integration and self-definition in Moroccan travel accounts, 1300–1800', in Dale Eickelman and James Piscatori (eds), *Muslim Travellers: Pilgrimage, Migration and the Religious Imagination* (London: Routledge, 1990), pp 69–84

Murata, Sachiko and William Chittick, *The Vision of Islam: The Foundations of Muslim Faith and Practice* (London: I.B.Tauris, 1996)

Netton, Ian Richard, 'Myth, miracle and magic in the *rihla* of Ibn Battuta',

Journal of Semitic Studies 29/1 (1984), pp 131–40

___, (ed), *Golden Roads: Migration, Pilgrimage and Travel in Medieval and Modern Islam* (London: Curzon Press, 1993)

Norris, Harry T., 'Ibn Battuta on Muslims and Christians in the Crimean Peninsula', *Iran and the Caucasus* 8/1 (2004), pp 7–14

___, 'Ibn Battutah's Andalusian journey', *The Geographical Journal* 125 (1959), pp 185–96

___, 'Ibn Battuta's journey in the North-Eastern Balkans', *Journal of Islamic Studies* 5/2 (1994), pp 209–20

Peters, F.E., *The Hajj: The Muslim Pilgrimage to Mecca and the Holy Places* (Princeton: Princeton University Press, 1994)

___, *Jerusalem and Mecca: The Typology of the Holy City in the Near East* (New York: New York University Press, 1986)

Renard, John, *Seven Doors to Islam: Spirituality and the Religious Life of Muslims* (Berkeley: University of California Press, 1996)

Richard, Jean, *Croises, Missionnaires et Voyageurs: Les Perspectives Orientales du Monde Latin Mediéval* (London: Variorum Reprints, 1983)

___, *Les Récits de Voyages et de Pèlerinages* (Turnhout: Brepols, 1981)

Robinson, Chase F., 'Prophecy and holy men in early Islam', in J. Howard-Johnston and P.A. Hayward (eds), *The Cult of Saints in Late Antiquity and the Early Middle Ages* (Oxford, 1999), pp 241–60

Schimmel, Annemarie, *And Muhammad is His Messenger: The Veneration of the Prophet in Islamic Piety* (Chapel Hill: University of North Carolina Press, 1985)

Seymour, M.C., *Sir John Mandeville* (Aldershot: Variorum, 1993)

Tatsuro, Yamamoto, 'On Tawalisi (as) described by Ibn Batuta', *Memoirs of the Department of Research of the Toyo Bunko* 8 (1936), pp 94–133

Taylor, Christopher, *The Cult of Saints in Late Medieval Egypt* (Ann Arbor: University Microfilms International, 1989)

Al-Tazi, 'Abd al-Hadi, 'al-Mara inda Ibn Battuta' ('Women according to Ibn Battuta'), in Conference Proceedings of *al-Rahhalat al-'Arab wa'l Muslimun* (Arab and Muslim Travellers) (Rabat: Moroccan Ministry of Culture (2003)), pp 55–68

Touati, Houari, *Islam et Voyage au Moyen Age* (Paris: Editions du Seuil, 2000)

Verdon, Jean, *Travel in the Middle Ages*, trans George Holoch (Notre Dame University Press, 2003)

Waines, David, 'Dietetics in medieval Islamic culture', *Medical History* 43/2 (1999), pp 228–40

___, 'Ibn Battuta on public violence', in A. Vrolijk and J.P. Hogendijk (eds), *O Ye Gentlemen: Arabic Studies on Science and Literary Culture* (Leiden: Brill, 2007), pp 228–46

Index